The Constitutional Divide

THE PRIVATE AND PUBLIC SECTORS IN AMERICAN LAW

William P. Kreml

UNIVERSITY OF SOUTH CAROLINA PRESS

© 1997 University of South Carolina

Published in Columbia, South Carolina, by the
University of South Carolina Press

Manufactured in the United States of America

01 00 99 98 97   5 4 3 2 1

Library of Congress Cataloging-in-Publication Data

Kreml, William P.
   The constitutional divide : the private and public sectors in
American law / William P. Kreml.
      p. cm.
   Includes bibliographical references and index.
   ISBN 1–57003–111–8 (cloth)
   1. United States—Constitutional history. 2. United States—Politics and
government. 3. Civil law—United States—History.
   4. Public law—United States—History. 5. Civil law—Great Britain.
   6. Public law—Great Britain. I. Title.
   KF4541.K66 1997
   342.73'029—dc20
   [347.30229]   96-10077

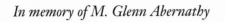

In memory of M. Glenn Abernathy

CONTENTS

ACKNOWLEDGMENTS

My deepest thanks to Zhenghuan Zhou and Arthur Vanden Houten, for their research assistance throughout this work. My thanks as well to George C. Rogers Jr. and Lacy K. Ford of the History Department, University of South Carolina, for their advice and counsel. Finally, my thanks to Nancy M. Kreml, for her proofreading of the manuscript. The responsibility for error is exclusively my own.

INTRODUCTION

Political science and jurisprudential scholarship on the American Constitution typically focuses on governmental institutions and the jurisdictional battles that go on between and among them.[1] Such a focus is understandable. Political scientists and jurisprudential scholars study public structures, and the U.S. Constitution lays out the fundamental structures of our government. The extreme decentralization of the U.S. Constitutional arrangement makes knowledge of each of these structures' prerogatives all the more necessary. But I suggest that even the most profound analyses of the United States' Constitutional arrangement are flawed in one important way. That flaw results from the relative inattention that is given to the balance between the private and public sectors. At best, structure is half the American governmental story. America's political structures are profoundly affected by laws, customs, usages, and traditions that are in turn the product of an evolution that went on within the private domain as much as it went on in the public domain for hundreds of years.

The English common law, that great body of judge-made case law, was supplemented by governmental statutes from time to time. But it was, and still is, largely a law of the private sector. The common law developed as a set of rules governing the individual ownership and sale of property, particularly land. It dealt far less either with the rules that governed the citizenry in a public way or with those rules that structured the governing institutions that would in turn govern that citizenry.

Growing out of the English common law, U.S. law developed in order to fulfill much the same function as the English law. It too concerned itself with the adjudication of private disputes about property and the contractual sale of property. No one can fully understand the U.S. political system, or the public domain in any general sense, without first understanding the still very private nature of U.S. common law.

Further, it is important to understand that the private law's twin pillars of property and contract are not simply implicit within the U.S. political order. They are explicit in the very words of the Constitution, Article 1's specific protection of the contract being only a single example. As property and contract have remained central to the U.S. political and legal systems throughout the country's history, political science and jurisprudential studies that deal only with the public law, and public structures, are at best inadequate and, all too frequently, misleading.

The Constitutional Divide attempts to demonstrate that the U.S. political system is in large part the product of both the private and public legal and political traditions of Mother England. It will examine these two traditions within the multiple contexts of Anglo-American jurisprudential history, the U.S. Constitution and the argument over its ratification, and the Constitutional case law of the last two hundred years.

Both the private and public tradition will be considered from two distinct perspectives. The first is historical. With its public and private provisions, the U.S. Constitution is anything but a historically idiosyncratic document. For all of its direct provisioning of the new American order, it is still much a product of the long and wondrous progression of the English jurisprudence that preceded it. Legal and political understandings crafted as early as Henry II's assizes and the private and public law facilitations of Edward I through the writings of those such as Edward Coke and William Blackstone are clearly reflected within the United States' principal governmental document. Early English legal and political landmarks were all necessary precedents for the design, and underlying rationale, of governance which the U.S. Constitution eventually adopted. Knowing the Constitution outside of its historical context is simply not possible.

The second perspective essential for Constitutional understanding is ideological. America's governmental design has typically been labeled as conservative, in contrast to the radicalism of the Declaration of Independence. Only recently, since the entire Anti-Federalist collection was published by Herbert J. Storing in 1981, has the ideology of the whole Constitution, the first seven articles and the Bill of Rights together, been laid out in stark relief.[2]

To be sure, Charles Beard, early in this century, argued that the U.S. Constitution was greatly influenced by the economic motivations of the framers.[3] Whether valid or not, Beard's position did not investigate the arguments of the Anti-Federalists, who both opposed various provisions of the original seven articles and specifically argued for a Bill of Rights. Neither did Beard assess the ideological balance of the Constitution and the Bill of Rights together. He merely described how the interests of the framers allegedly affected their support for the Constitution.

When looked at in its entirety, the Anti-Federalists wrote very credibly about their objections to the Constitution. These thoughtful Americans believed the Constitution to be seriously flawed from the outset, and their critique still echoes in the current, ideologically laden debate between the private and the public sectors. The writings of the Anti-Federalists on the Constitution illustrate what a vigorous dialogue the debate over the Constitution was.

Unfortunately, many otherwise informed citizens are still not familiar with the Anti-Federalist position. At a conference a short time ago a fellow panel member claimed that he "had read *The Federalist Papers* fourteen times." I could not restrain myself from asking him how many times he had read the Anti-Federalist papers. When he conceded that he never had, I allowed that his omission was far from unique. Not long ago a political science professor at a distinguished western university told me that there were no ideological differences between the Federalists and the Anti-Federalists. They differed, he said, only in what institutional arrangements they thought would best serve the new republic. The Anti-Federalist papers, in fact, offer that necessary ideological critique of the Constitution which drew its strength from the well-honed, predemocratic positions of English and pre-Constitutional American history. In its modern context that position is as significant today as it ever was.

Therefore, just as the Constitution cannot be understood without a full and concurrent treatment of the United States' private as well as public sectors, so too it is not possible to study the ideology of the Constitutional and post-Constitutional arguments without conscious attention to the U.S. Constitutional divide. Here I will trace the history of the United States' ideological conflict, focusing, after a brief review of the English experience, on the period that began just before the adoption of the U.S. Constitution and ending with the Warren Burger Court response to the Earl Warren Court, along with criticisms of the Burger Court. Parenthetically, I should add that I do not believe that the Rehnquist Court has sat long enough or has set its ideological direction sufficiently (in spite of what some interpret as a recent swing to the Right) to include it systematically within this analysis. I have included a few significant early Rehnquist era cases when I thought they fairly represented a continuation of Burger Court themes.

The ideological divide that I will describe here reveals itself in the never-ending battle over the boundaries between the private and public sectors as well as in the battles that have gone on over the institutional prerogatives of courts and legislatures and, to a lesser extent, state and federal jurisdictions. The principal thesis of this work, however, is that the first divide, the divide between the private and public sectors, is both historically and ideologically more significant than the separations between and among the United States' political institutions, whether within the federal government or between state and federal government. I believe that the principal indicator of ideological bias in Anglo-American law falls along the private-to-public divide, not on what have proven to be the more temporary alignments of particular ideologies with particular governmental institutions such as the Congress and the Supreme Court, or governmental levels.

THE CONSTITUTIONAL DIVIDE

CHAPTER ONE

A Framework for Analysis—
The Components

Nearly all scholarship on English and American law and government has focused on institutional prerogatives. Traditional Anglo-American institutional and legal writings, in other words, have typically asked themselves if certain interests have benefited from the favor of particular institutions, specifically the courts and the legislatures. Whether the political victory of one side or another of the ideological argument was facilitated by the institutional support of that position's advocates is frequently the crux of such work.

Even the writings of notable Constitutional interpreters such as the late Alexander Bickel at Yale and Laurence Tribe at Harvard have been marked by their almost exclusively institutional perspectives. In my view at least two components must be added to the traditional framework of Anglo-American Constitutional analysis. The battle between the private and public sectors must be the first addition, because it is the real key to Constitutional comprehension. But, almost as important, a knowledge of the *forms* of law, whether made by judges or legislated, is also essential to an understanding of English and American ideological history.

What do I mean when I speak of the forms of law? Let us look, for example, at the form of the contract as it exists today within the private sector. Does the contract concern itself with only the direct economic considerations that were important to the two contracting parties? Or are other concerns, the concerns of other citizens, included within the contract? The traditional contract, the contract of early post-Norman England, reflected how much of the public sector the economic realm embraced in those early days. By the close of the nineteenth century in the United States the contract was surely of a far different form. Then, it was almost wholly stripped of public considerations. Into the twentieth century the infusion of new considerations concerning employment conditions, compensation, consumer protection, and the like make contemporary contracts far different from their late-nineteenth-century counterparts.

The components of this study's framework, therefore, are fourfold rather than twofold. They include (1) the identification of the substantive, ideological positions of various political interests, (2) the progress of that great jurisdictional divide that separates the private and the public sectors, (3) the conflict that has existed and still exists between various institutions and jurisdictions (most important, the Congress and the Supreme Court but, secondarily, the federal and the state governments), and, finally, (4) the change in the forms of key legal and political concepts, again the contract being the most important. Such a fourfold analysis of the development of Anglo-American law and politics should offer a perspective on the U.S. Constitutional arrangement which is richer than analyses based solely on ideological and institutional components can ever be.

The Ideological Debate

I define the substantive, political debate here as simply the ongoing struggle between and among individuals, groups, interests, and, most important, ideas that have competed throughout the Anglo-American political and legal experiences. As some interests have won and some have lost throughout this experience, any review of Anglo-American Constitutional law must chronicle the record and describe the patterns that have existed within it. The ideological line that has drawn such a pattern, whether labeled a "liberal-to-conservative" line or whatever, has been remarkably evident, and more often than not predictable, over the centuries. The hurly-burly of politics, as disorderly as it sometimes seems, is actually far from random. The positions of the political players—commercial, governmental, worker, consumer, environmental, gender based, race based and others—more or less rationally define what it is that each wants from the political system.

By the "liberal" position, I refer to the generally egalitarian position on matters such as the distribution of wealth and the recognition of "underdog" community interests. By the "conservative" position, I refer to nothing more than the traditionally individualistic and competitive perspective that generally champions both a less egalitarian distribution of wealth and, at least traditionally, a less responsive attitude toward underrepresented interests.

The Private-Public Divide

It is, once again, the principal thesis of this book that the single most differentiating line within all of Anglo-American jurisprudential history, and within the U.S. Constitutional experience, has been the line between the private and the public sectors. From the American perspective, understanding the Constitution's principal dividing line turns out not to be difficult. The private-to-public line inexorably evolved as the principal jurisdictional divider during the English experience. It is only natural that it would continue during the Constitutional drafting and ratification debates as well as throughout the Constitution's subsequent history.

From at least the time of Aristotle the question of what belonged in the private domain and what was part of the public domain has been central to political philosophy. The issues surrounding the balancing of the general good with the individual good are at the core of political thought. I make no claim to an original perspective on such issues here. What I hope to demonstrate, again, is that examinations of the division between the private and the public domains has been either ignored altogether or improperly relegated to a secondary place within traditional American Constitutional scholarship. In fact, it is of primary importance.

Institutions

With respect to the public institutions I will examine, I seek merely to show the ideological positions of governmental bodies such as the United States Supreme Court, the Congress, and, to a lesser degree, the federal presidency and the various branches of the state governments. In the following chapter, for example, I will review the battles between the monarchy and the legislature in post–Magna Carta England within the context of the interests that each institution typically represented. In the bulk of the work I will describe the struggles between the U.S. Congress (and to a lesser extent the state legislatures), on the one hand, and the federal Supreme Court, on the other. Again, I will do so within the context of the interests that these institutions typically represented. The question of who gets to make the rules can never be far from center stage in any ideologically based Constitutional history.

As I have said, most of the arguments in U.S. Constitutional scholarship have focused on the formal institutions of the United States' federal and state governments. Though these divides do not make up the primary fault line of the Constitution, the Constitutional positions of James Madison, Alexander Hamilton, John Marshall, and the other Federalists—as opposed to the positions of Richard Henry Lee, George Mason, Elbridge Gerry, and the Anti-Federalists generally—did reflect deeply felt preferences for particular governmental institutions over others. Those institutional preferences reverberated throughout U.S. history.

Quite obviously, the institutional preferences of these individuals and others like them have their own history. Those preferences can be traced to the configurations of institutions and ideologies in the English experience, although the American experience subsequently changed the way that these institutions were, more often than not, thought of. It certainly changed the arrangement of these institutions within the political system. Significantly, the ideological positions favored by various institutions exhibited a degree of ideological consistency over a long period of time, the legislature favoring the "liberal" position, and the courts protecting property rights for much of United States' history.

In fact, even as the United States' ideological-to-institutional alliances present a pattern of differentiation which has proven to be less consistent than the ideology-to-private-to-public sector alliance, we cannot ignore the ideological biases contained within the institutional arrangements of the Constitution. Beyond the first three, institutional, articles of the Constitution, the ideological history of the Bill of Rights (without which our Constitution would be a very different document indeed) reveals interesting and largely consistent patterns. Placing the Bill of Rights into its appropriate sectoral (private-to-public) position within the U.S. Constitutional arrangement should be fundamental to Constitutional analysis.

Cognitive Form

The fourth component of this analysis, the cognitive component, will be investigated with less detail than the other three. Nonetheless, it will prove to be important. Discussions of the forms of the private sector's principal vehicle, the contract, will attempt only to make clear the degree to which the components of a contract are either more or less exclusively of an economic, or valuational, nature or are imbued with other, often more publicly directed qualities as well. As mentioned, the early history of the English contract reveals how traditional feudal bonds still dictated much of a contract's substance. Later, governmental involvement with internationally competitive productivity led to the forms of mercantilism which, in turn, ensured that the contract continued to be at least a marginally synthetic document, cognitively speaking. Then, by the nineteenth century, the contract's form had evolved into something far more analytic. That late century's contract was more purely bilateral in the sense of including only the immediately contracting parties in its negotiations and agreements. By the time of the twentieth century's concern with just distribution as well as a more recent concern with the environment, worker safety, women's role in the workplace, etc., once again synthetic—that is, nondyadic and not specifically economic—matters are included in the contract. Tracing the contractual form is a necessary part of any analysis of private-to-public sectoral patterns as they have evolved throughout Anglo-American history. The forms, in actuality, lie on a continuum. I speak of more or less analytic or more or less synthetic contractual forms throughout.

With regard to the rulings of courts, there can, of course, be no uniformly agreed upon distinction between the analytic and the synthetic cognitive modes. I believe that it is still possible, however, to differentiate rather clearly between the analytic nature of New Deal–denying rulings such as *Schecter Poultry* (1936)[1] and *Carter v. Carter Coal* (1936),[2] which strongly ratified traditional notions of property and contract, and the more synthetic form of contract found in a Supreme Court ruling such as *Muller v. Oregon* (1908).[3] There Louis D. Brandeis's inclusion of sociological, and even physiological, evidence concerning the fatigue of workers received its first judicial notice. The expansive, novel considerations of the *Muller* case added a new, qualitatively synthetic dimension to the employment contract. Later, in the twentieth century, the synthetic cognitive form plays an increasingly important role, one might say a historically dialectical role, in the adaptive strategies of the Earl Warren Court.

In short, my reference to the cognitive nature of a private contract refers to whether the contract in a given period of Anglo-American legal history is (1) more or less embedded in a context of social and political understandings or (2) "clean" in the sense that its provisions include only the immediate parties to the contract and the almost wholly economic purposes of their bargain and sale.

Regarding legislation, by cognitive differentiation I refer merely to whether the statutory law, like Brandeis's legal brief, encompasses new or as yet unrecognized social, moral, cultural, or other considerations. An example of the synthetic cognition can be found in the essence of Franklin Roosevelt's attempt to include considerations of working conditions, health, fair remuneration, and other such matters into statutory holdings. Analytic legislation refines previous understandings, such as those found in the Uniform Commercial Code, which ratified the position of a good-faith purchaser in the normal course of trade. Such legislation achieved only a higher level of evidentiary certainty. It added little that was new to the law.

Not wishing to unduly complicate an understanding of the Constitution, I briefly include considerations of these cognitive forms of public political positions, legislation, court rulings, and the like, because I have no doubt that cognitive preferences for either analytic or synthetic qualities of contract, cases, or legislation are so often a part of the ideology of the argument. When seen in the context of historically significant ideological arguments, these distinctions facilitate an even deeper understanding of the Constitution. That the important work of Constitutional interpretation has given virtually no attention to the internal, cognitive forms of the elements it habitually studies has always astounded me. Perhaps this work will encourage further attention to this important consideration.

Linkages

Of course, the four components that I have defined have been deeply intertwined within Anglo-American jurisprudence, even from the time of the Norman Conquest. Such an intertwining was not just predictable; it was necessary. It was hardly coincidental, for example, that the period of the Anglo-American contract's most thorough shedding of social and political encumbrances (the nineteenth-century's robber baron period) came at the same time that (1) the judiciary in the United States held its greatest sway over the legislature in rule making and (2) the private and public sectors underwent what was probably their greatest imbalance (in favor of the private domain) in all of Anglo-American history.

Should it be surprising that the cognitively analytic "cleaning" of the contract that reached its zenith at the end of the nineteenth century occurred at the same time that the federal Supreme Court achieved a clear dominance over both the federal Congress and those state legislatures that tried to introduce cognitively "synthetic" concerns, dealing with safety and worker welfare, into the private contract? At that time, the private sector, protected by highly creative "substantive due process" interpretations of the Constitution's Fourteenth Amendment, more clearly dominated the rule making of the American polity than the private sector ever had or ever would again.

Similarly, at the beginning of the twentieth century, or during the Progressive period, the inclusion of political and social considerations such as child labor and maximum-hour restrictions within a contract was achieved by the legislative branches of the government. In a few instances during this period the legislative branches even overcame the resistance of a well-entrenched, generally pro–private sector Supreme Court. The beginning of institutional rebalancing experienced during that historical period not only reflected the alteration of power among various substantive political groupings. It also reflected the slow rebalancing of the private and public domains in favor of the public domain.

The coincidence of the purely private contract's analytic form with both the highest ascendance of judicial powers and the highest ascendance of the private over the public sectors was in itself remarkable. But something else happened that revealed, and intensified, the ideological cleavage between the private and the public sectors. At the level of cognitive form the turn of the twentieth century introduced a radical redirection in the way that certain scholars thought about the entire process of judicial rule making. Although it was long understood that the engine of legislative rule making was much a part of the bias of political interests, it was not until the twentieth century that discussions concerning the internal components of judicial rule making gained credibility within debates over Anglo-American judge-made law.

The notion that the law might not be, and might never have been, "discovered," along with the corresponding idea that judicial law might be "made" in a way that legislated law was made, was at first a very radical idea. But, whether influenced by the advent of Freudian-like discoveries concerning the human subconscious or by the fierceness of the Populist-inspired battles over the nearly unbridled rights of contract and property at the century's turn, the mask of judicial neutrality, the illusion of scientifically arrived-at decisions coming from the bench, slipped away from the judicial ruling soon after the turn of the century.

What is known as the legal realist position, of course, is what has given rise to the so-called judicial behavior movement, or the study of motivations and ideology in the development of Constitutional law. Politically, the lessons of legal realism can be used as well as a departure for examining the law in terms of its analytic or synthetic cognitive nature. But, if legal realism deprived the courts of the semblance of neutrality, it has also permitted legislatures to claim that they are not alone in their own biases and ideologies. Legal realism, though technically a jurisprudential methodology, and not an ideologically laden school or position, has changed the ideological interpretation of all U.S. Constitutional law, wherever that law might come from.

Of course, to a degree all law, whether judge made or legislated, marks the triumph of one substantive political position over another. Even within a doggedly atheoretical jurisprudence such as that which Anglo-American law held onto for so long, a retrospective vision demonstrates that patterns presented themselves as political forces, confronted each other, competed for dominance, and, for at least a time, controlled one or both of the principal realms of rule making—the legislature and the bench.

Yet throughout history something happened to disturb any institutional equilibrium that might have appeared permanent but was, inevitably, only temporary. New issues, often the result of new political forces coming to the fore, brought themselves before the public. The proponents of new political perspectives challenged the reigning order, and, after a time, many succeeded in changing that order, and sometimes changing the institutional balances of the political system in the bargain. The Crown was dispensed with altogether in the United States, and was incrementally retired as a serious rule-making participant in Great Britain. Meanwhile, the power balances between Congress and sometimes state legislatures, on the one hand, and the federal Supreme Court, on the other, have fluctuated widely throughout America's political history. Presidents, and of course governors, too, have frequently played their role.

In short, the struggle that changed each legal-to-political order into something new was almost invariably linked to changes in all four components of the ideological, public-to-private, institutional, and cognitive form balance. This was true even though the combatants of the day never themselves defined their struggles using this quadratic analysis. Indeed, the political contest that has taken place between and among all of the four components I have listed have defined themselves more clearly as Anglo-American history has unfolded. A better understanding of the linkages among the four components can now lead both to a clearer definition of each component as well as a clearer understanding of how the aggregation of these components led to the political realities that they did.

Surely, the interactions between and among the four components ebbed and flowed in their intensity as Anglo-American history moved along. But, as the ideological conflicts that have framed Anglo-American jurisprudence have proceeded throughout history, these interactions have also become more complex. In spite of this growing complexity, I think that the various alignments of ideological, private-to-public, institutional, and cognitive components, like the pre-turn-of-the-century pattern of the Gilded Age and the post-turn-of-the-century Progressive pattern, have also become clearer. In part they have become clearer because the components that they were made of have rather consistently refined and intensified their own political identifications as time has passed.

Whether the political confrontation involved Alexander Hamilton's national bank, John Marshall's protection of the interstate commerce clause, Oliver Wendell Holmes Jr.'s *Lochner* (1905)[4] dissent on long hours worked in a bakery, or whatever other legal or political confrontation we will examine, something very important to the lives of ordinary citizens was being fought over in each controversy. The everyday seeking of po-litical and legal advantage has always been the generating force in the ideological struggle. But political and legal argument has frequently oc-curred on both the political and legal battlefields, often simultaneously.

If real-world battles begin with everyday political actors seeking ev-eryday political advantage, the arena that they choose, and the form of the argument that they create, increasingly reveals the ideological nature of the political and legal argument itself. The private-to-public sectoral contrast, the institutional contrast, and the contrast between cognitive forms are thus related to the conflict over ideology, although I will show how the sectoral and form variables have proven to be more consistently related to ideology than has the institutional variable. Using all four sets of components that I have described, let us begin to trace the ideological history of Anglo-American jurisprudence.

CHAPTER TWO

The English Contribution

Magna Carta

Magna Carta was as important to Anglo-American jurisprudence because of its impact on the emerging English *private* law as it was important to the emerging public institutions of the English government. Magna Carta is well studied for its portentous political nature. But, if the beginnings of political democracy can be found in Magna Carta, as evidenced by the guarantees of baronial election as well as other guarantees of political reciprocity between king and baron, the document also evidences the beginnings of private sector independence. Chapter 9's assurance that "Neither we nor our bailiffs will seize any land or revenue for any debt, as long as the chattels of the debtor are sufficient to pay for the debt" is far more a statement of a private-law principle than a statement of public law. Though Magna Carta is far less studied for its effect on the private law (which became the bulk of the common law), the document has succeeded in fostering a bountiful private progeny throughout the space of the last nearly eight hundred years. In fact, it may not be too much to say that Magna Carta's importance derives from its inclusiveness; it contained practically all of what needed to be a part of any political and legal system at that time.

What did the barons want at Runnymede? What they wanted, and what made their document so important from the outset, was far more than a recognition that King John had treated them ill and that they deserved redress. The barons demanded the recognition of an entire legal and political order that had already been established but which had recently been violated with impunity. In its still feudal yet already evolving way, that English order placed the everyday political and legal realities of the realm into a well-defined, largely self-contained context. That context was exemplified within a contract, even though it was a contract in the very broadest sense of the word. In its infancy the legal contract was necessarily weighted down with political considerations.

Though Magna Carta embraced an entire set of relationships between royalty and aristocracy (and to a lesser degree royalty and common subject), the grand contract that it represented also embraced the conventions that concerned themselves with land, attachments to the land, chattel or personal property, and the interactional conventions that transferred these interests from one party to another. All of these considerations, even before Magna Carta, were to at least some degree legally protected as quasi-private or, perhaps better, pre-private institutions.

From a modern perspective Magna Carta may be but a piece of paper without a "broad statement of principle or defined political theory," as Bernard Schwartz has put it.[1] But even without the full dressings contained in a more modern political document such as the U.S. Declaration of Independence or the Constitution, Magna Carta is still instructive in the modern era. As I have said, the entire legal and political order that Magna Carta both represented and resurrected is within the document. But it is the proximity of the legal to the political jurisdiction within the document which is so intriguing. For all of its wonder Magna Carta only strengthened the deep bonds of those purposes in England's law which in 1215 still did not demand neat distinctions between the private and public spheres.

Politically, Magna Carta dealt not only with that part of the law that assayed the political prerogatives of the Crown and the barons. Its pre-private notions marked that sense of the early English law that there would be limitations on what the government could do to any property holding. As Schwartz has said, there are "precise limits to scutage, feudal reliefs, wardship and the like" within Magna Carta.[2] Each of these limits, Schwartz assures us, was written in "legally enforceable terms against a king who had claimed to be all but a law unto himself."[3] Though deeply a part of what was still a feudal arrangement, Magna Carta's provisions, unlike those of Continental feudalism, were healthy forerunners both of today's private sector and, more particularly, of the contract as a private sector–facilitating document. The need for the private contract was found in the bonded relationship that some British citizens had with their own landed and personal property, not just with their king and their barons.

Subsequent refinements of Magna Carta witnessed changes in terminology that, for example, substituted *any baron* for *any free man*. Such alterations had momentous portent for the future constitutional development of English law. One of the most interesting divisions between these pre-private and a pre-public forms of ownership is defined by Charles Montgomery Gray in his review of the evolution of the common law. Gray distinguishes between those individuals who held their land title by a free tenure (and could therefore appeal to the common-law courts for protection of their title) and those who held only what was called "villein" tenure. Those who possessed only villein tenure were still very much a part of a feudal (manorial) political and economic system; they could not, accordingly, access the emerging common-law courts. This prohibition held true, according to Gray, because the lawyers of the day "thought naturally of an area in which [feudal] landlords were entitled to manage their relations with characteristically servile tenants."[4]

Again, it is Bernard Schwartz who, in characterizing the Great Charter, noted that the "breadth of the language used [in Magna Carta] has made it serve a far wider purpose" than just the resolutions of a momentary squabble between an obstreperous king and his offended barons.[5] Citing the great English jurist Sir Edward Coke, Schwartz argued that the chapter dealing with the rights of free men in their protection from being "captured or imprisoned or disseised or outlawed or exiled" (chap. 39) was anticipatory of precisely what Americans now call "due process of law."[6]

What, specifically, does due process of law protect in the modern sense? It protects life and liberty, but it also protects property. All in all, Magna Carta's chapter 39 protection of an array of private, largely landed rights not only strengthened the common law of property but was also illustrative of how the common law itself would stand as a bastion of protection either from arbitrary kingly intrusions or from any distortion of law that a king might use to intrude upon property and contract rights. The protection of those private rights has been a part of government and law within the Anglo-American tradition until the current day. But, as the private-to-public balance of those rights is not always well understood, we need briefly to trace the development of domains that became increasingly separate after the time of Magna Carta.

Henry II and Edward I

Magna Carta may have defined a realm, but, without question, it was a realm that had but recently evolved toward a universal law. The many localities of early post-Norman England had their own laws, and they possessed little inclination, or ability, to square them with anyone else's. The dispersion of political power during the reign of William I and his immediate successors, after William had awarded lands to his followers broadly throughout the kingdom, only barely represented political hegemony. Legal hegemony, a commonness of all the laws of a newly conquered land, was simply too much to ask of post-Norman England's early moments.

Little more than one hundred years after the 1066 invasion, however, it was clear to at least some of the barony, and fortunately to Henry II, that the realm would be better off if a legal reconciliation could be established throughout the land. What followed was a succession of assizes, French sittings, in which Henry hosted a number of conferences with his judges and legal advisors. Such conferences permitted Henry to slowly weave together the fabric of what is now the unified common law. As Sir William Holdsworth, a prominent English legal historian put it, the work of Henry II's assizes so firmly established the "centralized law" and placed it upon "the basis of fixed rules of practice" that it was possible for the law to immediately thereafter "stand the strain of an absent King (Richard I), a bad King (John I), and an infant King (Henry III)."[7]

Significantly, the noble work of real-world political and legal figures throughout the common law's history has almost uncannily been matched by the equally noble efforts of the great chroniclers of the law. Throughout English law these greatest chroniclers, as Holdsworth lists them, have included Glanvil, Bracton, Littleton, Coke, and Blackstone. Each of their contributions was unique and timely.

Glanvil, the first of the English giants of the law, captured the products of Henry II's assizes and made them into a readable and important history. It was Glanvil who wrote it all down, recording how a still very undeveloped common law had at least been bound into the single, reasonably coherent whole that Henry II had wished for. Significantly, Glanvil began to make note of the law's procedures as well as its substance. Though he dealt largely with the criminal law, as well as with the land law that was emerging as the bedrock of the medieval English legal order, he also scrupulously depicted the rules for attaining relief according to the law as those rules existed in a still very early age. How one gained access to the law that came from the courts, rather than from political pleading and favor in the king's courtyard, was already a significant part of the English legal tradition. Glanvil understood that, and he explained it well for those who wished to practice the evolving English law in increasingly routinized ways.[8]

But, if the English law was unified by Henry II and ratified in scholarly fashion by Glanvil, it was not until the thirteenth century that the writings of Henry Bratton, or Bracton, revealed the deep tensions that existed within the still only recently unified law. Those tensions, less than a century after Magna Carta, began to reflect the more decisive definitional boundaries between the private and public components of the law which the Great Charter had seemed to mingle so easily. Bracton's writings, unlike Glanvil's, were a spur to legal reform—specifically, a further freeing of the private law from the shackles of the public, still largely feudal order.[9] The reign of Edward I, at the close of the thirteenth and the very beginning of the fourteenth century, responded to both Bracton and the realities of the need for an increasingly facilitative private law.

Specifically, the tensions between the public and the private sectors of the law that Edward I dealt with were tensions between those elements of the law that regulated private business and those that maintained the political bondings of a still largely feudal political arrangement. Edward is the figure that he is in English law because of his artful rebalancing of those conflicting needs in favor of the private, not the public, sector.

With the Statute of Merchants in 1285, for example, Edward recognized the importance of debt enforcement for the creditor. With the Statute of Rolls of the same year, he ensured that debts would be both well recorded and easily redeemed. With the Statute de Donis, also passed in 1285, Edward dug even deeper into the land law, girding the private domain by guaranteeing that conditional titles would be invalid at the same time that he established the entail, which did permit family retention of land through succeeding generations.[10] The private-to-public balance was always to be precarious. But an entail, thought Edward, would permit only the kind of minimal encumbrance on the sale of land which protected family interests and then only while there were surviving heirs. The need for the ready transferability of land, in order to accommodate a fluidity of ownership, meant that encumbrances on the land would be far more circumscribed than they were with only a conditional title. Existing baronial families could continue to protect only their own family's lineage.

Slowly, as William Holdsworth has put it, Edward's reforms meant that "the jurisdictional and governmental elements in feudalism were being eliminated." The basis of the law, accordingly, became "more distinctly the law of property."[11] All of this happened at the time that common laws protecting procedures were being developed beyond those chronicled by Glanvil. As the greatest of the modern historians of English law, F. W. Maitland, has said, "That part of the law that is unenacted, non-statutory, that is common to the whole and to all Englishmen" (and is therefore a product of the courts even during Edward's reign), was beginning to regulate the land law.[12] By the end of Edward's reign the courts had begun to take their proper place as the institutional protectors of such law.

At the same time that he fostered the "liberation" of the private from the public law, Edward I also began to sort out the postfeudal arrangement of the English government. As Holdsworth has written, by the late thirteenth century "we see the beginnings of a House of Lords, consisting of the greater barons, and by its side a House of Commons in which representatives from the counties and boroughs take their places."[13] An embryonic parliament was coming into being.

Further, as Maitland noted, that parliament already possessed a bit of clout. Edward had conveniently responded to the churches' claim that he could revoke the Statute of Mortmain by pointing out that, since Parliament had passed the statute, which prevented landowners from burying their land titles in the tax-free church (but continuing to retain beneficial control), only Parliament could revoke the statute. Though the king was still "free to legislate without the Commons representatives," according to G. W. J. Barrow, "there was a distinct tendency in Edward I's reign for law-making by statute to be linked to meetings of Parliament."[14]

Edward I would have been secure enough in English legal history with his fostering of these pieces of common law–sustaining legislation and his fostering of the English government's institutional development. But, in order to further accommodate the merchants of the day and, more pointedly, to accommodate the alienation or sale of property which was the essence of commerce, Edward was responsible for one further piece of legislation which propelled the mercantile enterprise into what was soon known as the universal Law Merchant. In 1290 Edward passed the Statute of Westminster III: Quia Emptores. This statute, as Arthur Hogue has described it, was "clearly a compromise" between the feudal and the commercial interests of the day. On the one hand, it freely permitted "the complete alienation or sale of a tenure" in land. But, at the same time, it prohibited "the addition of new links in the existing chain of tenure." This latter provision, Hogue points out, would "tend ultimately to bring all tenants into the same relationship with the Crown."[15] Yet, even with this provision, Edward was not concerned with some abstract principle of the law. He was concerned primarily with the collection of escheats (a return of title to the Crown when there is no heir), which served as an assurance of the king's and the public sector's ultimate responsibility for the realm.

All in all, both the private sector and the public domain stewardships of King Edward I were noteworthy for treading that thin line between the feudal requirements of Edward's day and the necessity of encouraging wealth-producing private entities within the realm. The compromise between the private and the public sectors centered, above all, on the status of land. Another modern historian of the English law, Stephen Pollock, cites Sir Edward Coke's observation that Edward's timely revisions of the land law were far from being uncontroversial. "Infinite were the scruples, suits and inconveniences" of something like the Statute de Donis, said Coke, for, though de Donis certainly facilitated the alienation of property, Coke was quick to note that only the large landowners benefited from the setting up of such devices as the family-based interest of entail. Pollock noted, based on Coke once more, that from the time of the statute "legal ingenuity set to work to turn the position" of those who benefited from it originally to those who could also figure out a way around the statute.[16]

The commercial interest's strategy for circumventing the Statute de Donis (acting not just as the businessmen of their day but also as the principal users of a common law that would favor those who engaged in contract) was to figure out a way to provide "security to the purchasers" of any landed property. Put another way, commercial interests wanted to lessen "the danger of stale or fictitious claims of title" by guaranteeing that a title passing in the regular course of trade would always be good.[17] This guarantee, of course, would act as an incentive to trade; the commercially attained status of ownership would always be protected.

Thus, under Edward the ingenious common law–using, private sector entrepreneur facilitated the commercial transaction as vigorously as anyone had done so far. Such facilitation meant that the common law was to grow, particularly within the courts and not just from statutes devised by a king and his parliament. It was not to grow from the writings, however noteworthy, of those like Glanvil and Bracton. The common law, from Edward's time hence, grew principally from the creative uses of everyday business ventures and from the need for legal, court-generated protections of those uses. The disputes that were occasionally precipitated by these uses needed to be resolved. The appearance of these resolutions as early as the thirteenth century demonstrates that the hint of privatism found in Magna Carta had been well nourished by the latter part of the century. As Arthur Hogue states, by "the end of the thirteenth century the close personal relationships of lord and vassal had given way to more commercial monetary interests" in the law.[18]

Pausing for a moment, let us note here that what we see by the time of Edward I is not only a separating out of the private and the public sectors in a way that the Magna Carta had foretold but had not substantially accomplished. What we also see is that the institutions of the government, the courts as well as the king and the parliament, were beginning to develop themselves into the separate governmental, that is public, institutions that could and sometimes would oppose one another over their respective attempts to manipulate statutory and judge-made law.

Let us not forget that beyond his descriptions of the parliamentary institutions, Maitland also recounted the development of the courts under Edward I. By the end of the thirteenth century the King's Bench, the Common Bench or Court of Common Pleas, and the Exchequer Court, for example, had each formed their "own common sphere." Already the best friend of the commercial interests was the royal court, the court that could, by the inventiveness of new "writs," or pleas, give necessary relief to those whose dealings were undertaken in good faith. These were the purchasers who needed the title of what they bought to be good. Again, it was the royal courts that gave them clear title.[19]

By the close of the thirteenth century, of course, the common law was still not at the point in its development where the holder of a note for a debt would receive what the United States' modern Uniform Commercial Code (UCC) calls "holder in due course" status. Such status gives a high presumption of ownership to a seller who is acting in the normal course of trade, thus severely restricting what the common law knew as "personal" defenses against such ownership. Overwhelmingly, the modern UCC gives title to the good faith buyer who purchases something for value in the normal course of trade, without knowledge of any fraud or deception.

Yet we can already see that by Edward's time the courts in particular, and even the king and his parliament to some degree, were bending to the requirement that the commercial transaction needed to have a validity to it as something that transcended the still powerful feudal rigidities. Those rigidities often had bonded land titles to noble families and kings and even encumbered personalty. The dogged existence of these conventions, which tied property to a lineage and encumbered that property's sale, was something that Thomas Jefferson still needed to deal with in the eighteenth century on this side of the Atlantic when he outlawed landed entail and primogeniture.

Nonetheless, as the private and public sectors of thirteenth-century England slowly pulled themselves apart, so too the institutions of the English government increasingly drew themselves to one side or the other in the political debates of the time. The separation of these institutions was not permanent in the institutional-to-interest alliance, but it was sufficiently regularized that courts were rightfully regarded as the principal instrument of the emerging common law. While an institution such as the House of Lords, not unexpectedly, typically favored the barons, the Exchequer Court was the first court to have a separate, private law protecting legal jurisdiction, apart from the "government." Though it was made up of members of the king's council, this court had the distinction of not being required to route cases through the king's chancellor, even as early as the thirteenth century. Entrepreneurs liked that arrangement and used it regularly.

In short, it was the emerging common-law courts such as Exchequer, even if they were truly royal courts in their origin, which listened to the newly created, property-protecting writs of the declining English feudal period. These courts found ways around the rigidities of feudalism in order to give individual relief, and equity, to the industrious entrepreneur, not the rent-collecting landed nobility. The courts, though public institutions, were beginning to have a private identity and an increasingly private clientele.

Finally, if very tentatively, the private-law institution of the contract, although still encumbered compared to its modern-day form, was already beginning that process of "cleansing" itself from the bondage of feudal understandings. Still a long way off was the idea of a contract undertaken by parties largely separated from the public interest. But the movement in that direction was, by Edward's reign, not only clearly discernible; it was inexorable. The interests of those who engaged in contracts demanded contracts of this new nature, and commercial interests were beginning to be in a position to have their demands listened to.

Law and Equity

To be thorough, let us remind ourselves that the common law was not always the inventive and flexibly adaptive instrument of the entrepreneur which it was during most of Edward's reign and at other times in English history. Even toward the close of Edward's unusually productive stewardship, the common law was beginning to undergo a kind of a self-inflicted stagnation which would significantly change its role within English jurisprudence. The ossification of the law which occurred, in its own way, was as damaging to it as any return to the early feudal bondages might have been. By the close of the fourteenth century the common-law writs, originally devised to facilitate the legal enforcement of inventive private interactions, had become both so numerous and so arcane that those who came before what had only recently been highly accessible courts were increasingly frustrated by their inability to attain relief. What Holdsworth called the "decay" of the common law "into a rigid and technical system" unfortunately typified much of fourteenth-century English law.[20]

In great part the problem with fourteenth-century common-law courts resulted from a change in the profession of the individuals who

staffed them. Though the private members of the legal profession, lawyers and judges, were initially a healthy counterbalance to the often
overschooled, canon law and Roman law–loving scholars and judges of
an earlier time, the fourteenth-century common-law practitioners soon
began to suffer from their own brand of insularity. Thus, just as nominal-
istic scholars had fashioned a legal rigidity out of their attempts to maintain the principles of an earlier time on the Continent, the English lawyers
of the fourteenth century began jealously to protect their exclusive access
to the law. Not unexpectedly, they also lost the sense of justice which
earlier practitioners had attempted to infuse into the law.

As a result, writs multiplied. They also became less understandable
to the layman, and even experienced commercial practitioners were increasingly baffled over what they could do to attain fair and timely relief
within the context of the daily business rush. As a result of these difficulties, the common law's progress stopped, for a while. The "System of
Forms of Action or the Writ System" in England which Maitland noted
"was not abolished until its piecemeal destruction in the nineteenth century" would begin to encumber the law nearly as much as the feudal impediments had encumbered it before Edward.[21]

It is extraordinary that, during the one time when the evolving common law arrested itself from the necessary adaptations of a changing time,
another English political institution, the institution of the king's chancellor, arose in such a way as to continue the development of the English
law. Before the fifteenth century the chancellor was almost exclusively a
church officer, his obligations with regard to the law being essentially
those of a record keeper. But, as the law became less friendly in the fourteenth century, a century when the Crown itself was less accessible (and a
century when both the Hundred Years' War and the Great Plague bedeviled the nation), the chancellor found it simpler to give substantive legal
advice, though quietly, to those frustrated commercial interests that could
not locate the correct writ before a common-law court.

It was not long before it became obvious to the chancellor that his
own granting of some direct, if informal, judgment about the equities of
a dispute would facilitate the resolution of that dispute far better than his
procedural advice on how the labyrinthine common-law courts could be
approached. After that realization it wasn't long before the chancellor's
office simply transformed itself into a separate, highly effective court.

That chancellor's court, of course, was soon to become known as a
court of equity, a place in which an expeditious, and usually quite fair,
legal result could be garnered. Merchants liked this easy and just access
to whatever helped them get on with their business. Even today, though
the equity jurisdiction largely has been remerged with the law courts,

equity pleadings still place the requirements for "clean hands," "the exhaustion of legal remedies," and other fair-minded notions before those who seek equitable forms of relief. Equity's full legitimation by the time of the fifteenth century has never been reversed. As Maitland summed it up, it was "becoming plain that the Chancellor is doing some convenient and useful works that could not be done, or could not easily be done, by the courts of common law."[22] Its indispensability was enough to make equity a permanent part of that forever practical English sense of justice.

And so, even if the private English law needed to march on without the common law for a while, it sojourned rather well. The private law's needs, and the needs of those commercial interests that most used the common law, were only temporarily impaired when that law became rigid and restrictive rather than dynamic and commercially facilitative. With all of the trauma over the arcane writs, it was the institution, the court, that was paralyzed, not the law itself. The common-law courts, in a sense, were but temporarily defaulting to the chancellor and the equity courts.

As the private sector's laws continued to grow unabated, their need to be increasingly separated from the encumbrances of the last vestiges of feudalism, or to some extent from government generally, grew as well. The private sector, and the increasingly cleansed, postfeudal contract that the private sector used to transact its business, merely found a home in another place. Both the equity court and the law court prospered under this new relationship. Something that was particularly apparent in the areas of landlord and tenant law, as Pollock points out, was that Chancery had "created a true right of property in the tenant."[23] By the end of the fourteenth century "the farmer's possession was as secure while his estate lasted as the freeholder's."[24] Such certainty was also evident in the area of trusts. Often, as Pollock puts it, judicial recourse with regard to trusts "was had to the extraordinary jurisdiction of the Chancellor, a power still fresh, flexible and ambitious."[25]

Thus, even with its fourteenth-century jurisdictional detour, the record of the common law as a flexible and facilitative set of substantive doctrines, and as a set of procedural regularities which made those doctrines useful, was most laudable. Hogue puts it nicely, noting that, while "at times practitioners of absolutism, both royal and popular, threatened to sweep aside the substance of common-law rules" and while "at other times civil wars interrupted the operation of common-law courts," the common law redoubtably survived.[26] "More than once the common-law system has been in peril of its life," Hogue said.[27] But even the War of the Roses, and even in spite of the "reception" of certain tenets of the Roman Law in the sixteenth century and the outright disregard for the common law which followed Elizabeth I's death in 1603 (bringing on the Stuart absolutists, which we will attend to in the next chapter), the private sector–dominated common law continued to be the law of the land.

Then, after the Stuarts—that is, in the early days of democracy with England's increasingly institutionalized Parliament and the threats to the common law brought by the increase of legislative statute—the judicial law still endured. If their writs were abolished, as we perhaps should have expected, more flexible causes of action took their place. As Hogue said, the common-law system survived democracy because "so many Englishmen, common lawyers, country squires, and city merchants [had] been drawn into the operation of a legal system which has borne directly on the incidents of their daily life."[28] And, as he put it again, "in their minds, title to property and enjoyment of personal liberty have been intimately associated with the perpetuation of the common law."[29]

In sum, the law's "technical complexity," its early linkage to the land, and, perhaps more than anything, the "ability of [the law's] practitioners to adapt the legal system to new conditions," is what saved it.[30] Inevitably, that law, in its turn, saved the evolvingly separate private sector, and particularly the twin pillars of property and contract, which would forever remain the buttresses of the private domain.

CHAPTER THREE

Revolution
and Counterrevolution

Coke's Revolution

Not unexpectedly, it was the newly well-developed common law that was to stand, nearly four hundred years after Magna Carta, as the principal bastion of liberty against the Stuart king's political outrages. Under the Tudor king Henry VIII, the Crown, according to George Trevelyan, had set itself "in alliance with the strongest forces of the coming age—London, the middle classes, the seagoing population."[1] These now powerful commercial interests, emboldened by the favorable attentions of the sixteenth-century Tudors and armed with their increasingly liberated understanding of the common law, were fully prepared to challenge James I and his seventeenth-century Stuart successors. The key figure in the challenge had been the figure whom virtually all common law observers point to as understanding England's political and legal arrangements better than anyone: Edward Coke.

Sir Edward Coke is properly known for many things, not the least of which was his brave personal confrontation with James I and the consequent loss of his judgeship, which nearly brought an end to a distinguished career. Yet we should not forget that Coke was, before all, a private lawyer. Moreover, he was the lawyer who assured himself of early notoriety by arguing every law school freshman's bugaboo exercise, *Shelley's Case*. In *Shelley* Coke took a complicated will in which the proper disposition of real property was not clear and found a rationale for the case's decision which made the case central to Anglo-American jurisprudence forevermore. Coke's reasoning in *Shelley* was difficult, sometimes tortuous. The Court's opinion combined the remainder interest with the life estate and thus ensured the payment of the feudal reliefs, on the one hand. But, on the other hand, it also merged the two interests into an easily alienated, fee simple title. This facilitation of property alienation is what made *Shelley's Case* so important.[2]

Thus, though Coke's treatment of the *Shelley* testator was at best questionable, the case's ruling was clearly a commercially favorable decision. Whatever the justice of the dispute between those who had dealt with different branches of the Shelley family, the case crystallized the legal sanctity of the land-based business interaction, Coke ensuring that the buying and selling of real property through the institution of the contract, without the encumbrances of feudally descendent, testator-generated restrictions, would be inviolable.

Apart from its contractually facilitative aspects, the meaning of *Shelley* for the law today is one that Hastings Lyon and Herman Block properly note accents the certainty of the law over legal uncertainty. "While it was arbitrary, so are many other fundamental rules of law," say Lyon and Block. If "the title would be in suspension or abeyance," the condition of that title would be something "the law did not favor."[3]

So it was, again, the certainty of the law—the law's predictability and the furtherance of commercial enterprise which that certainty encouraged and still does encourage—which was the hallmark of the early-seventeenth-century legal challenge to the Stuarts. If any challenge to the political abuses of the king was to be justifiable legally, the law, even in cases that had nothing to do with the government, must stand close scrutiny as something that spoke with reason far better than the king.

Just as in *Shelley*, Coke's successful argument in *Dr. Bonham's case* (1610) further advanced the progress of reason in the common law. Here Coke was arguing something that directly impacted government. He contended that anyone's benefiting from a case upon which he stood as a judge simply defied reason. Since the London Board of Physicians stood to benefit from a decision against Bonham, Coke's position, at a minimum, would stand as an example of the common law's search for simple fairness. But, even more important, the case is an example of how a common-law court could strike down an act of Parliament. As Coke himself put it, "when an Act of Parliament is against common right and reason, or repugnant, or impossible to be performed, the common law will control it and adjudge such Act to be void."[4]

By 1616 both Coke and the reason of the common law were ready for full battle with the Stuarts, who themselves were not easily reasoned with. Coke and the first Stuart, James I, struggled openly over the king's appointment to an office of someone who may well have not been popular with the citizenry. As Lyon and Block point out, the holding of a public office had typically been "regarded as substantially a vested property," or something that could be "bought and sold," even before the Stuarts.[5] James's outrage at Coke's opposition to a kingly appointment, expressed through the king's fawning chancellor, Francis Bacon, is instructive for understanding the nature of much of the struggle between law and government as well as the private law's role as the preserver of personal liberty into the seventeenth century.

James's response to Coke's advice on the king's appointment was pungent at the least, boasting in the first sentence that "we have never studied the Common Law of England." James was responding to Coke's mock solicitation informing the king that "in case letters come to us contrary to law, . . . we do nothing by such letters" because the law is concerned with things like "the case between two for private interest and inheritance earnestly called on for Justice and expedition." As Magna Carta had made plain, the law, in substance as well as in method, should stand in opposition to public officers who violated it. Coke's comfort with such a role for the law was precisely what caused James such upset.[6]

All of this, of course, is prelude to Coke's greatest achievement within both the development of the law and the development of democracy in England. That achievement was the Petition of Right. It was this marvelous document, penned in 1628, which responded to the indulgences of Charles I, who had assumed the Crown in 1625 and immediately exceeded his predecessor in attacking the liberties, private as well as public, of the English citizenry. One of Charles's greatest excesses concerned a forced loan from the public coffers which even Parliament rejected and about which Coke exclaimed, "Shall I be made a tenant-at-will for my liberties?"[7] Note the real-property metaphor in this protest. Note as well the language within the petition itself which attacked the loan proposal as being "against reason and the franchise of the land."[8] These two cardinal elements of the law, of course, were close cousins in the eyes of Sir Edward.

In sum it was the common law itself—more private than public and far more legally defined than statutorily enacted—which Edward Coke both relied upon and contributed to throughout his historic career. From *Shelley* to the petition it was Coke's continued use of legal reason—as reason had evolved throughout the common law's substantive protections, procedural remedies, and the writings of Glanvil, Bracton, and more recently Sir John Fortescue[9]—which both stood up to the unlawful acts of the Crown and advanced the notion of a private law that was beginning to be altered by a public, legislative institution. Coke, the great upholder of reason in the law, encouraged that reason to grow beyond its private moorings and expand into a public domain that might properly call itself democratic within the lifetime of this solitary figure. The quality of that public law, and even the quality of those institutional mechanisms that were soon either created or enlarged upon to create the public law, would continue to be in dispute as history evolved. But the sanctity of the element of reason within the law, and the certainty in the minds of Coke and others of his time that the law and its reason were superior to a king's law, was the spur to England's parliamentary, wonderfully democratic progress.

At one level the growing tension between the private and the public sectors during this seventeenth-century period was in good part the result of the argument over rationalism's institutional sources. The question of whose reason was to be used in the determination of disputes, and what difference it made, was not yet fully on the legal or political table. But the debate over whether the court or the government would best approach reason was at the heart of a great deal of seventeenth-century English political, and legal, history.

In the seventeenth century, more than at any previous time, tensions between the private and public sectors threatened to unravel the peace of the commonwealth. A struggle between the institutions of the Crown and the legislature surely existed too, but the legislature's opposition to the Tudors in the previous century had largely been subdued by an alliance between the monarchy and Parliament during at least the early part of that century. In the seventeenth century the real institutional struggle was therefore between the private common law, with its courts and its adherents among the commercial orders, on the one hand, and the public, political institutions of a Stuart England, on the other. James's 1616 response to Coke, noted earlier, marked that century's ideological-to-institutional alliance.

In a modern time many still see the government or the public domain as standing in opposition to private rights. But in the seventeenth century it was the private sector's law that underpinned the uneven but inevitable progress of democracy within England's public governance. In a manner of speaking, Coke's arguments constituted a generous "lending" of the reason of the private, common law to the political law. Coke's 1616 suggestion concerning a linkage between public preferences and a public appointment insisted that the government utilize the quality of reason that was already found in the private law.

If Coke, in his time, was not successful in making mandatory that lending of the private law's reason to the public law, the events that marked the close of the century—particularly those surrounding the Glorious Revolution of 1688—made the institutional imperative clear to the political branches. Institutionally, the revolution's now secure beachhead for democracy ordained the permanence of the legislature. And the substantive political results of this legislative repositioning marked the final ascendance of the mercantile class to at least some importance in politics, just as it marked the checkmating of Crown, church, and aristocracy. As Barrington Moore Jr. has pointed out, after the Glorious Revolution "Parliament was more than a committee of landlords; urban commercial interests had at least some indirect representation."[10]

With regard to the private and public sectors, England's institutional repositioning after 1688 made clear not only that the reason of the law would control public governing but also that the government's principal purpose, in the mercantile era, would be to serve the private sector. Looking for a moment at the cognitive variable defined in chapter 1, we should note that the nature of the seventeenth-century contract was still far from the even purer forms that the contract of two hundred years later was to assume. The franchises, subsidies, and monopolies given to such mercantile mainstays as the East India Company, the Hudson Bay Company, and other enterprises charged with enhancing the English balance of trade all reflected a relationship between government and business which was quite synthetic in its form. Nonetheless, the seventeenth-century mercantile understanding confused the private and public sectors far less than the encumbering relics of a feudal England had confused the sectors centuries earlier. The cognitive nature of the contract and the property that it sold had largely shorn itself of those public relics.

Blackstone's Counterrevolution

The legal and political lessons of the great Coke had an important influence on the founding fathers. In many ways, they exceeded both (1) the political lessons of someone like John Locke on the founding fathers (note Gary Wills's reflection on the relative unimportance of Locke to the founders)[11] and (2) the real-world lessons of the immediate period of the American Revolution. Though the direct influence of William Blackstone's *Commentaries*[12] on America's new government may have been great, the evolution of the substantive history of Anglo-American law and politics, along with the evolution of the institutional, private-to-public, and cognitive nature of the law that Coke was responsible for, contributed in no small way to the success of the American political experiment.

The four volumes of Blackstone's *Commentaries* are turgid stuff. They chronicle, classify, define, and occasionally exhort, and they do so with an overwhelming confidence that the common law had, by the mid-eighteenth century, reached that final stage of development which, almost by definition according to Blackstone, required no further modification. But, if what happened throughout the period from Magna Carta to the eighteenth century was the development of an intellectual and real-world legal rationalism (without much room for differentiation among the various kinds of rationalism), then Blackstone's writings mark the end of any claim to rationalism's neutrality.

Apart from their content the *Commentaries* are nothing if not intellectually pretentious. They claim a "science" for themselves, and for the common law they claim something that needs to be distinguished from the Continental civil law, with the latter's necessity for professorial lectures "upon the institutes of Justinian and the local constitutions of his native soil."[13] Blackstone, from the beginning, was not above patronizing, bowing to say, "Far be it from me to derogate the study of the [European] civil law, considered . . . as a collection of written reason."[14] But, though Blackstone might be "persuaded of the general excellence of its (the civil law's) rules," he cautioned his English brethren not to "carry our veneration so far as to sacrifice our Alfred and Edward to the manes of Theodosius and Justinian."[15]

The burden of this position, again, was that Blackstone thought the English common law had gone about as far as it could go, or needed to go. The emerging English law, and particularly the law's housing within the legal profession rather than within the academy, as well as the common law's having come directly to the tenets of the natural law through the reasoning of daily decisions rather than the directions of political rule, all made the English law superior to the Continental law for Blackstone.

At the institutional level such mid-seventeenth-century immodesty was music to the ears of the now politically empowered English mercantile interests. At one time this vision of the English law conveniently kept the legislature, a harbinger of democratic progress as it increasingly worked against the Stuart kings, from getting too powerful and from thus turning against the mercantilists. At the same time, it kept the private protections of the original common law intact; the court-to-legislature line of institutional demarcation still paralleled the private-to-public line of jurisdictional separation. Substantively, a well-circumscribed legislature meant that the mercantile class would have little to fear from overly egalitarian levelers. The rights of landowning Englishmen and the process of rule making concerning these rights should remain in the legal jurisdiction, or in the hands of the courts. It should never fall to a political jurisdiction and certainly not to a parliament.

But, again, if Coke's seventeenth-century legal rationalism was relatively uncontroversial, and ultimately predemocratic, it was Blackstone, in the eighteenth century, who slammed the democratic gears into reverse. As a result, the newly empowered merchants could cheer on someone who decried the fact that the English "statute book is swelled to ten times a larger bulk" than it was but a short time earlier.[16] Such a position also revealed how Blackstone's preferred form of that law, the increasingly lucid, increasingly analytic form of the contract, dominated the law. Just as there was exactitude to the Newtonian world and just as there was precision in the Copernican heliovision, so too there would be what Blackstone called "a discipline so wise and exact that it need not be further tinkered with or in any way disturbed."[17] Very important for the merchants of the late eighteenth century, not to mention for the industrial capitalists of the coming nineteenth century, a precise and certain vision of the common law meant that little would have to be done by Parliament to keep the legal and political equilibriums of England precisely where they were. These equilibriums were now balanced where the newly vigorous private sector wanted them to be. Blackstone assured the mercantilists that, just as the private sector would have no further need (per Coke) to loan its reason to the public sector for democracy's improvement, so too there would be no need for the public sector to loan what might be its own reason back to the private sector. The necessity for public legislation, as a result, should be minimal.

A discernible shift of legal and political bearing was therefore at work in Blackstone's writings. With his talk of "science" and of "the wondrous involuntary manner" of so much of the universe (reminiscent of not only Newton but also of Adam Smith's "invisible hand"), Blackstone's sense of legal perfection gave to the common law something that would later be regarded as sterile, even brittle.

More than anyone, the United States' former librarian of Congress Daniel Boorstin criticized Blackstone's bearing on the common law, specifically citing Blackstone's use of the notion of "primitivism" as a bulwark against innovation.[18] This primitivism, according to Boorstin, not only limited "man's freedom to change the law" (through public institutions) but also gave to the law's structure, as Boorstin explained it, "the primitivistic conviction that the original form of the legal system had been one pure and rational simplicity."[19]

Of course, Boorstin considered such a depiction of an original, primitive kind of law to be sheer nonsense. According to Boorstin, the law and its underlying reason became something that was "mathematically demonstrable" only under the rigid structures of a chronicler and particularistic definer of the law like William Blackstone.[20] For Blackstone, as Boorstin put it, the law was nothing more than a "science of logic," a set of rules which was complete, to be sure, at one level because of those rules' "internal coherence."[21] But, at the same time, the law was also something that tragically represented a tautology, or what Boorstin called a "closed legal system."[22] Once "logic and symmetry" became its attributes, Boorstin argued, the common law itself, not just those growing legislative improvements to the law, became utterly immune to experience.[23] It became immune to growth.

From another perspective, what Daniel Boorstin argued about Blackstone's writing was that "it was [only] the very coexistence of the prescriptive and the descriptive in the concept of natural law that had made it possible for him to rationalize the law" in the first place.[24] Blackstone's mechanical, static vision of the common law, according to Boorstin, would have put an end to the law's growth and progress had the chronicler had his way. Clearly, with regard to the cognitive nature of this vision of the law, the internally coherent, predictable vision of the law, or its *certum*, is successfully opposed to the dynamic vision of the law, the vision in which the law is open to the accommodations of justice in an ever-changing world. This, of course, is the law's *verum*.

Though the *certum-verum* distinction takes on even more importance as the Anglo-American experience continues, for now let us merely consider that in a political, specifically ideological, context, it is those who search for, and argue for, the superiority of a law that is certain, predictable, and unchanging—that is, those who argue for the law's *certum*—who by the late eighteenth century most often supported the private, contractual, and largely economically oriented interests of society. Their preference for *certum*, a term for the law's predictability, contrasted with the preference of those who searched for a law that could embrace the justness of the novel circumstances of a different time. The law's continued quest for *verum*, in other words, maintains the justness of the law, even if the formal rulings of the law must be changed. The term *verum*, akin to *truth*, often implies a role for public, democratically oriented political interests as certain interests infuse the law with original, if sometimes overdue, considerations. That alignment of private interest with the law's *certum* and public interest with the law's *verum* typified the British legal-political condition at the time of the American Revolution. It surely had an impact on the American revolutionary and postrevolutionary experience as well.

Once more, the cognitive nature of these *certum* and *verum* visions of the law should always be kept in mind. It is the *certum* vision of the law and the corresponding preference for the pure, almost invariably private contract that was increasingly free of the social encumbrance which utilized the cognitively analytic cognition. The synthetic cognition's sense of the law's *verum*, including the complexities which so often make up modernity's requirements for justice in the law, is what so often comes from public legislation.

Blackstone's analytic cognitive vision of the law and Boorstin's synthetic criticisms of that Blackstonian vision, apart from their substantive, indeed ideological, differentiations, embody this analytic-synthetic contrast quite clearly. The private law's ongoing separation from the social encumbrances of an earlier day certainly heralded the degree of sectoral separation that existed by the time of the eighteenth century. But after Blackstone the analytic-synthetic distinction in the law, particularly the law of contracts, became even more apparent.

Blackstone's analytic and undynamic notion of the law surely contrasted with Coke's vision of a growing law that would assist, not retard, the development of democracy. The contrast between Coke's and Blackstone's preferred forms of the law portended very different notions of how far democracy was to go.

CHAPTER FOUR

The American Experience

Democracy's Framework

Let us now examine the American experience. Virtually all writings concerning the U.S. Constitutional tradition refer reverently to the American democratic tradition's English origins. It was a tradition of restrained government, one that relished its penchant for a limited public sector, which the framers took from the Mother Country.

Regarding institutions, the emphasis on restrained government was manifested most clearly in the separation of powers arrangement of the United States' political branches, that arrangement being rationalized by James Madison in *The Federalist Papers* (nos. 46–51). The fact that Madison either deliberately or unconsciously misinterpreted Montesquieu's misunderstanding of the British separation of powers has had little impact on American commentators. Montesquieu talked with Bolingbroke and the Country Party (the Tories) on his English trip. He did not talk to Walpole and the Whigs, who were quietly constructing what would become modern cabinet government under Bolingbroke's nose. With a cabinet government, of course, the prime minister and the Parliament's majorities are fused in order to create an unseparated arrangement of legislative-cum-executive powers. The Tories, intentionally behind in their understandings of democratic governments, spoke of separated powers within the seventeenth-century context of that term—the separation of the Crown from both the prime minister and Parliament. Montesquieu, like the Tories, never quite imagined what the separation of a nonmonarchical executive and a democratic legislature might look like.

In a larger sense, of course, the U.S. Constitutional arrangement can only be understood within its historical and ideological context, and not all of that context is English. America's own immediately postrevolutionary period was crucial as well in providing both the incentive and the rationale for the final Constitutional design.

What happened in the former colonies during the Articles of Confederation period was that democracy flowered as it perhaps had never flowered anywhere. The franchise often included not only those of great property but sometimes those of little as well. Legislatures met with frequency and without fear of dismissal. A small state like Rhode Island, for example, may have achieved a level of popular democracy unmatched by any political jurisdiction, anywhere in the world, until well into the next century.[1]

By "democracy" what do I mean with regard to the institutional and private-to-public arrangements of the newly sovereign states? Although it is typically denigrated, the Continental Congress, the loosely constituted and underpowered legislature of the thirteen states, was not a wholly inactive or ineffective body. Shortly after its convocation it urged all states to write their own formal Constitutions in order to ensure sound government as well as protect citizen's liberties. Yes, states would more than likely have done it anyway, but it is relevant that in the wake of the British expulsion, and in the afterglow of the deeply democratic implications that the Declaration of Independence had left for the new republic, a federal body exhorted each American polity to capture that democratic spirit before it perished. That spirit was much in keeping with what Gordon Wood has called the "classical whig" position, that is, that rulers "derived their power ultimately from the people; election only made explicit what was always implicit."[2]

Though there was considerable variance among the states, their respective Constitutions, charged with protecting their state's fledgling democracies, frequently opened with a Bill of Rights. Such language ensured at least a minimal protection against potentially overbearing government. But crucial to what the Constitution responded to soon after, these state Bills of Rights provisions were not designed to retard the public will within states which had overwhelmingly prescribed for strong, legislatively dominated governments in those same Constitutional documents. There was a reason for legislative dominance within the early states. Essentially, the Bill of Rights provisions of the states guaranteed rights that were not exclusively individual or private. They guaranteed the very gateways to democratic, public participation in government.

As Akhil Reed Amar notes in his 1991 *Yale Law Review* article,[3] it was public rights that guaranteed the citizenry of continued participation within their government after the Revolution. I cannot overstate the importance of the differentiation between what are often called individual or private rights and those public rights that ensure the effective action of the citizenry as a whole. The repeated, ill-taught notion that somehow the guarantees of the federal Constitution's Bill of Rights were designed to protect individuals *from* their government is simply not true. To be sure, rights can protect individuals in the *legal* sense that they shield an individual citizen from impediments to political activity such as those the Stuart kings imposed on their citizenry. The denial of free speech, the searching and seizing of the records and correspondence of citizens, the denying of due process of law in trumped-up trials, for example, all violated citizens rights. Those rights, again in a strictly legal sense, wrap themselves around individuals who might have complained of, or sought to change, their government.

Yet the larger purpose of the Bill of Rights was, and still is, decidedly *collective* and *political*. Its purpose was to ensure the right of the citizenry to govern itself through the passage of public law. As Amar rightly points out, the "dominant approach" to the Bill of Rights—the proposition that the bill was designed "to vest individuals and minorities with substantial rights against popular majorities"—is simply incorrect.[4] The principal purpose of the bill, Amar argues, was not to "impede popular majorities, but to empower them."[5] Without question, Amar contends, the Bill of Rights is "centered on protecting a majority of the people within a possibly unrepresentative government."[6]

For at least the more democratic states of the new American Republic, the new and vast legislative powers that these states enjoyed, coupled with those state's Bills of Rights, enabled what many considered to be democratic excesses within the legislative halls. Classic debtor-creditor politics frequently took place there, with debtors, for one of the rare times in the long history of ower and owed, winning more than their share of the battles. Debt foreclosures were statutorily postponed, sometimes indefinitely. Paper money was generously printed, causing the inflation that substantially diminished the value of a creditor's return. Often heavy taxes were laid against the most expensive properties.

And then, when hard times hit the new nation in the middle 1780s, a dramatic confrontation sparked an important reaction. Shays's Rebellion, though a short-lived and easily suppressed armed protest, was thought so dangerous by those like Henry Knox that Washington's old Revolutionary War comrade ran to his former commander with the tale. Knox suspected that many citizens quietly approved of Shays's action against mortgage foreclosures. Knox knew that citizens approved of those debtor-favoring legislative actions already mentioned. Small landowners typically believed their state governments should at least pass moratoriums in hard times. If the legislatures wouldn't do so, at least some small land-owners felt that the prevention of foreclosure, even by force of arms, was fully justified.

Curiously, this new and virile brand of American democracy, institu-tionalized by those legislatively dominated state Constitutional arrange-ments, found the public challenging neither the government of a king, who had been excused, nor an overbearing federal government, which of course did not exist. What it found was a successful public challenging of the private sector's most cherished institutions of property and contract. In many states the private sector interests had substantially lost govern-mental control.

The alignment of political ideology, institutional bias, and particu-larly the private-to-public sector balance was as clear to creditors as it needed to be after Shays's Rebellion. What latter-day political commen-tators would call a "redistributive" public policy thrived within that leg-islative jurisdiction and, of course, within a public domain that often limited the tenures and salaries of property-protecting judges. The extracontractual considerations of hard economic times had been legisla-tively imposed upon the exclusively contractual, analytic considerations of money loaned and money to be repaid. This weighing, in a nutshell, is what gave such impetus to the quiet meeting at George Washington's Mount Vernon home in 1785, the somewhat more visible meeting of representatives from five states at Annapolis in 1786, and the full con-vention in Philadelphia the following year. With the shutters closed, that convention wrote the U.S. Constitution.

The Constitution

The U.S. Constitution's procedure-guiding structure, its tripartite institutional arrangement, is well studied. But the openly private sector–protecting, substantive nature of the Constitution, illustrated in specific references to private property and contract which I will refer to at the close of this chapter, deserves full consideration as well. The absence of a full-blown Bill of Rights also clearly illustrates the framers' fear of exces-sively popular government.

With reference to a Bill of Rights, the Constitution's drafters did not favor a statement of rights because they realized that a hearty declaration of citizen liberties at the federal level would imperil the same private rights there which had been imperiled at the state level by debtor-con-trolled legislatures. As we will review, those who were not happy with the Constitution—the Anti-Federalists—spoke more critically of the absence of a Bill of Rights within the document than they spoke of anything else. Indeed, the eventual acceptance of a robust Bill of Rights by the Constitution's drafters was the price that the dissenters placed on their reluctant acceptance of the original document.

Recall that four states, most notably New York and Virginia, appeared as though they might not ratify the Constitution, even as late as the summer of 1788. North Carolina had voted the document down in its first convention, in the spring of 1788. For a time Rhode Island would not even consider it, passing it only in 1790 and then by two votes. The Anti-Federalist dissenters got what they wanted, once more, because they focused not on what the Constitution included but on what it did not.

Beyond the argument over a full-blown Bill of Rights, one common misunderstanding about the Constitution must be dispelled if the great Constitutional debate is to be properly understood. The protection of citizens' rights in the Constitution did not begin with the first eight amendments to the document. The fact is that the framers of the first seven articles of the Constitution, anticipating Constitutional rebuttal to the effect that at least some protection of citizens' rights would be expected in the new political order, specifically included limited citizen protections in their own seven articles. The framers knew all too well what the state constitutional conventions had written into their principal documents, and they suspected from the outset that they would not achieve passage of their own governmental design unless they could point to some protections of rights within their own document.

The Philadelphia framers placed their civil protections into section 9 of Article 1. That section should be examined in detail, particularly in the context of the balance of the private-to-public sectors within the U.S. political arrangement. Section 9 made it clear that the new federal government would not impose certain restrictions on the American citizenry. So, just as section 8 of Article 1 enumerated what the new government could do and just as section 10 enumerated what the states could not do within the new federal arrangement, section 9, by enumerating what the federal government could not do to its public citizens, served as the "reassurance" corner of the Constitution. Section 9 was designed to keep the states' citizens from worrying about the more powerful national entity that would soon be governing them. Specifically, the section reminded the states, and their citizens, that the drafters had not forgotten the abuses of George III or the Stuarts.

The first provision of section 9, protecting slave ownership, is perhaps the most artfully drawn of the provisions. Its background reflects the reality of those years immediately preceding the Constitution when

Southern landowners, to some extent of rice plantations (principally in South Carolina) but to a larger extent of cotton plantations, had come to the conclusion that African slavery was the only practical way to make their labor-intensive enterprises profitable. They had tried prison labor, indentured labor, even the bringing of London prostitutes over to the new world. Such contrivances did not pan out, and, as a result, Southerners reasoned, additional years of importation would be needed to fill the needs of an already westward-expanding South. Twenty years was so allotted.

Yet there is more to the first provision of section 9 than simply the political satisfying of slave-holding interests. Only ninety miles from Philadelphia, in New York, the Continental Congress was in session at the same time as the Constitutional Convention. It had an important piece of legislation before it, one that it eventually passed, gathering the often difficult unanimity under the Articles of Confederation to do so. The legislation was the Northwest Ordinance, bringing into the Republic a vast area west of the Alleghenies and north of the Ohio River, or what was to become nearly five and a half states. The achievement of bringing this large an area into the new nation's jurisdiction was notable enough, but just as notable was the provision within the Northwest Ordinance ensuring that slavery would never be allowed in the region.

Constitutionally significant is the Continental Congress's inclusion in the ordinance of a formal slavery ban in the territory, this being one side of a broad series of hard-fought but very significant agreements that were hammered out between the Northern commercial interests and the Southern landed interests at the convention. The latter were often supported by New Englanders from states such as Connecticut. Among a variety of understandings dealing with fugitive slaves, navigation acts, export fees, and the like, one Constitutional quid pro quo guaranteed that the southwestern portion of the new nation, essentially western Georgia and what is now Alabama and Mississippi, would be permitted to adopt slavery.

Much of the study of the North-South conflict in the Constitutional convention properly centers around bargains such as the so-called three-fifths compromise. This agreement allowed the Southern states to count their slaves as 60 percent of a person for purposes of House of Representatives allocation. But the events that followed, particularly the Civil War itself, as Christopher and James Collier point out, may support the argument that the first paragraph of section 9, Article 1, marked an even more significant North-South compromise.[7] Those sitting in the Constitutional Convention knew that what was going on within the Northwest Ordinance ninety miles to the north was not an attack on slavery. They knew it represented but one more portion of that series of understandings that would allow slavery to exist beyond the immediate borders of the Carolinas, Georgia, Virginia, and the Tidewater region.

What does section 9's first provision mean when it artfully says that the "migration and importation of such persons as any of the States now existing shall think proper to admit shall not be prohibited by the Congress prior to the year one thousand eight hundred and eight"? The language is a bit disingenuous, is it not? The kind of "migration" the framers were writing about was not some voluntary migration from England or wherever. It was the forced migration of African slaves which that first provision unmistakably protected. It is a provision, I suggest, that amounts to a Constitutionally created "Southwest Ordinance," a guarantee to one significant region of the country that it would get what it wanted out of continental expansion, just as the New York meeting of the existing government guaranteed that the other significant region got what it wanted. Such dealing between the North and the South, at this moment in history, was invariably brisk, if not invariably subtle.

Institutionally speaking, how should we interpret the Constitution's guarantee that African slaves could be imported into the expanded as well as the original South for another twenty years? At a minimum the guarantee is bolstered by the promise of institutional federalism. The new, clearly more powerful federal government was promising the states that this government's new legislature, the Congress, would not imperil what the Constitution granted as a fundamental right. Paradoxical, and painful to acknowledge though it may be, the first "civil liberty" protected by the Constitution (much in contrast to the public right protecting provisions of the later Bill of Rights) was the liberty to continue the importation of slaves after the passage of the document. The protected retention of those slaves already in the Southern states, of course, did not even need to be mentioned.

As a result of what I have just outlined, the deeper meaning of paragraph 1, section 9, reaches well beyond the balance of state and federal authority. It may be best to typify paragraph 1 as a property and contract–based protection, the kind of protection which had been the burden of traditional, English civil liberties, even though the "persons" referenced in paragraph 1 were not yet owned. They were not yet property. Contracts for their future ownership, as a result, were merely anticipatory.

Of course, the nature of such a property and contract protections was not public in the sense of assuring what became the Bill of Rights or other political kinds of liberties. They were barely public only in their design to win favor from those governing publics who controlled state politics, again in the South. These citizens were well ensconced within, and were anticipating the growth of, their plantation, slave-based economies. In the American context, as it would have been in the English context, what was protected was still the private right of ownership. Again, the purpose of section 9's opening guarantee may have been barely political in the sense that it appealed to a public, again the politically dominant public, within certain states. In the seventeenth century such a government might have been feared as a Stuart-like, autocratic political entity. But, in the eighteenth century in America, the first Constitutional civil liberty assured the dominant political interests of certain states that it would not betray their private rights.

I spend some time on this, the first civil protection of the Constitution, because the provision must be clearly set off from the remaining, truly public protections of both section 9, Article 1, and the later amendments known universally as the Bill of Rights. As the Philadelphia framers, not the authors of the Bill of Rights, were largely concerned with individual, overwhelmingly economic, rights and with the protections of those rights that the private law of property and contract ensured, the remaining provisions of section 9 are but bows to the anticipated clamor of state publics whom they rightly suspected of being jealous of losing their political rights.

Looking briefly at the remainder of section 9, we find that all of its other provisions are indeed more public than they are private. Knowing that opposition to the Constitution would focus on the powers of the new government, the framers' assurance to the public sought to guarantee specifically that political activity could continue as it had before the Constitution. The assurance of the section—that the writ of habeas corpus would be suspended only in times of rebellion or invasion; that no bill of attainder or ex post facto law would be passed by the general government; that no direct tax would be assessed that would circumvent the proportionality of the state's populations; that no tax would be assessed on articles exported out of states; that no state would be given preference in interstate commerce; and that no money would be taken from the general treasury except as provided for by law (and well accounted for at that)—were all protections of the public. They were general, not specific, in nature, and, although individual, legally protected citizens would be expected to exercise them, it was a promise by the federal government to state citizens that theirs would be a government very different from that of the Stuarts. If America's new leaders ever became like the Stuarts, the listed rights would ensure public redress.

Finally, in the provision that some today would smile at, the Constitution assured the citizenry that there would be no separate, elevated class of citizenship, with an elevated set of perquisites. The prohibition against the granting of titled nobility may, perhaps, be the most obviously public and political protection of the totality of section 9's rights. For all their innate conservatism, and for all of their favor for the private sector as well as for the courts that would protect that sector, the Philadelphia conventioneers were aware that their opposition would brand them as aristocrats. If there had been talk of George Washington becoming a king, something Washington himself consistently discouraged, there was talk too of a kind of aristocracy which would not be unlike what had aligned itself with the Stuart kings in the previous century. The Constitution assured the larger citizenry that groups like the Washington officer core–based Order of the Cincinnati would never claim nobility.[8]

In sum, what all of these protections of section 9, taken together, demonstrate is that the framers were astute enough about the difficulty of Constitutional ratification that they willingly guaranteed a degree of protection to those citizens whom they knew would expect rights to be a part of the new political arrangement. It was hoped that section 9's olive branch, and that is exactly what it was, would persuade the still state-grounded citizenry of the American Republic to accept the Constitution as they, the national framers, had written it. As it turned out, the barely democratic provisions of Article 1, section 9, proved to be an inadequate peace offering to that citizenry. But in a small way the provisions laid a foundation for the later adoption of those public, political rights covered by the full Bill of Rights.

The Remainder of the Document

Feeling that they had provided sufficiently for the public's protection, in great part by including civil liberty protections in their Constitution, the framers carried on with the rest of their institution building. After granting the legislature the status of being the subject of Article 1, the framers proceeded to weaken that potentially overdemocratic institution as much as they could. Principally, they did so by bifurcating the Congress, this task being done so thoroughly that, even in a day of weakened upper houses throughout Europe (in which titled aristocracy did and sometimes still sits), the United States Congress remains the only fully bicameral national legislature among the industrialized states.

Roger Sherman's bicameral compromise, immortalized in textbooks, was hardly a radical solution for a Constitutional Convention that certainly felt more comfortable with land-centered than population-centered legislative houses. Pennsylvania's unicameral legislature, still in operation in 1787, and the Georgia unicameral legislature, which had only recently converted itself to bicameralism, were considered as dangerous precedents for the conventioneers. The staggering of senatorial and representative terms further weakened the Congress.

Article 2, dealing with the chief executive, worked somewhat more of a compromise with the states. Here the Constitution assured them that their electors would choose the nation's presidents. The framers compromised again by limiting the presidential term to four years, longer terms having been vigorously argued for by some in the Convention. That left Article 3, the provision that created the federal Supreme Court and "such inferior courts as the Congress may from time to time ordain and establish." This article's protections of any federal judge from popular disapproval, achieved by not having judges subject to removal so long as they practiced "good behavior," as well as by not having their emoluments "diminished during their continuance in office," had enormous consequences for the protection of the private law's dual bastions of contract and property.

The above, I hope, shows that the location of the boundary between the private and the public sectors was the single issue that most inspired the arguments of both the Constitutional framers and the Constitution's detractors. The absence of a comprehensive Bill of Rights within the original Constitution particularly was a direct reflection of the kind of private-to-public balance that the Philadelphia framers preferred. The later inclusion of the rights amendments merely rebalanced what so many among the citizenry considered to be a clear diminishing of the public domain in the original seven articles.

Regarding the institutional arrangement of the new government and how those arrangements reflected the same struggle, what needs to be added is a reference to those other provisions in the original seven Constitutional articles which also demonstrate the primary importance of the private-to-public boundary to both the Constitution's framers and its opponents. These provisions, notably, have nothing whatever to do with the institutions of the government. Though it is frequently assumed that the Constitution is but a procedural document, and that little of a substantive political nature therefore exists within it, these less-studied provisions are in fact glaringly substantive and important. They specifically protect the private sector, and, in doing so, they darken the private-to-public line in the Constitution.

Forrest McDonald notes that the key "limitations" on the federal government concerning "property rights in one fashion or another" include "the prohibition against interference in the slave trade before 1808, the ban on export duties, the restriction regarding direct taxes, the prohibition against preferential treatment of ports, the ban on taxation of interstate commerce, and the prohibition of corruption of the blood."[9] True enough, but I would argue that limitations on the *federal* government with respect to private property were not what the framers were concerned about. It was the states that frightened them.

Regarding the states, McDonald properly notes that they "were forbidden to coin money, [and] to emit bills of credit," the creating of a federal monetary structure surely granting some of the stability that the federalists so desperately sought.[10] There was the search for stability, too, in the making of "anything but gold and silver coin legal tender in payment of debts," the provision responding to the soft-money habits of many state legislatures.[11] More directly, as McDonald points out, section 10 of Article 1 declares that no state shall pass any law "impairing the obligation of contracts," this provision being "designed exclusively to prevent infringement of property rights."[12] The historically evolved shield that the common law gave to the private transaction had been jeopardized in English history well before it had been jeopardized by American state legislatures. It would be jealously reinforced in the Constitution.

With all of these features, however, McDonald fails to mention one of the most important of all state-related demarcations of the private-to-public line in the Constitution. That provision rests in the fourth article, the article which ensures that "Full faith and credit shall be given [by all states] to the public acts, records, and judicial proceedings of every other State." Institutionally, of course, this is one of the many Constitutional provisions which binds the states into something beyond a confederation. But the provision is far more than institutional, for, like the contract clause, it speaks directly of the private-to-public distinction, protecting creditors from the most frequently used debt evasion strategy of that and any other time. Tiptoeing from the jurisdiction in which a judgment of debt had been rendered, and in which its enforcement was far more certain than it would be anyplace else, had always carried the fresh-start promise that encumbered debtors sought. Ensuring that debts would be made good nationally was a key Federalist counterstrategy.

Even beyond the contract clause, the framers chiseled one more provision into the Constitution's private-to-public divide which commentators have almost universally overlooked. The marking, to be sure, is implicit, never stated, it being found in Article 6's stating that "All debts contracted . . . before the adoption of this Constitution, shall be as valid against the United States . . . as under the Confederation." The specific provision, of course, only ensured that bondholders after the Revolutionary War would be far more secure in their creditor status after Constitutional passage than they were under the old government. But that is not all that the provision meant.

There has been a great deal written about the motives of the framers concerning their self-interest with regard to securing the war bonds' value. I make no original contribution to that debate, but I do ask that we not let the explicit wording of Article 6 obscure that implicit ancillary assumption that underlaid the article itself. That assumption meant that all private debts were to be honored after the ratification of the Constitution, just as certainly as they were to be honored before the Constitution. A land contract, a contract for chattel, a personal service contract, or whatever, would carry as much force after Constitutional ratification as it did before. The formation of an altogether different government—the public movement from the Articles to the Constitution, in other words—was to have absolutely no bearing on any private obligation. That understanding, resting on the same rationale of the inviolability of contract which underlay the public bond redemption, was so widely held that, unlike the provisions involving the private and the public divide, it never needed to be mentioned. That all contracts would be honored among private citizens was that obvious to the framers, and to everyone else.

In sum, it is not just the Constitution's absence of a full Bill of Rights and not just the dispersion of the institutional arrangements of the public sector's government which are central to the private-to-public balance within the Constitution. In the context of their seeking to preserve the private prerogative behind the wall that separated the private and public sectors, brutally simple Constitutional provisions made it obvious to all that the common law's historically distilled private protections would remain sacrosanct in the new order.

In short, the framers made it clear that the brief interlude wherein several individual states visited too much democracy upon the common law's private sector would now be dramatically, and irrevocably, terminated. Even Blackstone's fear of his day's parliamentarians never led to such English restrictions on democratic institutions as the North Americans would put into place soon after the publication of Blackstone's *Commentaries* on the Atlantic's other shore. The American polity might be free to seek its destiny, but only on one side of those very clear, private domain–protecting understandings that were indelibly etched in the Constitution from the outset.

CHAPTER FIVE

The Federalists
and the Anti-Federalists

Madison's Government

First out of the chute with arguments geared to ensuring Constitutional ratification, the Federalist drafters of the great document sought out friendly New York newspapers for what are still the United States' best known op-ed pages. Eighty-five generally well-reasoned pieces were written in all, their three authors hoping to bring quick ratification for the Constitution they had crafted so carefully in Philadelphia.

The most prominent of the Federalist's offerings is James Madison's no. 10, still regularly cited for its spirited rationalization of the overall Constitutional plan. To stifle altogether "the mischiefs of faction," or to stifle "liberty," was not the framers' intent, Madison protested, if a bit too much. Such a course would not be wise, Madison argued, but then it would not be necessary either. It would do simply to control the effects of faction, keeping within bounds the majoritarian wave of citizen activity which had frightened the Federalists in the first place. The three-pronged strategy of the Federalists included the structurally centrifugal devices of (1) separated federal powers, (2) the division of powers between national and state sovereignties, and (3) the "extending of the sphere" of the government in such a way as to make it next to impossible for majoritarian democrats, America's state-based egalitarians, to organize nationally.

These arguments are well covered in traditional treatments of the Federalist argument. But, just as the Constitution itself contains far more than the institutional structure of the document's first three articles (as argued in the last chapter), so too many of the Federalist arguments dealt with far more than Constitutional structure. In no. 10, for example, Madison openly referred to "public and private faith," to the "alarm for private rights," to the "different and unequal faculties of acquiring property," to "the possession of different degrees and kinds of property," to the "landed interest," to the "manufacturing interest," to the "monied interest," and to the "many lesser interests." Do we wonder why he so feared the passage of laws "concerning private debts?"[1]

What the Constitution did, as Madison candidly conceded, was "secure the public good and private rights."[2] Of course, there was a balance to it, Madison claiming that in the Constitution, as with all things, there was "a mean, on both sides of which inconveniences will be found to lie."[3] But, for the Constitution's framers and for Madison in no. 10, that mean had been distorted by state legislatures in the too-recent past. The repeated mention of private rights in this most central of all *Federalist* papers confirms the purpose of the Constitution as much as anything in the document itself.

There is one other revealing segment of Madison's no. 10 which, from both a historical and an ideological perspective, makes the purpose of the framers crystal clear. Still early in the offering, Madison argues that "No man is allowed to be a judge in his own cause: because his interest would certainly bias his judgment."[4] The argument should be familiar; it is Coke's point in *Dr. Bonham's case*. Looked at more closely, however, Madison's use of the reason he and Coke both found in the common law points in the opposite ideological, and institutional, direction from the way Coke used it. Recall that shortly after *Dr. Bonham's case*, as mentioned earlier, Coke had attempted to loan the reason of the law to James I, and to the government generally, by suggesting that James consider the opinions of those served by a public official when appointing that official. Coke's argument for reason, in both the matter of *Dr. Bonham* and the matter of the kingly appointment, in other words, was facilitative of democracy, not an impediment to it. Institutionally, Coke was dealing in one case with the rules of judicial decision making and in the other with executive prerogative. Madison, however, was countering legislative, sectorally public overreach. It was the people assembled who might be unreasonable in their laws, not a judge.

Continuing in no. 10, Madison wrote bitterly about the dangers of legislatures, noting that popularly elected legislatures invariably pandered to their own and their constituents' desires rather than to the necessities of an ordered society. Of course, representation is what democratic institutions have always sought to do. Nonetheless, it is noteworthy that by the close of the eighteenth century the reason-based pleas of James Madison and the American Federalists needed to reverse the sectoral balance between the private and public law which Coke in England had more than nudged to the democratic, public side. Such a reversal demonstrates again that the framers' primary goal was the preservation of the private domain, however the public institutions might be arranged or however those institution's prerogatives might be allocated. Though Blackstone's specific notion that Parliament was loftier than any king was ultimately mooted by the colonies' revolution, the American framers spoke more urgently even than Blackstone about the need for legislative restraint. The legislatures of unkinged and sometimes ignoble state governments had trampled private interests. To keep these legislatures, and now the federal legislature, in their proper places in order to preserve the private domain, was how the framers would protect themselves from such democratic hubris.

Hamilton's Judiciary

If Madison's best writings in *The Federalist Papers* offered the rationalization of the overall Constitutional plan found in no. 10, perhaps accompanied by the specific explanation of the separation of powers found in nos. 46–51, Alexander Hamilton's best writing dealt specifically with the Supreme Court and the Supreme Court's principal task of interpreting the law. Hamilton's calling the Supreme Court "the least dangerous branch" was disingenuous at best. He wished for nothing less than that ultimate judicial check on legislative rule making which was so evident in his arguments for judicial review.

As a result of the framers' favor for the propertied citizenry over the unpropertied citizenry, Constitutional provisions such as the lifetime appointment (with good behavior) and the forbidding of emolumental reduction, protected federal judges far better than judges had been protected at the state level during the pre-Constitutional period. Madison had argued that his Constitutional arrangement afforded protection for those who, because of "different and unequal faculties," had already acquired property."[5] Hamilton's *Federalist* no. 78 through no. 81 explained why a truly independent court system was needed to protect such property. Article 3, among other things, was written to guarantee that independence.

And so, just as Madison borrowed from Coke in arguing that no man should be a judge in his own cause, Hamilton also borrowed from the common law in arguing that the Supreme Court would be free of political ideology. Because of such purity, he continued, the Court should be permitted to engage in judicial review. The Court's law, in extending the private-domain protection of the common law of England which had itself been sui juris since at least the time of Edward, was clearly superior to any law coming from a government.

Think of it. The English Blackstone, for all of his fears over statutes "swelled to ten times a larger bulk," never suggested that the king's courts had any right to overturn Parliament's law. But Blackstone, as I suggested earlier, spoke within a context that still tolerated a monarchy and, more important, possessed no written constitution that would specifically limit the representative powers of Parliament. The pre–Glorious Revolution memories of a parliament much abused by a king and frequently run out of town after the king had gotten his way with it were less than one hundred years old when the *Commentaries* were written.

Yet in the United States, if Madison's Constitution had restricted a legislature as well as forbidden the return of a king who might in Stuart fashion have swung round to oppose the mercantilists and their business interests, who would be left to protect the courts? Madison, again in tune with *Dr. Bonham*, had argued against the mixing of courts with legislatures, claiming that "With equal, nay with greater reason, a body of men are unfit to be both judges and parties."[6] But Alexander Hamilton, in writing of the federal Supreme Court and the need to preserve its independence, used the reasoning of the law of agency, a derivative of contract law, to argue for the supremacy of the Constitution and its interpreters. That "the prior act of a superior," [the Constitution] "ought to be preferred to the subsequent act of an inferior and subordinate authority" (a legislature) was the core of Hamilton's position.[7] The argument is ultimately a fiction—the people when ratifying a Constitution somehow lifting themselves to a level that they never again reach when selecting agents to pass legislation. But the purpose for creating such an intellectual skyhook was clear.

As Hamilton put it, when "a particular statute contravenes the Constitution, it will be the duty of the judicial tribunals to adhere to the latter, and disregard the former." This "least dangerous" hierarchy of definitional authority not only placed the judiciary above the legislature with regard to the ultimate interpretive role in the Constitutional law.[8] It also kept the private law where the government—and all of the American Federalists and Chief Justice John Marshall, through thirty-four years on the bench—very much wanted it. The Federalists not only favored the Supreme Court as an institution over the political branches. They also favored the broadest possible jurisdiction for that Court. Not surprisingly, the Court was the institution that invariably received the most criticism from the Anti-Federalists.

The Democratic Response

If the progression of Coke's private law-to-democracy sojourn which had gone through *Shelley's* case, *Dr. Bonham's* case, the 1616 appointment dispute with James I, and the *Petition of Right*, was slowed by the Federalists in this country, as Blackstone had attempted to slow it within England, those same Federalists had no difficulty referencing Coke in the service of *court*-guaranteed legal reason. It was left to the Anti-Federalists, therefore, to continue the progress of Cokeian reasonings that had indirectly underpinned the legislative democracy of the pre-Constitutional states.

The Anti-Federalists, of course, are best known for their successful insistence that the Bill of Rights be immediately affixed to the Constitution. They knew that a formal Bill of Rights had been purposely left out of the document, and they were not mollified by what they considered to be the insufficient guarantees against ex post facto laws, bills of attainder, and the preservation of habeas corpus which were written into section 9 of Article 1. In the earlier compromise the Federalists may have understood the justice, and no doubt the political necessity, of preserving a modicum of democratic protections within the Constitution. But the Anti-Federalists were unsatisfied with such short rations.

What, in fact, were the Anti-Federalists most concerned about? As the preceding chapter pointed out, the Anti-Federalists were *not* principally concerned with so-called individual rights when they demanded that a Bill of Rights extend beyond the minimal civil protections of Article 1's section 9. In their concern for the continued progress of the same majoritarian democracy that Madison spoke so frighteningly of in *Federalist* no. 10, the Anti-Federalist price for Virginia and New York's perhaps reluctant ratification of the Constitution spoke to something far different from those common law–derived rights that were part of what all but the first subsection of Article 1, section 9, guaranteed.

First and foremost, it is necessary to remind ourselves that as the protections that the Anti-Federalists' Bill of Rights sought were overwhelmingly public and political in nature, the Anti-Federalists sought to ensure that collective, democratic groupings within the citizenry could balance the private interests that had been favored by those who wrote the original document. As a result, the Bill of Rights that responded to the institutional and private law–protecting arrangements of the Constitution was individual in only one sense. As I have said, it did legally wrap each citizen in a protective cocoon during oppositional activity.

But also, the Bill of Rights is openly aggregational and public, as

Akhil Amar properly describes it in his *Yale Law Review* piece. Beyond what I have already referred to, Amar pointed out there that the protections of free speech, free press, petition, and assembly in the First Amendment were all designed to permit the citizenry *as a whole* to engage in political activity without fear of retribution. As Amar reminds us, "for Anti-federalists, the Constitution was at heart an 'aristocratic' document."[9] What the Anti-Federalists feared was "that the aristocrats who would control Congress would have an insufficient sense of sympathy with, and connectedness to, ordinary people."[10]

Amar also reminds us that the original First Amendment had to do with the numerical smallness of the public's institution, the legislative body. This was something that the framers, and particularly the Convention president, George Washington, had considered important enough to act on by expanding the ratio in the House of Representatives from one representative per forty thousand citizens to one per thirty thousand. The second original amendment dealt with what was eventually passed as the Twenty-seventh Amendment in 1992, it forbidding Congress from boosting its compensation while in session.

Yet, in what became the opening stanza of the ratified Bill of Rights, Amar correctly notes that "an even stronger kind of majoritarianism underlies our First Amendment" than the two amendments previously cited would show.[11] As Amar puts it, "The body that is restrained is not a hostile majority of the people."[12] In fact, Amar properly notes that the original first two amendments and what became the first successful amendment were all concerned with the probability that the Congress may in fact have turned out to "have 'aristocratical' and self-interested views in *opposition* to views held by a majority of the people."[13]

Going on, Amar argues that even such thought-to-be individual rights as the Fourth Amendment's protection from unreasonable searches and seizures, the Fifth Amendment's right not to testify against one's interest, and the Sixth Amendment's right to be represented by counsel were each designed to forestall the kinds of impediments to political activity which the Stuarts, and reactionary British aristocrats, had utilized. The U.S. Bill of Rights in this sense goes well beyond the British Bill of Rights, which largely protected the parliament only in its relationship to the Crown.

As for the political battle itself, the Anti-Federalists were simply much later in getting to the public with their arguments than were the Federalists. Knowing that they needed to catch up, the Anti-Federalists played their strongest suit first. Demanding a comprehensive Bill of Rights, they pointedly cited those state Bills of Rights that I have alluded to. To be sure, the Anti-Federalists' institutional preference for legislatures over courts was almost as significant for them as was their concern with a Bill of Rights. George Bryan's original Anti-Federalist argument, in fact, had been that there was nothing wrong with the Articles of Confederation government which a strengthening of the Continental Congress could not fix. Bryan considered that a return to "the unanimity of the country [of] a few years past," or to a time "*when Congress governed the continent,*"[14] would be sufficient for the country to prosper. But that time, and its option, had passed.

It was therefore left to Anti-Federalists such as George Mason to speak more directly to the Constitution's proposed institutions, beginning with Mason's own preference for a legislature. Placing his primary faith in this most democratic of governmental bulwarks, Mason noted that, as prescribed under the Constitution, "there is not the substance, but the shadow only of representation" in the Constitutional legislature. As a result, the House of Representatives, which was to be the only repository of truly democratic legislation as Mason and the other Anti-Federalists understood it, would "never produce proper information in the legislature, or inspire confidence in the people."[15]

As for the Senate, Mason expressed his fears openly, noting that members of the "Senate have the power of altering all money bills, and of originating appropriations of money, and the salaries of the officers of their own appointment, in conjunction with the President."[16] Neither of these latter kinds of offices, specifically the cabinet and the presidency, Mason pointed out, "are representatives of the people, or amenable to them."[17]

Yet, if the Senate, along with the presidency and the cabinet, frightened Mason somewhat, it was the judiciary that truly terrified the Virginian, one of the few Anti-Federalists who had come to Philadelphia and actively engaged in the Constitutional debate. For one thing, he thought, the federal judiciary was constructed so "as to absorb and destroy the judiciaries of the several states." Specifically, like England in those times when the common law was overwhelmed with inaccessible writs or an undue influence from the Crown, Mason felt that the new nation would find the laws to be rendered "tedious, intricate, and expensive, and justice as unattainable, by a great part of the community." As in England too, such a condition here would only "enable the rich to oppress and ruin the poor."[18]

Even beyond his institutional fears, and beyond his fears concerning the unnecessary intricacy and the sometimes deliberate inaccessibility of the common law, George Mason had one even greater trepidation. As he stated it, there was "no declaration" in the new Constitution that would ensure "trial by juries in civil cases."[19] That omission, along with the fear that the new Congress might "grant monopolies in trade and commerce," could lead only to further oppression of the indebted poor.[20] The new government, aided as well by the constitution of "new crimes" which would permit its officers to "inflict unusual and severe punishment," should appropriately be labeled a "moderate aristocracy."[21] Mason even feared that it might degenerate into "a monarchy or a corrupt oppressive aristocracy" within a few years.[22]

Richard Henry Lee, Mason's fellow Virginian, grandfather of the Confederate general but not in attendance at the Philadelphia convention, was for a long time considered to be the author of the Anti-Federalist work "Letters from a Federal Farmer." Recent scholarship has shown that the true author was "more probably the New York anti-federalist Melanchton Smith,"[23] but, whoever the author was, he obviously had been granted generous permission to write of Lee's fears regarding the proposed new government.[24] Noting that the convention would have been better served if "eight or nine other people had been present,"[25] he, like Mason, focused to a considerable degree on the Constitution's omission of a Bill of Rights. But, significantly, Smith, for Lee, also focused on the Constitutional protections of the judiciary. It was the absence of the jury within the judicial system—not just in civil cases, as Mason had emphasized, but in criminal cases as well—which rankled Lee. As Amar has noted, Lee knew that the criminal charge had been used to oppress dissent in the English past. In that same past it had only been "the unanimous consent of twelve of his neighbors and equals" which at least could protect dissenting English citizens and, later, dissenting American citizens from an oppressive state government.[26]

If, according to Lee, that same form of protection was needed against the new federal government, or if the "great end of civil society" came down to nothing less than "the impartial administration of justice" which Lee thought it did, provisions for a jury would have to be a part of the political order.[27] And if, as Lee (through Smith) also suspected, justice was to be "entrusted to the magistracy," and if that magistracy, inevitably, was to be "selected by the prince," then the decisions of the courts "will have frequently an involuntary bias towards those of their own rank and dignity."[28] A man of unquestioned social rank and dignity himself, Lee could not be taken lightly when he suggested that "trial by jury in [both] criminal and civil cases, and the modes prescribed by the common law for the safety of life in criminal prosecutions shall be held sacred."[29]

And so the Anti-Federalist argument, tardy and fragmented to be sure, eventually did take shape. In concert, another even more prominent Virginian, Thomas Jefferson, suggested from his ambassadorial post in Paris that only nine states ratify the Constitution and that the other four should hold out for the adoption of a Bill of Rights. In that way, Jefferson wrote, a more equal balance between the prerogatives of the government and those of politically active citizens would be guaranteed.[30] As it turned out, four states did exactly what Jefferson proposed, although not all in response to Jefferson. Those states, predictably, included Virginia, where James Madison, in a hard-fought campaign, defeated James Monroe for a place in the new House of Representatives by pledging to introduce Constitutional amendments there. Jefferson's strategy, if not carried out by someone who lived next to him, as Monroe did, would be carried out by someone whose political philosophy would move ever closer to Jefferson's as the years went by.

I have already mentioned the Bill of Rights' Fourth (search and seizure), Fifth (due process), and Sixth (right to counsel) Amendment protections of the citizenry in the context of their ideological balancing of the Constitution. Let me close this section by pointing to the little-written-of Seventh Amendment in the Bill of Rights. This amendment instituted at a federal level, as it already existed at state levels, the change in the courts which so concerned George Mason. First, the amendment provided that "suits at common law," that is civil suits, would always enjoy "the right of trial by jury." Second, the amendment assured each citizen that "no fact tried by a jury shall be otherwise reexamined . . . than according to the rules of the common law." What the twelve good men and true of the new American Republic concluded about whether someone did or did not in fact owe a personal debt would not be questioned outside of the jury room, even at a higher court level.

With the above provisions the Anti-Federalists addressed (1) mild institutional revisions that brought protections to citizens against potentially unfair courts, (2) general protections concerning the working of the courts, and (3) general civil protections that allowed citizens to criticize their government. The Bill of Rights succeeded, at least to a great degree, in permitting democracy to restart its evolutionary progress, now at the federal level. Institutionally, the fragmentation of the government's design would be at least partially balanced by permitting aggregated citizens (Madison's "factions") to speak, write, petition, and assemble without fear of unjust interference by the government, particularly by its executive and courts. With regard to the private-to-public balance, a liberated public, at least to some degree, would be permitted to speak out against private monopolies and those other privileges that the Anti-Federalists suspected would nestle themselves into the new political order.

The Contract: Form and Class

Before leaving the Federalist/Anti-Federalist contrast, I will return briefly to a key Constitutional matter. It is a matter that demonstrates the nature of the Federalist's and Anti-Federalist's very different perspectives on both the Constitution's institutional arrangement and the private-to-public balance of the American Constitutional design. In spite of section 9 of Article 1's protections against ex post facto laws, the bill of attainder, and any revocation of habeas corpus, the Anti-Federalists argued that the Constitution's fragmented design, along with its specific protections of property and contract, still tilted the instrument toward the day's private interests. Their Bill of Rights, therefore, responded to the original seven articles at a level even beyond the mere institution-balancing and private-to-public domain–balancing considerations that I have mentioned so far.

To understand this final response thoroughly, let us first acknowledge that the Federalists designed what they considered to be an adequate system of balances between private and public interests, on the one hand, and institutional effectiveness and cautionary decentralization, on the other. They also felt comfortable with the balance in the *form* of the business contract which they foresaw as being necessary to the well-being of the new nation. They were comfortable, in other words, with the expectation of profitable mercantilist cooperation between the government and industrious entrepreneurs.

It is easy, from a modern perspective, to misinterpret the nature of the contractual form as it existed even well into the early years of the Republic. It is also easy, after the political revisions of early-twentieth-century progressivism and President Roosevelt's New Deal, to think of the early Republic's contracts as existing in the almost purely analytic form. Put another way, one could think of the contract as being overwhelmingly analytic in the sense that it merely concerned the economic necessities of the immediate contracting parties, wholly unencumbered by the social or governmental order of which it is a part. But this conception of contract, as we have reviewed it, was surely not the form of the contract which existed throughout most of the history of Anglo-American jurisprudence. And it was still surely not an accurate description of the business contract as late as the Constitutional era.

Recall that the original Magna Carta–era contract was overwhelmingly synthetic in form. The Magna Carta's "scutage, feudal reliefs, wardship and the like" all represented the deeply interwoven private and public sectors that made up the embryonic English common-law contract. It was, again, as political an instrument as it was an economic instrument. Coke, as late as the seventeenth century, still had no cause to think of the contract as being without political import, and even Blackstone, more than one hundred years after Coke, assumed that private property as the subject of a business contract was at least partly imbued with public purpose. This, after all, was the residual and still virile legacy of Magna Carta and of all the subsequent English experience. It continued with the mercantilism of a time that promised wealth for an entire nation, even if that nation be new and economically jejeune.

In a very important sense, as we shall see in the next chapter, the Anti-Federalists never successfully challenged Article 1, section 10's enshrining of the mercantilist form of contract. As a result, the Constitutional provision that ensured the protection of the contract within the original seven articles represented a kind of balance within a balance. To the framers the contract itself, as Blackstone had enshrined it, had reached a finished state, a perfection, with its public utility and its private equity complementing each other within Blackstone's much-loved legal symmetry.

But within the Constitution when looked at as a whole, the nod to citizen protections which section 9's attainder and habeas corpus protections provided were designed to balance what the framers expected would be the continued acquiescence of the citizenry toward governmental favor for selected commercial enterprises. What is important to understand here is that the Anti-Federalists may have spoken harshly of such privileges, but they were never able to change the *outcomes* of the new government's protections of private interests during the Constitutional or the immediately post-Constitutional period.

In short, though the Bill of Rights was designed to quiet citizens' fears concerning the most heinous governmental restrictions possible on public, antigovernmental activity, it was not designed to allay the frustrations that an aroused citizenry might feel with regard to its government's support for selected private businesses. In this sense the preferred form of mercantilist, government–to–private sector economic activity, as represented in the governmentally inspired contract for such major projects as the building of toll roads and canals, the improvement of harbors, and such things as shipbuilding (not to mention the eventual creation of the national bank) was never effectively countered by the Anti-Federalists.

To be sure, the Anti-Federalists had voiced their opposition to the privileges of the commercial class, just as they had spoken to the institutional arrangements of a government that could halt the progress toward institutionalized democracy which active governments had supported in order to reduce privilege in their states. They had also voiced opposition to those contracts that led to abusive mercantile advantage. But though the Anti-Federalists felt strongly that government-assisted mercantile contracts were deeply biased, they created no Bill of Rights-like counterbalance to them.

Thus, the bias of the mercantile contract for privileged, government-subsidized enterprises, continued well into the nineteenth century. It did so in large part because of the judicial (it could not have been legislative) hand of one man, Chief Justice John Marshall, who very much wanted it to continue. And that bias with regard to the mercantile contract not only substantively favored government-supported entrepreneurs in a way that the Anti-Federalists felt discriminated against the citizenry's least-fortunate citizens, but, as Richard Henry Lee (through Melanchton Smith) argued, the mercantile contract even discriminated against the rising middle class.[31]

It was Lee, after all, who had feared the role of a "consolidating aristocracy" in those deceptive steps that led up to the Constitutional Convention.[32] It was Lee who spoke out against those "dangerous men" who "avariciously grasp at all power and property."[33] Lee preferred the political position of "men of middling property."[34] He even preferred something close to what was to become the Jacksonian (nongovernmental and egalitarian) encouragement of private enterprise. But, during the Marshall period, the relationship of entrepreneurs to government, with their usage of still somewhat synthetic contracts, would be protected. The separation of the private and public sectors was still nowhere as far along as it would be one hundred years later.

CHAPTER SIX

The Interpretive Period

John Marshall's Court

Both the sectoral (i.e., private-to-public) analysis and the institutional (i.e., legislative-to-court) analysis of the Constitutional period are more intelligible when they are placed into the context of the cognitive forms of that time's contractual modes. The contractual form that typified post-Constitutional private-to-public sector cooperation actually helped to shape the Constitution's principal divide.

Early cooperation between the government and the nation's productive enterprises certainly worked to the advantage of the day's substantial private interests. The mercantile contract's synthetic condition could have been anticipated after what Madison and Hamilton wrote in the *Federalist*. But, ideologically, predictions on the direction of the U.S. government would have been more tenuous. It is customary to typify the first years of U.S. Constitutional interpretation as years of expansive national authority. In part, to further that synthetic, mercantilist contract, the powers of the government were expanded significantly by the Supreme Court rulings of the United States' fourth, and still longest-serving, chief justice, John Marshall. The powers of the new government were extended well beyond the printed word of Article 1, section 8, when Marshall finished with them.

Who benefited from the new government's enlarged powers? Predictably, the same people whom the Constitution sought to assist with its words were now being helped by the government, through Marshall's broad constructions of the document. Before dealing with specific powers of that government, we need to review, if only briefly, the usual textbook opening case of *Marbury v. Madison*.[1] *Marbury* is still an important case, its importance lying, of course, in the procedural table setting for the federal government which it helped to solidify. But on its merits the case was a contrivance, created out of a Constitutional problem that did not need to have been examined. The Federalist-passed Judiciary Act of 1789 had laid out the operational protocol of the Third Article of the Constitution, adding other courts and jurisdictions. It also added a provision concerning the right of the Supreme Court to issue a writ of mandamus, a writ that forces the government, or more precisely an official of the government, to do something left undone. The mandamus provision in the Judiciary Act was attached as what appeared to be an addition to the original jurisdiction of the Supreme Court.

The Federalist Chief Justice Marshall could have granted the mandamus and thereby ordered that Jefferson's secretary of state, Madison, give Marbury his commission. But Marshall used the case for something more important. He threw Marbury and three other potential Federalist magistrates to the wolves, declaring that the Supreme Court would claim the power of judicial review in their place. Marshall cited the improper addition of an original jurisdiction provision that the chief justice found to be inconsistent with the Constitution. As a result of *Marbury*'s ruling, the Supreme Court would be able to declare acts of the Congress unconstitutional.

The argument over judicial review in the U.S. experience, as we noted earlier, is the core of Hamilton's *Federalist* no. 78. But, if the addition of a new arena of original jurisdiction could be accomplished only by a Constitutional amendment, as Marshall declared, Marshall succeeded in ensuring that the Supreme Court would stand as a bulwark against the newly elected president, Thomas Jefferson, and perhaps other non-Federalist presidents, as well as Jefferson's newly victorious allies in the Congress. By so doing, *Marbury* clearly positioned the Supreme Court so that it could protect the private sector prerogatives guaranteed in the Constitution. In the remaining thirty-two years of Marshall's tenure on the bench, the chief justice and his Federalist colleagues on the Court engaged in just such protection of those private prerogatives.

The Private Sector Cases

With the institutional subflooring of the Supreme Court's jurisdiction secured, Justice Marshall and the Supreme Court soon moved on to cases that were directly relevant to the new country's entrepreneurial arrangements. The most famous of these cases is *McCulloch v. Maryland* (1819),[2] the case that protected the national bank from the encroachments of state governments. The state of Maryland had tried to tax the bank, arguing that the state was in no way interfering with it or with the greater powers of the national government.

Marshall would have none of it. For him the Constitution did not merely list the national government's powers; the great document surely imported that certain means would be available to the government in order to achieve its ends. The larger purposes of the document were subsumed within provisions such as the "necessary and proper" clause. This provision, according to Marshall, permitted the government to be creative in divining how it should accomplish the Constitution's greater goals. Implied powers were certainly intended by the Constitution, they being directly related to a Constitutional goal in the same way that the national bank was directly related to the power to lay and collect taxes, borrow money, and regulate commerce.

Beyond the direct argument of *McCulloch* with respect to the Constitutionality of a national bank, a brief comment on Marshall and the Bill of Rights may be helpful here as well. Referring to the Tenth Amendment, the last among that list of public-protecting additions to the Constitution which the Anti-Federalists argued for, Marshall noted derisively in *McCulloch* that the motivations for the amendment were "framed for the purpose of quieting the excessive jealousies which had been excited" by the Constitution's passage.[3]

In 1819 Marshall still had forgotten neither the argument for, nor the ideology that lay behind, the Bill of Rights. Noting that the framers of the Tenth Amendment had omitted the word *expressly* in ensuring that powers not given to the federal government remained with the states, Marshall needled the Anti-Federalists, pointing out that "the men who drew and adopted this amendment, had experienced the embarrassments resulting from the insertion of this word in the Articles of Confederation."[4] As a result, they "probably omitted it to avoid those embarrassments."[5] Marshall's biting reference sarcastically recalled the weaknesses of the pre-Constitutional Articles of Confederation to the Anti-Federalists.

Institutionally, *McCulloch* was a confirmation of the federal government's powers over the states as well as a reconfirmation of the Supreme Court's role in advancing the federal government's sense of mercantilism. Marshall, in perhaps the most famous of his declarations, asked that we "never forget, that it is a constitution we are expounding." We might also never forget that it was a bank that Marshall was protecting. The national bank, then in its second charter, was the quintessential mercantilist institution. It was beneficial to certain interests, financial interests of course, as well as to creditors and hard-money people generally, not to the yeoman debtors of the day. The bank had only been granted its second charter after the debacle of the War of 1812, a period when the dying Federalist Party's argument for financial stability, along with its favor for New England mercantile interests, regained a measure of legitimacy for a time. Once more, the private-to-public balance was central to the Constitutional argument, and the linkage of ideology with that private-to-public balance was clear. But it was a strengthened federal government that upheld that divide, and it clearly favored the private over the public interest.

If *McCulloch v. Maryland* presented John Marshall with an opportunity for federal institutional expansion, in furtherance of the private sector's protection, the case of *Gibbons v. Ogden* (1824)[6] presented the chief justice with an even more direct opportunity to link the federal jurisdiction to preferred business interests. Gibbons was a steamboat operator whose craft crossed the Hudson River into New Jersey. But, because of state monopolies, increasingly common in the rush of the state-centered economic protectionism which occurred in the 1820s, the New York State Supreme Court declared Gibbons ineligible to compete in the river trade.

Marshall's opinion in *Gibbons* thus spoke not only to the substance of the interstate commerce clause and the institutional supremacy of the federal jurisdiction when it came to such commerce. It spoke just as vigorously to the process of Constitutional construction itself, decrying those who would "contend for that narrow construction which, in support of some theory not to be found in the constitution, would deny to the government those powers which the words of the grant . . . import."[7]

Substantively, Marshall's opinion spoke to the necessity, responded to by the Congress in furtherance of a commercial need, to foster unimpeded navigation. Referring to the federal act concerning such matters, Marshall wrote "that regulation is designed for the entire result, applying to those parts which remain as they were as well as to those which are altered."[8] This was the crux of it. The Constitutional purpose was to promote the best of national commerce, not what states felt they needed to protect their employments and state-centered businesses.

But, even beyond its institutional implications, *Gibbons* was an unabashedly pro-business case. Though it seemed to strike down monopoly, apparently an anti-business position, it in fact favored the grander competitor in business, the national competitor of this case. It anticipated, correctly, how America's commerce would expand and how it would become truly national in scope. The case facilitated that historical progression in favor of the largest, and the most promising, economic interests that the still-young national economy could muster.

And so, with the institutional preparation of *Marbury* as well as with the two private sector–supporting and federal jurisdiction–supporting cases of *McCulloch* and *Gibbons*, John Marshall interpreted the Constitution as broadly as he could. The powers of the new national government would be expansive. But that expansion was performed in the service of the private sector, which at this time was represented by a comfortable, early-nineteenth-century conviviality between government and business. The Marshall Court's rulings were unmistakably pro–private sector rulings in spite of, or even because of, their federal government–enhancing character. Like the original Federalists, all of whom he survived by many years, John Marshall was consistent to a fault in supporting such interests.

The Contract Cases

Before leaving Chief Justice John Marshall and his Supreme Court, we should briefly consider three more pro-business cases. Two spoke to Marshall's direct support of the nineteenth-century version of the English common-law contract. The third spoke to the allocation of authority between the national and state governments in a way that still impacts Bill of Rights interpretations at the state level.

Specific protections of the contract in the Constitution were consistent, as we've seen, with the deepest motivations of the founders. Chief Justice Marshall's opinions in the cases of *Fletcher v. Peck* (1810)[9] and *Dartmouth College v. Woodward* (1819)[10] were also consistent with the framers' larger, and decidedly private, purposes. Neither of these cases approaches *Marbury*, *McCulloch*, or *Gibbons* for the brilliance of their legal reasoning, or for their legal mendacity, depending on one's point of view. Indeed, it is almost as if the directness or the lack of guile within Marshall's two contract opinions deliberately mirrors the directness of the common-law contract itself. "A deal is a deal" is the crux of what both cases said, but Marshall said it emphatically both times.

In *Fletcher v. Peck*, Marshall spoke pointedly to the problems surrounding the use of t2he Bill of Attainder in a way that would jeopardize someone's life, liberty, or property. Marshall could not pass up the opportunity to review the historic record of legislatures that had passed acts depriving people of their private rights. But, in the context of this ideological lecturing in *Fletcher*, the case focused on the nature of the contract that the state of Georgia had entered into. It had granted land ownership in the Yazoo area, what is now part of Mississippi, to cronies of legislative members. And it did so in return for a bribe, a fact that everyone knew and which was ostensibly corrected when the next year's more honest legislature attempted to cancel the sale.

But Marshall, tongue firmly in his cheek, declared, "it is not intended to speak with disrespect of the legislature of Georgia, or of its acts. Far from it."[11] All we are doing, Marshall said, was assure the repurchasers of the land, those who bought it from the bribers who got it from the first legislature, that they would be protected in their title. The case's discussion of private contract law was all the more powerful because it concluded by saying that "the rights of third persons who are purchasers without notice, for a valuable consideration, cannot be disregarded."[12] If such rights were not protected, "all titles would be insecure, and the intercourse between man and man would be very seriously obstructed."[13] The contract, and the reasonable expectation of those who entered into it, would be preserved. This strategy of ensuring the right of the good-faith purchaser for value in the normal course of trade, as we have reviewed, is but a modern outgrowth of common-law court protections regarding land that date back to the thirteenth century. The case of *Fletcher v. Peck* is taught less frequently today than it deserves to be. It no longer appears in many undergraduate Constitutional law texts. It is still an important case, particularly because of its discussion of the private law and its declaration of the supremacy of the private law over what even an honest legislature might do to correct a less than honest legislature's misdeeds.

Again, a deal is a deal, and that reasonable expectation of a purchaser in a private setting takes undeniable preference over the most honorable and best intentioned of legislative acts. As Marshall said, "The rights of third persons who are purchasers without notice, for a valuable consideration, cannot be diminished."[14] He added, "Titles which, according to legal test, are acquired with that confidence which is inspired by the opinion that the purchaser is safe" will be held to be good.[15] The private-to-public line was rarely drawn more clearly, or more generously toward the private side, in U.S. Constitutional law.

Another private sector case, *Dartmouth College* (1819), was even simpler on its facts than *Fletcher.* The New Hampshire legislature's attempts to reconfigure the governance of Dartmouth College ran afoul of what was not a pure buyer-to-seller contract but, rather, a grant from a political sovereign. In this case, however, the political sovereign was His (former) Majesty George III. We had excused George III in 1776, and if the Revolutionary War bonds were being made good by Article 6 of the Constitution, wasn't it strange to maintain the validity of paper such as a college charter which came from the other side of the conflict, in this case the losers'?

Not for Marshall. Even an arrangement created by old opposition would be upheld, Marshall's legal rationale in *Dartmouth College* being that "the circumstances of this case constitute a contract."[16] That "large contributions have been made for the object [the college]" in reasonable reliance on that contract was irrefutable.[17] Traditional common-law notions of reasonable reliance were rarely better illustrated, Marshall saying that "the contract is granted, and on its faith the property is conveyed."[18] Any impairment of that contract, not by something as trivial as having a king removed as the nation's sovereign but by something as pernicious as having a sitting legislature try to reconfigure a contract, would not be tolerated.

Beyond these contract-related cases, Marshall's final important Constitutional case, decided but two years before the last Federalist's death, grew out of a civil liberties protection dispute that became the landmark case of *Barron v. Baltimore* (1833).[19] Barron was but a small businessman, hardly a Francis Biddle or someone involved with an institution like the national bank. Barron owned a wharf in Baltimore's harbor, and, when the city of Baltimore (a legal entity created by the state of Maryland) improved its streets, silt ran toward the harbor, filling Barron's slips. This put him out of business, Barron's suit against Maryland claiming that he had been deprived of his property without due process of law. He based his claim on the Constitution's Fifth Amendment.

If there is one case among all of the great Marshall Supreme Court cases, or indeed among the cases of any chief or associate justice, which reflects the conflict between the private and the public sectors of the government and at the same time reflects the Supreme Court's willingness to protect federal prerogatives within the private domain, it is *Barron*. At first glance the case is ironic. Marshall does not hold for Barron, the private businessman. But why not?

For better or for worse, Marshall's bitter memory of the Anti-Federalists was as alive in 1833 as it was in 1819 with *McCulloch* or at the time of the Bill of Rights itself. Marshall had not forgotten who had fostered the Bill of Rights, and he had not forgotten their denigration of the document that Marshall so revered. Thus, in response to Barron's plea nearly forty years after the Constitutional debate, Marshall did no more (and no less) than remind a new generation that it was "universally understood" that it was the Anti-Federalists who as "part of the history of the day," had greeted "the great revolution which established the Constitution of the United States" with "immense opposition." [20] Continuing, when "serious fears were extensively entertained that those powers which the patriot statesmen who then watched over the interests of our country deemed essential to union" were expressed by the Anti-Federalists, when these Anti-Federalists "demanded security against the apprehended encroachments of the general government—not against those of the local governments," it was this Bill of Rights that they came up with.[21]

Not only had Marshall not forgotten these contrarian citizens and what they had tried to do. He would make sure that the Anti-Federalists' ideological descendants did not forget, or eventually triumph, either.

Barron, a small businessman who sought to use what the Anti-Federalists had used to balance the Constitution's protections of private rights at the state level, was quietly told that neither the federal Bill of Rights, nor the federal government in any guise, would shield him. He would have to go to his Anti-Federalists' beloved state to find his remedy.

In this chapter what I have described is how the United States' interpretive period, the period immediately following the passage of the Constitution and the Bill of Rights, continued essentially the same ideological-to-institutional arrangements that had centered the Constitutional ratification debate. The impact of the Supreme Court opinions of the great Chief Justice John Marshall on the institutional arrangements of the new U.S. government is a well-studied subject. But it is only half the story, and it is, I suggest, the lesser half. More than anything else, John Marshall's opinions ensured that the private sector–protecting devices within the federal Constitution were also maintained, as the federal government's powers were maintained, in the interpretive cases that followed the ratification.

That Marshall succeeded in protecting the private sector as well as he did is, of course, a testament to the brilliance, and the judicial daring, of the author of the United States' foundational judicial opinions. But that success is also a product of the residue of those balances between the private and public sector which had been accumulating for so long in both English history and the American experience. Those who put the U.S. political system together did their work within the context of a very pointed history. That history had protected the private sector vigilantly through the early years of Coke, Blackstone, and those that came before them. A Federalist-dominated Supreme Court in the United States' interpretive period could hardly ignore that history.

Whether or not one is in sympathy with the perspective of the Federalist drafters and those ratifying Marshall Supreme Court opinions I have reviewed, it is impossible to read the provisions of the Constitution highlighted in previous chapters or the Marshall opinions reviewed here without acknowledging the framers' profound commitment to a historically steeped and ideologically seasoned perspective. At least through the time of Marshall, the private sector continued to be the privileged sector in the United States, just as it had emerged as the privileged sector over the long pull of English history after the seventeenth century, and particularly after that century's mercantilist successes over the Stuarts. This new country, the Federalists and their latter-day interpreters felt, must do no less than continue that private dominance, and they successfully charged their federal government with doing just that.

CHAPTER SEVEN

The Taney Revision

The Federalists' Last Stand

Chief Justice John Marshall's greatest cases stretched the enumerated powers provisions of the Constitution's Article 1, section 8, as well as other provisions of the Constitution. It is interesting to speculate that, had the Anti-Federalists foreseen Marshall's interpretive rulings, Constitutional ratification might have been even more difficult than it was. Yet, in a larger and more historically sensitive way, Marshall's cases represented nothing more than the continuation of a long Anglo-American history that currently embraced a highly mercantilist view of the relationship of government and private sector.

The early interpretive period of the Constitution, at the same time, marked that period of solidification for both the United States' political system and for the national economy that is associated with the country's coming of age. It is obligatory, therefore, to assess Marshall's great Constitutional cases, as we started to do in the last chapter, as not only furthering the sanctity of the Constitution but also as continuing English mercantilism's judicial acceptance on this side of the pond.

Both the contract cases of *Dartmouth* and *Fletcher*[1] had dealt with grants—that is, permissions from a government. If Sir Edward Coke's notions of reason were to be extended to U.S. mercantilism and if they were to continue to be a part of United States common law well into the nineteenth century (as Marshall surely wished for it), then the law's protection of private property was mandatory. Marshall was no abstract theorizer. What he sought were actual political *and* economic communities that each worked well because they worked together. The other nationalist figures of the time were hardly stargazers either. They saw the elements of property and contract for what they were, still the core of a practical, wealth-producing mercantilist system.

In James Kent's late 1820s *Commentaries*, for example, lecture 19 of part 2 uses no less than six terms that bracket contract within a government-to-entrepreneur, rather than a private offerer–to–acceptor, form of understanding. *Grants, donors, rights, franchises, patent,* and *license* all mark Kent's work, shoring up his affirmation for whatever protections a private, preferred economic entity could garner from the state.[2]

Of course, if the mercantilist form of contract was governmentally inspired or if, at a minimum, it represented an agreement between a government grantor and an entrepreneurial grantee, then the government itself would need to be strong enough to both make and enforce such arrangements. Therefore, the legacy of federalism, beyond that of Chief Justice Marshall's thirty-four years of Constitutional rulings, should be seen as more than just a legacy of contract and property, no matter how supportive of those two fundaments they were. Marshall's bequest was also, necessarily, a legacy of strong government, that government actively assisting the nongovernmental sector.

Beyond Kent, the legacy of strong government support for America's core businesses was still argued well into the 1830s, after Marshall had left the Court. The *Commentaries* of Supreme Court Justice Joseph Story, the great nationalist of the Jackson period, for example, spoke as approvingly of the private sector's receiving support from the national government as Marshall ever did.[3] Further, the emphasis upon the national-to-state balance in Story's writings was every bit as real as it was for Marshall. Fervent nationalist that he was, Story, like Marshall, recognized that the supremacy of judicial law over legislated law was as much a part of profitable mercantilism as was the supremacy of the national government over state governments.

In point of fact, a fair portion of the mercantilism of the pre-Jacksonian and Jacksonian periods did exist at the state, not the federal, level. As George Brown Tindall has noted, it was states who "plunged heavily into debt to finance the building of roads and canals, inspired by the success of New York's Erie Canal."[4] Except in cases like *Gibbons,*[5] in which state mercantilism interfered with federal mercantilism, Marshall did not interfere with private-to-public cooperation at the state level. He would accept the states' doing what he believed the federal government should also be doing, so long as there was no national interference from below. Story, in Marshallian tones, reminded the citizen that *"the people do ordain* and *establish,* not contract and stipulate with each other."[6] In such ordaining of a federal "'*constitution,*' not a '*confederation,*'" Story also reminded the citizenry that the federal Constitution was a "supreme law," a law that, as he put it, "imports legal obligation, permanence, and uncontrollability by any but the authorities authorized to alter, or abolish it."[7] Courts at both the state and federal levels were the institutions that had traditionally supported private law.

Story's borrowing of the "ordain and establish" phrase from the Constitution did indeed import the supremacy of one level of government over another. But, again, it was not just national and state jurisdictions that Story was writing about. Still much in the Federalist mode, he was concerned as well with the supremacy of the judicial over the legislative determination of law. It was judicially interpreted, private sector–supporting law that for Story should continue, in the post-Marshall era, to grow out of a federal jurisdiction that was, in turn, something more than a compact among the states.

Of course, the contracts that Jacksonian small-*d* democrats would argue for in opposition to Story did not contain the synthetic form of the grant, franchise, etc., which writers such as Kent of the National period or the Marshall Court or even Story favored. The judicial successors to Marshall, generally being opponents of the nationalist vision of Story, foresaw that the more purely competitive private contract, not the mercantilist grant, would foster a more egalitarian society. As Richard Hofstadter has pointed out, "The Jacksonian movement grew out of expanding opportunities and a common desire to enlarge those opportunities still further by removing restrictions and privileges that had their origin in government."[8] Hofstadter further noted that Jacksonianism "was essentially a movement of laissez-faire, an attempt to divorce government and business."[9] As Sidney Fine put it, "The Jacksonians would tolerate government intervention to remove monopoly, but such intervention was designed to restore a situation where competition would once again prevail and where government intervention would no longer be necessary."[10]

Like Marshall in *Barron*[11] on the Federalist side, therefore, the Anti-Federalists' successors too had not forgotten the arguments of the Anti-Federalists to the effect that the power of the national government would inevitably lead to economic as well as political favor. They did not ignore the fact that, in the years since the Constitution's passage, federal government–encouraged mercantile contracts had often resulted in very profitable relationships for segments of the private sector. The post-Marshall Supreme Court's attack on a more than half-century-old economic-to-political arrangement marks one of the key sectoral, and institutional, milestones of U.S. Constitutional history.

Justice Taney's Reasoning

Though Roger Taney honestly believed he had resolved the nation's by then deeply festering regional conflict, this chief justice's name has been remembered above all for the devastating impact of his *Dred Scott* (1857) opinion.[12] The shock of the *Dred Scott* decision, particularly as it settled in on the abolitionists of the North, still overshadows a Taney Supreme Court decision that was far more important than *Dred Scott* to the long-term development of U.S. jurisprudence.

On its facts Taney's decision in *Charles River Bridge v. Warren* (1837)[13] negated a state-granted monopoly held by someone who assumed the permanence of that monopoly for carrying traffic over the Charles River. The city of Boston had grown, extending itself up the Charles River. A new toll bridge, a bridge that would compete with a previously chartered bridge closer to town, was licensed by the state of Massachusetts to accommodate the upriver population. The ruling of Chief Justice Taney, upholding the right of the Bay State's legislature to alter the expectations of a prior monopolist, marked the judicial acceptance of at least a modicum of egalitarian, legislatively directed involvement in the economy. In contrast to John Marshall's rejection of legislative interference with private rights in such cases as *Dartmouth* and *Fletcher*, *Charles River Bridge* permitted the public sector's most democratic institution to impinge on previously secure private rights.

Just as important, *Charles River Bridge* also marked progress in the historic separation of private and public domains. Whereas the mercantilism of Hamilton and Marshall had helped ensure governmental protection for private entrepreneurship, Taney placed the private interest into a position that was more competitive with other private sector entities at the same time that it was more divorced from government. From the standpoint of productivity, as well as from the standpoint of distributive fairness, Taney felt as many in the executive and legislative branches of both state and federal legislatures did during the Jacksonian period. Competitive enterprise now better suited a nation that was more secure about its economy than it had been at any time since the Revolution.

If the public sector was now frequently to encourage competition, as it had encouraged early mercantilism, so be it. The grant for the second bridge in Boston came from a government after all, just as the grant for the first bridge had. A full divorce of the private sector from government, of course, was never completed within a national experience that included late-century support for grants of land to the railroads and stiff tariff protection, and even twentieth century water, farm, and other subsidies, particularly in the West, that continue today. But the historic trend of separating economic, private sector entities from the protection of the government accelerated during the 1830s. And, as a result of business's decreased involvement with the government after that time, the contract itself correspondingly moved a healthy notch toward an analytic cognitive form. A lessened involvement with the government often turned Kent's mercantilist "grant," "license," "monopoly," and so on into more of a party-to-party, private contract.

With the Taney Court, in sum, the pro-mercantilist, pro–federal government judicial activism of the John Marshall period substantially came to an end. Whereas Marshall was expanding the federal Constitution by way of broad constructions, and sometimes negating what the political branches at the state level had been doing since the time of the Articles of Confederation, Taney was far more accommodating to legislative rule making generally and to state legislative rule making in particular. In that sense the Taney Court, at least while it was dealing with economic issues (i.e., before *Dred Scott*), cannot be classified as an activist Court in the sense of reversing legislative creations. It was generally sympathetic to such creations.

To a large degree the Taney Court was less activist than the Marshall Court because the small-*d* democrats firmly controlled the remainder of the government under both Andrew Jackson and Jackson's mostly large-*D* Democratic Congress. Why would a chief justice who was both a small- and large-*d* democrat himself want to interrupt the promised, and frequently realized, egalitarianism that the ending of the "three-cornered hat" period brought to the still-new country?

The progress of Jacksonian democracy should be understood at another level as well. There was a subtle but very real relationship between the alteration of the private-to-public boundary and the alteration of the institutional alliances of the Jackson/Taney period. The movement to a more unfettered private sector, with its accompanying movement to a more analytic, non–publicly engaged contract, had a very real impact on the nature of the balances between both the states and the federal government, on one hand, and legislatures and the courts, on the other.

Yes, the retreat from Marshall's judicial activism placed legislatures in a more powerful position vis-à-vis the Court during Taney's reign as chief justice. The Anti-Federalists' domestic successors in this era were much happier with Taney than they ever were with Marshall. But, beyond the realignment of legislative-to-court power, the Taney period also marked a change in the balance between states and the federal government which went beyond the acceptance of those state-generated, antimercantilist policies that I have referred to.

By the time of *Charles River Bridge* the restrictive tariffs that hurt Taney's native Southern portion of the country were renewing Constitutional-era suspicions between the Northern and Southern regions of the nation. Similarly, they were lessening the possibility of economically based, Constitutional-era-like political alliances such as those of a Charles Cotesworth Pinckney from South Carolina with either the merchants of Connecticut, for example, or an Alexander Hamilton representing the Schuyler family from New York. At the same time, an alliance such as the one between latter-day Anti-Federalists from North Carolina, whom we saw voting down the Constitution in the first ratification convention, and latter-day successors to a family such as the anti-Constitution Clintons from New York was now more likely to be supplanted by a different kind of political identification. That identification was based on region.

In short, the Taney alteration of the private-to-public balance and the legislative-to-court balance coincided with, if it did not in fact encourage, an alteration of another important balance, the state-to-federal balance now reflecting the strains of a growing regional conflict. The Taney who reversed the trend of Marshall's economic opinions and who held off the nationalist bent of his well-written contemporary on the Court, Joseph Story, was unwittingly laying the groundwork for the exacerbated tensions of the 1840s and 1850s, long before *Dred Scott*. A federal government that did not require mercantilism to fend off the economic threats of an England or a France perhaps did not need as strong a federal government in other matters either. As a result, activist state governments that did not need to be reined in by a private sector–protecting federal Supreme Court could begin to think of their new independence within more than merely an economic context.

Do not misunderstand. No one would argue that the tensions that grew up between the two great regions of a nation more confident on the world stage than it had ever been occurred because of the decline of mercantilism. The clash between a relatively egalitarian, commercial, and industrializing North with an agricultural and slave-holding South would have carved the political fault line of the bitter 1828 and 1832 tariff disputes, even without the decline of federal private-to-public cooperation.

Similarly, all would acknowledge that the small-*d* democratic alterations that occurred in much of the nation's politics in the late 1820s and the 1830s, with the ending of the Congressional nominating caucuses, the beginning of local and state nominating conventions, the beginning of public campaigning, and the strikingly vigorous political energy of an increasingly expanded franchise, also impacted the sectoral division. These events played an important role in the movement from a closed and centralized national politics to a more open and decentralized governmental arrangement throughout the northern and western portions of the country in contrast to the South. But these political developments too would not alone have fired a divisive regional debate.

Finally, no one would doubt that the diminished quality of national leadership, both in the Senate with the passing of Daniel Webster, John C. Calhoun, and the "Great Compromiser," Henry Clay, by the early 1850s, as well as in the White House with the indolent presidencies of Zachary Taylor, Millard Fillmore, Franklin Pierce, and James Buchanan surely played no small role in the building crisis. The absence of leadership is invariably a part of any political fissure, but this too did not of itself further the regional schism.

But, with due consideration for the factors described here, it is hard to deny the fact that subtle but very important shifts in the configuration of state-to-federal and legislative-to-judicial power in the post-Marshall era not only were represented by but were to at least some degree facilitated by the antimercantilist rulings of Chief Justice Taney in cases such as *Charles River Bridge*. Such cases both acknowledged and fostered the growing separation of the private and public sectors. Some thought that they rebalanced state-to-federal power. Though the Roger Taney of *Dred Scott* was twenty years older than the Taney of *Charles River Bridge* and though that latter-day Taney was neither a well man physically because of his age nor a well man emotionally because of the recent deaths of his wife and a daughter, the second great Taney case (*Dred Scott*) relies in a great part upon the movement away from the private-to-public sector linkages of John Marshall that is represented in *Charles River*.[14]

Let us closely compare the two great Taney cases. First, note that the balance of state-to-federal power in *Charles River Bridge* and *Dred Scott* is identical. Both deprecate federal power in favor of state authority. The case's judicial-to-legislative alignments, on the other hand, are reversed. Taney's ruling in *Dred Scott* was a clear judicial declaration of legislative unconstitutionality, the case overruling a national legislative agreement, the Missouri Compromise, and doing so by implicitly embracing a plethora of state legislative actions that permitted the "peculiar institution" to continue unfettered in the South. In its institutional underpinnings, therefore, *Dred Scott* countermanded all John Marshall stood for. And sectorally, the Taney Court in *Dred Scott* now protected the private sector in a way that would divide the nation, not ensure its bonding. The federal lawmaking that created the Missouri Compromise and which had implicitly recognized the federal, public citizenship of African Americans had been representative of that bonding. *Dred Scott* rended that bond, moving well beyond the passive acknowledgement of public power in defense of the private sector in *Charles River.*

In short, it is the private-to-public sector alignment of *Dred Scott* that is so grotesquely extended beyond *Charles River.* Dred Scott, after all, was private property: he was a slave. Taney would protect that slave property's ownership, well in keeping with Article 1, section 9's first civil liberty, as well as in keeping with Article 4, section 2, subsection 2's guarantee that escaped slaves should "be delivered up." Taney would certainly oppose any public sector attempt at that private ownership's mitigation. Article 1, section 9, recall, was the only civil liberty in the original seven articles which protected such a private property-related right.

Thus, if the substantive ruling in *Dred Scott* (finding the thought-to-be-free Scott to be still a slave) shocked the nation, the Court's wholesale denuding of the federal government's powers in favor of the nation's most challenged private right, the ownership of a slave, outraged what was by then a hearty abolitionist element in the North. With its specific declaration that the Missouri Compromise was unconstitutionally passed by the general government, along with its ruling that no federal citizenship existed for the nation's largest minority, the case revealed that Taney had engineered a thorough jurisprudential about-face and ironically resurrected a Marshall-like Court stance on the power of the Court versus a legislature in order to substantially unbalance the domains of private-to-public rights. If the immediately post-Marshall Supreme Court, with its pro-legislative and antimercantilist biases, had found its home with Taney, the chief justice's preference for the power of state governments placed both the institutional (legislature-to-court) and the sectoral (private-to-public) dichotomies into as exaggerated a set of castings as it had ever known.

Put another way, when the central issue of the day became one of the power of state governments versus the power of the federal government, Taney's favor for the former jurisdiction led him to abandon the institutional (legislature-over-court) allegiance that had marked his early cases. Competitive economic interests, when promoted by legislatures, might still be encouraged, of course. But when a legislature, even the federal legislature, threatened a private interest held by a state's politically dominant citizens, that is, when a sectionally specific private interest such as slavery was threatened by a broad implementation of federal legislative powers, an institutionally redirected Taney Court would intercede to protect the private, state-centered interest regardless of the institutional consequences.

All along, the evolution of the private-to-public domain's separations, as found in cases such as *Charles River Bridge,* had lain at the heart of

Taney's original jurisprudence. But in *Dred Scott*, when the regional debate had begun in earnest, Taney affirmed an extreme commitment to the private sector, that position accommodating the Southern aristocracy's position. The Tidewater Marylander's judicial accommodation of the Southern aristocracy requires reference now to another aristocratic Southern family, one from Virginia, and one even more notable than Taney's.

The Lees of Virginia

In my earlier discussion of the Federalists and the Anti-Federalists, I cited the writings ascribed to the Virginian Richard Henry Lee as among the most noteworthy of the Anti-Federalist arguments. Lee's position, at the time of the ratification, was of course what would later be called the "states' rights" position. It reflected the traditional Anti-Federalist preference for a considerable independence of state governments from federal political instruction.

One of the most important public choices in all of American history was the choice of Richard Henry Lee's grandson, General Robert E. Lee, to side with his home state of Virginia in opposition to the national government once his state had seceded from the Union. The younger Lee, of course, was already a notable military figure, having served bravely in the Mexican War as well as having commanded the army contingent that captured and disarmed John Brown's Harpers Ferry abolitionists in 1859.

It is well-known that President Abraham Lincoln offered command of the Union armies to Lee, whose refusal resulted in Lee's overmatched involvement with a series of incompetent Union generals through the early years of the war. Lee wretchedly paced the floor the night of Lincoln's invitation and, much later, eschewed Jefferson Davis's suggestion to continue guerilla activity at the end of the war. There is little doubt, however, that the Confederacy lasted far longer than it would have had the general chosen differently when the hostilities began.

The secession of the state of Virginia, along with the other "border" states of Arkansas, Tennessee, and North Carolina, occurred several months after the secession of the seven Deep South states. History reminds us that only shortly before its secession Virginia's citizenry was still evenly divided on the issue. What is now West Virginia, of course, engaged in its own secession from the state that finally departed the Washington government, General Lee failing to recapture the lost hinterlands of his native state in one of the war's earliest campaigns.

All of these developments seem to reaffirm the great sectoral and institutional themes that were left behind by Federalists such as Alexander Hamilton and Anti-Federalists such as the Civil War general's grandfather. If Richard Henry Lee, and those like Elbridge Gerry from Massachusetts and many others had stood for the supremacy of the states, it would seem to be understandable why the Virginian Robert E. Lee made the choice that he did, for his state and against his nation.

But it's not as simple as that. Were the states of the 1860s, particularly in the South, in an analogous position to that of the states of 1788, or even of the 1830s, vis-à-vis the federal government? To a considerable degree they were not, and the evidence for this is apparent when one considers what had changed *within* the states that were ready to embrace the Confederacy's proximity of private and public sectors, as opposed to what had changed in the Northern and Western states.

The use of the title Confederate States of America, of course, was no accident. The secessionists were harkening back, if not entirely, to the time when states were the sole sovereign. Though the Confederate Constitution is identical to the federal Constitution in many places, the return to a state-dominated league of national identity was clearly the plan in Montgomery and, later, Richmond. But history never returns to exactly the same place. Though the coastal states of the South were more dominated by the planter class than were states on the other side of the Appalachians, the balance of power throughout the South still overwhelmingly reflected the influence of the planters at the time of the secession. Tocqueville's chronicling of democracy's ascendancy in America always had an asterisk.[15]

As Clement Eaton put it, "The Jacksonian movement . . . was slow in bringing about change in the undemocratic practices of the older states of the South."[16] Though the Southern Anti-Federalists at the time of the Constitution were overwhelmingly made up of either backcountry yeoman farmers or those who spoke up for the South's small middle class, such as the elder Lee, those middle-class interests were still politically marginalized at the time of secession in at least the older Southern states. As Eaton noted, "An important criterion in determining whether the state government was controlled by an aristocracy or by the people was the basis used in apportioning representation in the legislature."[17] States such as Maryland, Virginia, North Carolina, South Carolina, Georgia, and Louisiana, according to Eaton, were still grossly malapportioned in favor of the aristocracy. "In 1860," Eaton concluded, "South Carolina was the most aristocratic state in the nation, the only one that continued to choose presidential electors, the governor and state officials by the legislature and to require a high property qualification for its chief executive."[18]

Thus, the configuration of support for the national government had changed by the time of the secession debate. National separation was overwhelmingly proposed by those same low-country interests that were

generally Federalists in 1788, their allegiances to the national government having been whittled away over a time of unfavorable tariffs during
the Jackson period as well by the threatening abolitionism that immediately preceded separation. As a result, the dominant economic and political figures of the South had long been on the side of state as opposed to
federal power by 1860. By then they had long opposed a strong federal
role over a variety of issues such as assistance to homesteaders and assistance to land-grant colleges, the Homestead Act and the Morrill Act being approved by the federal Congress only during the Civil War.

All in all, the Southern secessionists of 1860–61 believed they were
speaking for the same social, cultural, and political interests of the South
which Richard Henry Lee had been quite uncomfortable with at time of
Constitutional ratification. But, though a solitary look at the issue of state
versus federal power must score an event such as General Lee's siding
with his state as institutionally consistent with his grandfather's wariness
of federal power, the younger Lee's decision, within the context of the
arrangement of economic and political interests in the general's time,
may have been anything but consistent with his grandfather's position.
The elder Lee had supported emerging independent yeoman and
nonmercantilist, competitive, middle-class interests. Grandson Lee fought
for the agricultural, slave-based politics of a rural mercantilism that in
1860 still dominated Southern politics.

The secessionist position, of course, opposed the prewar position
that made up what there was of Unionist sentiment in the South. This
sentiment was typically expressed by a growing middle class in states like
Virginia and, particularly, North Carolina, the last state to secede. The
strongest of these middle-class commercial and financial interests most
often resided in the still small cities of the Upland South such as Char-
lotte, Greenville, Atlanta, and Carrolsville (later Birmingham). In a few
rural upland counties, such as Yadkin County in North Carolina and
Winston County in Alabama, the citizenry went so far as to rebel against
their state governments during the Civil War. They rejected their state's
secession from the Union and waited for the Confederacy to pass away in
the shadows of their Appalachian hills. East Tennessee, as far west as
Knoxville, also remained loyal to the Union. But the commercial,
nonmercantile interests of this upland region were no stronger politically there than they were in the other Southern states.

In contrast to these upland perspectives, it may be that Robert E.
Lee's choosing of the secessionist position in the Civil War supported the
very type of private sector–dominant mercantilism *within* Southern states
which his grandfather had opposed seventy years earlier. More modern,

commercial interests became either caught up in the emotion of the secession or (as in Virginia) simply lost out in the struggle to have their states remain loyal to the Union. Once more, the secession debate winners were those interests whose wherewithal depended upon the continuation, unlike the North, of a highly synthetic form of social, economic, and even cultural contract that was only partly marked by the continuing endorsement of slavery. What an irony it was that Richard Henry Lee's position on the middle class and on antimercantilist private enterprise was so repudiated by Virginia's secession. And what an irony it was that Taney's separation of the private and public sectors (and preference for the private) in cases such as *Charles River Bridge* was so perverted by the aristocratically led secession that institutionally and sectorally dominated his opinion in *Dred Scott.*

Majorities and Calhoun

At their foundation the pre–Civil War arguments of the secessionists rested on a distinct political as well as economic position. That position, in turn, rested particularly on the issue of political majorities. In briefly examining these arguments, I will not detail the positions of those who ultimately founded the Confederacy. I will focus instead on that one writer and political figure who served as the intellectual underpinning for the Confederacy's creation. That figure, of course, was the South Carolinian John C. Calhoun. At the outset let us look at Calhoun's argument not from the standpoint of its substantive positions on a variety of the day's issues but from the standpoint of how Calhoun's sectoral and institutional preferences compared to the perspectives of those who chose not to take a similar, minoritarian view at other times in Anglo-American history.

I use the word *minoritarian* here in obvious contrast to the term *majoritarian.* The history of the Anglo-American legal and political experience, until the Southern secession, demonstrated time and again that the whole of the Anglo-American political community almost invariably came to accept the consequences of constitutional struggles that went on between competing interests. Whether it was the War of the Roses, the battle between the Houses of York and Lancaster, or the English Civil War, which pitted the Stuart monarchy against Cromwell's republicans, there was never a sense in England that even these greatest of political confrontations would be settled by carving English sovereignty into geographic parts. No one suggested letting one position's advocates live under a fundamentally different set of arrangements than some others.

Throughout the English experience, in other words, the majority position, or at a minimum the *aspiring* majority position, simply strove to replace the previously accepted arrangement. It did so without threatening to leave the overall community or without threatening to evict those who lost if the evolutionary majoritarian position they supported gained favor. Similarly, the losing side of history, so to speak—that is, the side whose position lost out to the aspiring, eventually successful, position—invariably folded itself, if reluctantly, back into the larger polity.

Outside of the great struggles for power represented by the earlier English conflicts, English political and legal debate often concerned that liberation of the private law from the feudal law which we have reviewed. Further back, the ascending commercial interests of the twelfth and thirteenth centuries demanded, and eventually received, what they needed from what were still often feudally responsive authorities during the centuries immediately following William. The losers in that struggle, incidentally, never asked that England be dismembered, or confederated, between feudal and freehold lands.

Succeeding English political and legal conflicts witnessed the evolving position of the private law, along with the mercantile arrangements that sometimes fostered it, as they ascended through the millennium's middle centuries. By the time of the seventeenth century the Stuarts, as we have also examined, attempted to reverse history for a time, compelling the private law and its advocates, such as Coke, to battle for what they felt were their rightful legal and political prerogatives. If the aspiringly majoritarian political position of the seventeenth-century mercantilists eventually won out in the Glorious Revolution of 1688, Parliament's permanent status only made the day's mercantilists feel more secure. Though the voting franchise was still much restricted by today's standards, it was this commercially dominated Whig period that saw Walpole triumph over the Tories and Bolingbroke, creating that majoritarian cabinet form of government I have described. Once more, the losers did not retire from England or seek to dismember their country for having lost.

Within the American experience, although the Revolution may well have been supported by only the one-third of Americans so frequently referred to in the textbooks, the Revolution's success was soon accepted by a vast majority of formerly English colonists. A few on the losing side fled to the Canadian colonies, to be sure, but they never sought to rend the thirteen which had recently liberated themselves. As colonialism withdrew from this middle ground of the North American continent, the country's Articles of Confederation most certainly captured the majority American political position in the years before the Constitution. Shortly after, even if the Constitution was a minoritarian document that was approved in great part because of the influence of a small number of framers and their ratification allies, it was soon accepted by all.

Then, only a historical moment later, the Bill of Rights spoke again to a majoritarian sentiment. It assured the American citizenry as a whole that democratic political progress would continue within both the public, specifically legislative, institutions of the Congress and their own state legislatures. In doing so, the Bill of Rights actually ratified the Constitution as much as did the states' ratifying conventions by giving the Constitutional debate's losers in the ratification struggle cause to stay within the community. Similarly, those who had opposed the Bill of Rights did not retire, or suggest national dismemberment, when the Bill achieved Constitutional status. In the next generation the early moments of Andrew Jackson's presidency represented an additional stage of majoritarian progress. The fuller democratization of the American political system reinforced the strength of the public sector as well as the legislative and executive branches of both the state and national governments. But older, mercantile economic interests invariably folded themselves into the new order.

During the Jacksonian period, pre–Civil War tensions had begun in earnest. While the nation's majorities grew out of evolvingly democratic processes, along with the acceptance of a more egalitarian society within the northern and western sections of the nation, an ever more isolated Southern aristocracy saw itself as losing its influence in the face of a faster-growing and increasingly wealthier North. The Southern aristocracy's sense of the permanence of its minority status, reinforced by the issue of slavery, brought a greater intensity to the Republic's politics than any issue before it. It led the Southern leadership to a different form of response to its status from any that the Anglo-American experience had yet witnessed.

In short, the Southern regional acceptance of Calhoun's arguments concerning what he called the "concurrent majority" meant that a portion of a nation wished now to dismantle the whole. Seeing itself as a permanent minority (which it needn't have) was surely part of Calhoun's, and the Southern aristocracy's, sense of self. Refusing to see how the South could ever be part of the historical evolution—that is, a part of a majority again—just as surely led to the Southern aristocracy's unique antimajoritarian position.

Why did the aristocratic South not envisage how it might continue to be a vital part of the Union? The growing population of the North and the West, Calhoun figured, would if anything extend its majority position whether the national argument included (1) the admission of new states, slave or free, (2) tariff policy and the dominance of Northern protectionist interests, or, most tellingly, (3) the eventual disposition of the slave population within the South itself. Calhoun's structural response to all of this, his argument for institutional disengagement, was ultimately expanded by Chief Justice Taney, who included the clipping of the Congress's legislative wings regarding North-South "settlements" such as the Missouri Compromise in his infamous *Dred Scott* decision.

In the northern and western sections of the United States the political accession of the latter-day successors to the Anti-Federalists, particularly the political accession of the 1830s small-*d* democrats under Jackson, brought forth new, uniquely American examples of how a political order might peacefully move aristocracy aside and involve the citizenry in its government. This, after all, was what Tocqueville was describing so vividly in *Democracy in America*.

Yet the fact that democratic progress proceeded farther in the North than it ever did in the South meant that by the 1830s the Southern aristocracy was only more frightened than ever. The South's leadership's inability, or unwillingness, to envisage how it might have continued to be a full partner in the national union had a great deal to do with the fact that its leadership greatly feared the rise of its own commercial middle class and the political clout that would have accompanied it. In a sense the aristocracy of the South therefore feared precisely what Richard Henry Lee had favored. Rather than support a potentially competitive private sector within its own region which would gradually replace the agrarians, a position not only consistent with the progress of the remainder of the country but in keeping with the entrepreneurship of the South's own Taney in *Charles River Bridge*, the dominant figures of the South chose even more vigorously to defend their slave-based, agricultural mercantilism. As I have said, it was a social and economic order that resembled eighteenth-century mercantilism in its *form* far more than anything that existed elsewhere by the fourth decade of the nineteenth century.

Let us not forget that non-slave-based, commercial areas existed throughout the upland South, Lacy K. Ford pointing out that a state like Georgia, for example, had but 10 percent of its cotton produced in its upland counties.[19] As John C. Inscoe has observed, by the late 1850s Southern upland "residents' increased independence and self-confidence in the role as suppliers" led them to pull away from the political lead of those in the lowcountry who had dominated their regions economically and politically.[20] As Inscoe put it, "Mountain Masters" were "Chiefly professional men, shop-keepers and men in office."[21] Indeed, there was "diversification" even among the few slave owners of the upland region, with those slaves being involved in "manufacturing and mercantile enterprises," not just agriculture.[22] As a result, as Steven Hahn has written, the South's commercial bourgeoisie was rooted in the up-country, where a gathering "process of democratization . . . grew out of extended agitation" for political independence. The up-country became "more of a yeoman stronghold" than other parts of the South, a place where "self-sufficiency," specifically the moving away from dependence on the lowcountry plantation system, was the order of the day.[23]

From the perspective of the antebellum lowcountry planters, to permit those non-slaveholding areas and their interests to be better represented within the Southern states would jeopardize their own control. As a result, the slavocracy never let it happen. Thus, whereas minorities within the American and the English polity before the American Civil War had chosen to accept their fate within the larger political system, most recently within the context of an increasingly democratic American tradition, the reluctance of the Southern leadership to follow in that tradition and permit their up-country citizens to form natural, majoritarian, alliances with their Northern opposite numbers required an institutional and sectoral stance that was wholly outside of the Anglo-American jurisprudential tradition.[24] The subsequent chapters of this work will continue to trace the development of that experience, but suffice it to say here that there is a configuration of private-to-public power, as well as of judicial-to-legislative power and state-to-federal power, which both permits the achievement of acceptable legal and political results for temporary political minorities and imposes far less severe penalties than the Southern secession did on the general American polity. Such minorities, I will suggest, can ensure redress even when a legislative majority is temporarily foreclosed to them.

I have spent this time on Calhoun's position, and placed it within its historical and ideological context, for reasons of a later contrast with a more successful, and not incidentally far more politically integrative, strategy for the achievement of potentially majoritarian political and legal goals. At the point of the greatest political tension in all of American history, however, it was Calhoun's anti-majoritarian and anything but politically integrative strategy that soon carried the day in the South.

The Private-to-Public Pattern

In a sense the nineteenth-century pre–Civil War period was almost too neatly divided. John Marshall's thirty-four post-Constitutional years as chief justice were followed by the twenty-nine-year reign of a very different chief justice, Roger Taney. The two chief justiceships spanned nearly the entire period from the adoption of the Constitution through the first three years of the Civil War.

Typically, the contrasts between Marshall and Taney have been described in institutional terms. The former was, indeed, a staunch nationalist, the latter a defender of states' rights. The former was deeply suspicious of popular legislatures, the latter more accommodating (at least in the early going) to the wishes of an increasingly democratic people's representatives.

But the analysis cannot stop there. There are other layers of analysis, and those layers reflect deeply ideological, and historically quite consistent, themes regarding the balance between the private and the public domains as well as the balance of cognitive forms. They concern the Southern lack of continuation of the private sector's centuries-old pattern of continuing separation from the public sector, specifically the reduction if never the complete cessation of mercantilism in the American North and West as it contrasted with the continuance of a broad synthesis between the public and private sectors in the South. Further, the private sector held to an increasingly egalitarian notion of contract in the North and West, along with the inexorable if incremental change in the cognitive form of the contract toward the more purely analytic device. These were the private-to-public and cognitive form changes of the Jackson/Taney period which the South never participated in.

Obviously, the northern and southern regions of the country differed in many ways by the time of the Civil War. It is a truism to say that the existence of an emerging industrial region within the same polity as a doggedly agricultural region surely heightened the interregional strains that led to the war. But there has always been more to the Civil War than the differences between an industrial and an agricultural, a free labor versus slave labor, society. The war's coming was also colored by the South's continuation of an essentially eighteenth-century synthetic *relationship* between its private and public sectors, a relationship that had changed little in the lowcountry South during the first six decades of the nineteenth century.

In that context, it is not altogether a coincidence that Chief Justice Taney was ruling on a Boston case in *Charles River Bridge*, the bridge over Massachusetts' river to the sea. In New England the private-to-public balance had encouraged a more democratic public sector, through a state legislature, to enforce a more competitive private sector protocol on someone who had previously benefited from mercantilism's privileges. But in the South that kind of thing never happened. The near constancy of private-to-public sector *proximity* within the Southern states (i.e., the still mercantile, if agricultural, arrangement that bonded the economics, politics, social systems, and even cultures of the Southern states) was as much a part of the eventual separation between the North and the South as were the interregional differences over tariff policy, the admission of Western states, or even the disposition of slavery within and outside the South.

Because the politically powerful aristocracy of the South declined to let the proximity and the balances of the private and public sectors in its region proceed according to Anglo-American history's progress practically everywhere else within the common-law nations, and because, in doing so, it thwarted the incipient majoritarianism of its own region's internal politics, as discussed earlier, the South's aristocracy not only locked the region into the national political minoritarianism that the secessionists used as an excuse for dissolution. It also guaranteed that the South's remaining mired in its sectorally confused mercantilism would ensure the continuation of inordinate private sector privilege. A slave-based economy meant that only the Supreme Court's most embarrassing case could momentarily rescue the South from what the federal legislature had done (in the Missouri Compromise)—ironically, to *accommodate* the region in an earlier time. A slave-based economy ultimately meant that states would not only have to be equal to but eventually would need to be superior to the national government in a way that went far beyond what would have been necessary for competitive, modern enterprise to prosper anywhere in the country.

In these last pages, I have but briefly described the well-known strategy of the Southern states' Bourbon leadership as it sought to defend itself from a majoritarian, increasingly Northern-dominated federal government. I have also portrayed Calhoun's fear of majoritarianism within the South and the impact of that fear. In contrast to that rolling evolution of Anglo-American majoritarian history which typically replaced the old order without thought of rending the political entirety, John C. Calhoun's arguments over separation from the Union provided a selfish solution to the problem of any temporary minority within a larger polity. The costs of these arguments, as we all know, were enormous.

As I have said, I have spent some time on Calhoun's arguments here because subsequently I will describe how latter-day, seemingly frustrated potential majorities and aspiring majorities achieved their political and legal goals *within* the national polity, without threat to that polity's unity. I hope that the analysis I have offered here, with its tracing of the private-to-public jurisdictional boundary and its nearly as important tracing of the institutional boundaries between legislatures and courts, and ultimately the states and the federal government, will help to highlight the contrast of latter-day minority positions with Calhoun's position.

CHAPTER EIGHT

Dissolution

The Grand Compromise

What did the Civil War decide? Of course, the Civil War decided that states were not free to leave the Union and that the African-American slaves of the eleven seceding states were finally to be liberated. Soon after the war the four states that had permitted slavery but had not seceded were told that they could not hold onto their slaves either. That notification would not have been forthcoming if the North had not won the war.

Though an event of such momentous proportions as the American Civil War decided other things too, the rest of the changes, both in the South and in the nation as a whole, resulted from a combination of the war's outcome and a continuation of a variety of trends that had long been part of the historical progression. Let us examine, first, that body of Constitutional law which reflected the combined postwar anger and righteousness which so often invades the perspective of any war's winner. Three amendments to the Great Document, the first amendments since the 1804 attempt to clean up the framers' bungling of the presidential selection process, stand as the postwar Constitutional landmark. The Thirteenth Amendment was simple enough. It expanded the Emancipation Proclamation beyond the wartime strategy's parameters. As even Russia had freed its serfs in 1861 and as other nations around the world were freeing whomever was bonded in a variety of ways, the Thirteenth Amendment declared that the United States would be free of its slavery, within both the states of the old Confederacy and those "border" states (Missouri, Kentucky, Maryland, and Delaware) which had remained loyal to the Union. The Thirteenth Amendment was ratified in 1865.

Yet, sensing the South's attempt to restore its antebellum social and political order, radical Republicans of the Congress, by the year 1868, decided that something more than the simple abolition of slavery was Constitutionally necessary. The Fourteenth Amendment was nothing if not ambitious. It attempted to set matters straight about what the winner of the war wanted from the loser.

The first section of the Fourteenth Amendment is straightforward enough. It directly reverses *Dred Scott*,[1] affirming citizenship, federal citizenship, for all who were born or naturalized in the United States. Just as no one need spend time wondering who was the object of Article 1, section 9's "Migration" or "Importation" provision, so too no one could doubt who the "persons" were that were being assured they were "citizens" if they had been "born or naturalized in the United States."[2]

The third section of the amendment (I shall return to the second shortly) was more punitive than any other. It lopped the names of the Confederacy's founders from consideration for federal offices, while section 4, almost a replay of the sixth article among the original seven, guaranteed the payment of the war's bonds. It made clear that only the bonds of the winning side were going to be redeemed, of course. The fifth section of the amendment merely permitted Congress to enforce the above provisions. It was in the second section that the meat of the amendment could be found.

Recall that one of the first harbingers of North-South tension within the American political experience had occurred during the convention's consideration of Congressional representation. The issue revolved around how the Southern slave would be counted. The so-called three-fifths agreement struck a balance between the Northern position, which argued that these unfortunates should not be counted at all, and the Southern position, which argued that the slaves' existence, regardless of their status, should guarantee full counting. In spite of the logical difficulty of representing those whom their governments would never enfranchise, the Southern position gained more than a splitting of the difference in the Constitution's three-fifths compromise.

Section 2 of the Fourteenth Amendment attempted to change all that. With the exception of Native Americans, the disenfranchised Confederate leadership, and, of course, women, all citizens of the Old South were to be full political participants after the war. Also, section 2 provided that the representational allocation of any state would be proportionally diminished within the national House of Representatives should any disenfranchisement occur.

During the Reconstruction period, which varied in length from state to state but which was ended in the last state by the 1877 Hayes-Tilden presidential election compromise, section 2 pretty much had its way. The former slave did vote and sometimes even held office. His expectation of full participation in the politics of each penitent sovereignty had at least a chance at realization. But, alas, such hopes were soon dashed in the context of what is called the "Restoration." Though some Black voting continued after Reconstruction and though some Black office holding sustained itself within a few areas of the South through the end of the century, it was only in the state of North Carolina that Blacks were briefly sought out (during the Populist period of the 1890s) as part of a transracial coalition of voters and officeholders which retained full Black membership in the polity. Section 2 of the Fourteenth Amendment was the first Constitutional casualty of the Restoration period. The second was the Fifteenth Amendment, passed in 1870, which specifically attempted to ensure the right to vote. By the turn of the twentieth century, after nearly universal implementation of the Jim Crow laws, it too was not worth the paper it was written on.

Very soon after the Civil War the vanquished planter class had attempted to regain the same political and economic dominance that had led the South to war in the first place. As I mentioned, Reconstruction did not begin immediately after the war, beginning only when the North's Radical Republicans feared that the South's old order would return to power and thus in part reverse the verdict of the war. The social tumult of Reconstruction has been well described, but we should consider the impact of Reconstruction, and its ending in 1877, on the balance of the private-to-public domains.

The disputed presidential election between the Democrat Samuel Tilden and the Republican Rutherford B. Hayes in 1876 led to the famous Compromise of 1877. A presidential commission charged with looking dispassionately at the two sets of ballots which came from the states of Louisiana, South Carolina, and Florida (and Oregon) wound up voting along party lines. Some in the South, fearing Hayes would continue Reconstruction, threatened to secede again. The 1877 compromise ensured the departure of the last Union troops from the South in return for letting the less-than-radical Republican Hayes benefit from what may have been the sole stolen presidential election in American history.

When the federal troops left the South, however, they abandoned more than former slaves, Northern "carpetbag" interests, and the native Southern "scalawags" who had cooperated with the intruders. The troops' leaving marked how much of the Civil War the South had won. It ensured that the traditional social, economic, and political protocols of the antebellum period would be restored and that the entire South would be granted a kind of semiautonomous status for the foreseeable future. Beyond what happened within the South, in other words, the 1877 compromise acknowledged the willingness of the national government to recognize the considerable differences that existed between one region of the country and the remainder of the still-growing nation. That acknowledgment, of course, was one of the reasons that the period of the post–Civil War national government remains as the weakest period of the national government in the over two hundred years of the country's history.

The acknowledgment of a post-Reconstruction South was not the only reason that the national government of the nineteenth century's last decades was so weak. In part that weakness was the result of the kind of officeholder who peopled the government in that day. The Congress was led by men like Richard Conkling, James G. Blaine, and Richard Bland, men whose talents (and ethics) were a far cry from the Websters, Clays, and Calhouns of the prewar period. But if the Congress's horsepower was diminished during the post-Reconstruction period, that period's White House fully rivaled the immediately prewar presidencies in ineptitude, the talents of Presidents Ulysses S. Grant, Hayes, James A. Garfield, and Chester A. Arthur equaling those of Taylor, Fillmore, Pierce, and Buchanan. One end of Pennsylvania Avenue failed to glitter on both sides of America's greatest trauma.

Although the weakness of the national government's leaders added to the acknowledgment of a semiautonomous region within the country, two other factors contributed just as significantly to the further weakening—one might almost say balkanization—of the national government and its powers during the postwar period. The first was the continuation of westward expansion. Even until just before the Civil War there was a degree of intimacy to the geography of what was by worldly standards still a very young nation. We were then made up of little more than what was east of the Mississippi, extended only by the West Coast states of California and Oregon—distant, underpopulated outposts from which little political influence came.

But the postwar expansion of the West meant the devolution of sovereignty into many new jurisdictions. At first these new states were frequently controlled by powerful mining, ranching, railroad, or other private interests, even if, and sometimes because, they were so underpopulated. We know that the South's check on national power before the war was for a time ensured by the Missouri Compromise, which balanced Northern and Southern state admission and thereby guaranteed equal representation in the Senate. After the war westward expansion led to an influence for the new states which, combined with the private, Eastern economic interests to which they were so often tied, also encouraged the weakening of national political power.

In short, westward expansion added to the power of private interests through the added clout of states (and particularly their senators) which often over-represented the nation's private interests. Westward expansion, and its further weakening of the federal government, thus only complemented Southern semiautonomy in further disassembling the national government.

Another important factor that contributed to the reduction of what was left of federal power after a successful war was the Industrial Revolution. Beyond the causes already reviewed, the principal reason for the federal government's newfound weakness may have been that the newly industrialized private sector in all regions except the South radically strengthened itself during the postwar period. The rise of the great industrial and financial empires of post–Civil War times might have successfully overwhelmed the national government within any configuration of internal sovereignties, regardless of the quality of its leadership and regardless of its settlement with the recently chastised South. To be accurate, the Industrial Revolution began before the Civil War, when America's railroads began to reach out from Baltimore and Charleston in the early 1830s.

But within the geographical hinterland U.S. industrialism exploded after the war—Leland Stanford's railroads, Andrew Carnegie's steel mills, John D. Rockefeller's oil wells, and the great Wall Street empires of Jay Gould and J. P. Morgan all sporting their newfound wealth. With Southern semiautonomy came the politically decentralizing impact of the westward expansion, the weakness of America's political leaders, as well as the truly national alliances of industrialism and commercialism as they stretched from New York boardrooms to the great American plains and beyond. All contributed to the greatest period of private-to-public imbalance in the country's history. Within a few years after its greatest conflict, the national government that had organized itself so brilliantly to prevent the secession of virtually half of its territory had become a helpless giant.

Private Sector Dominance

What impact did this new, postwar imbalance of the private-to-public sectors have on the law? And what impact did it have on the legislatively generated and contractual forms of law that we have been tracking? To understand fully the inordinate imbalance between the private and the public sectors during the latter decades of the nineteenth century, as well as demonstrate the impact of such imbalance on the law, let us first review the institutional imbalances that accompanied, if they did not result from, the private-to-public imbalance.

I have referred to the weakness of the federal government vis-à-vis the states during the Gilded Age. But by the 1880s and 1890s many states, particularly in the West, had gained sufficient population to allow some citizens who were not directly tied to the dominant mining, railroad, and industrial interests to think about regulating those frequently indulgent industries. As John O'Sullivan and Edward Keuchel have written, it was the states who pushed reform first because "the Grange movement, which favored anti-business legislation, tended to be strongest at the state legislative level."[3]

In short, many citizens, horrified by the excesses of powerful private interests in their state legislatures and their governors' chairs, began to assert control over their state governments. They started to use the police powers that were Constitutionally reserved for the states to deal with what they considered to be threats to their health and safety. Finding the federal government disinclined to engage in such regulatory conduct, these states attempted, at the behest of the Grange movement and other insurgencies, to right the sectoral imbalances that exploited their citizens.

Unfortunately, as George Brown Tindall has noted, the political issues of the robber baron day led both major parties to engage in "a policy of evasion." As Tindall put it, "On questions of the currency, regulation of big business, farm problems, civil service reform, internal improvement, and immigration, one would be hard put to distinguish between the parties."[4] The weakness of these indistinguishable parties, like the weakness of the general government, also meant that statutes addressing these kinds of issues could emerge only from state legislatures.

Overwhelmingly, state-level reformist efforts failed in their early years. The principal Constitutional interpretation that assured that failure was found in those tortuous interpretations of the Fourteenth Amendment which twisted the amendment's word *person* to include corporations. Though the amendment had undeniably referred to the just-freed slave, the Court's "substantive due process" doctrine obliterated many of the states' early attempts at regulation of the new industrial and railroad powers of the period.

The substantive due process doctrine originated with Supreme Court Justice Stephen Field's dissent in *Munn v. Illinois* (1877).[5] This influential justice rejected the majority's notion that property "becomes clothed with a public interest when used in a manner to make it of public consequence."

The decision had permitted Illinois' regulation of grain elevators. Field reasoned that "one might as well attempt to change the nature of colors" as change the nature of property.[6] Then, in subsequent cases such as *Wabash Rwy. Co. v. Illinois* (1886), *Chicago, Burlington and Quincy R.R. Co. v. Chicago* (1889), and, finally, *United States v. E. C. Knight* (1895),[7] the famous sugar case, the substantive due process doctrine and other property protecting doctrines received majority support in the Court.[8] The result was the purest embodiment of private enterprise which has ever been adjudicated, either within the United States or any other common-law country.

The inviolability of the private contract, the sanctity of private property, and the need for the protection of the private sector generally from what a popular legislature might attempt to do to reform it were the essence of the Gilded Age. At that moment in the history of the private-to-public balances that we have chronicled, the United States Supreme Court's power filled the vacuum of the other two national branches. In doing so, again, it crushed virtually all state legislative attempts at correcting the sectoral imbalance.

At the same time, ironically, the Court heartily approved of much of what a state legislature might do to accommodate some states' leadership's local interests. The restoration of the Southern social order, as permitted by the 1877 Compromise, surely made the infamous "separate but equal" case of *Plessy v. Ferguson* possible, if not inevitable.[9] This case permitted the state of Louisiana to divide its passenger train accommodations according to race. With the notion of "state action" being ruled as including only the public activity of a state institution, a state statute was thus classified as not violating "equal protection" guarantees when it merely separated the races. Laws that mandated racial separation, as opposed to laws that restricted the private sector in its economic dealings, were found throughout this period. Whether the Supreme Court would intercede at the state level was foretold by the extreme Court-enforced separation between the private and the public sectors (and the favoring of the private sector in the balance), not just the imbalance between the state and national jurisdictions.

At first glance the dominance of the federal government in the person of the Supreme Court over states' legislatures with regard to the private sector would seem to negate any need for the decentralization of the government I have been describing. But look more closely. If the private-to-public division had been the principal division in American politics since the time of the Constitution, as I think it had, the alignment of the federal Supreme Court against "reformist," non-Southern, state legislatures should also seem familiar. The federal Court's protection of private interests mirrors almost precisely the protection of the private interests which came about during the chief justiceship of John Marshall, though the form of the private interest was not at all the same. Indeed, that Court-led protection was not very different from the private sector–supporting rulings of the pre-war Roger Taney Court, when the legislatures of his time encouraged competitive private business.

Yes, the robber baron period evidenced far less economic paternalism than did the English-like mercantilism of the Marshall post-Constitutional period. But that was true because paternalism wasn't needed any longer. To be sure, the railroads were given their land for westward expansion. Mining interests had "mineral rights" thrown into their leases of public land. Even today, as I've mentioned, Western water subsidies, comfortable cattle grazing fees, farm subsidies, and the like dot the federal budget. But those who received federal assistance in order to build the U.S. economy after the Civil War still had a far different relationship with the public sector than their counterparts in Alexander Hamilton and John Marshall's time did in theirs. They were in control of both an increasingly wealthy private economy and a weakened national public sector.

Of course, there had been self-interest in the post-Constitutional period, too, Hamilton's Wall Street friends having done well with the redemption of the war bonds, while others made money on the building of post roads, harbors, canals, and the like in the immediate post-Constitutional period. But the weakness of national public leadership during the Gilded Age still stands in sharp contrast with the post-Constitutional period, not only because of the relative strength of the early government but also because of the sheer corruptness of Congressional leadership during an era in which industrial expansion was at its height. "The best Congress that money can buy" was, indeed, privately bought and sold in the last three decades of the nineteenth century. The largesse that flowed from the hands of the robber barons in order to influence the Congress and the officers of a weak executive branch permitted a kind of profiteering which Hamilton and Marshall would never have condoned.

Once more, a merely institutional analysis of what happened in late-nineteenth-century America is simply not adequate for an explanation of the robber baron's position vis-à-vis the government in the late nineteenth century. Only an understanding of the private-to-public balance tells the true story of who was winning and who was losing in that historical moment. The federal Supreme Court's activist role in supporting the most unbridled private sector ever to exist in this country should have been predictable. The result of such support was that this judicial activism also ratifies the primacy of the private-to-public divide, demonstrating that the private sector was the greatest stimulus for (1) the semi-autonomous status of the Southern region, (2) the geographical dispersion of the national sovereignty, (3) the weakness of national public leadership, and (4) the growth of truly national industries.

One final point must be touched on with regard to the fin-de-siècle power of the private sector. The public role in the economic entrepreneurship of the robber baron period was a pale shadow of the mercantilism of the post-Constitutional period; and if indeed late-nineteenth-century entrepreneurship was prompted not by paternalistic admonitions from public institutions but by an aggressive and well-funded private sector, these changes must have led to further change in the form of the economic contract. What was the cognitive form of the robber baron contract? Without question, the contract of the Gilded Age was the most analytic of all U.S. contracts not only because it represented an almost pure separation of public and private interests but because it also displayed an almost complete disregard for the health and safety of workers as well as for the equity of the industrial wage. In spite of early attempts at unionization in some industries, issues surrounding the industrial wage had not yet been successfully focused in the public forum. As the private and the public sectors were more separated, and the private sector more dominant, than at any time in U.S. history, the country was sitting directly between the very different phases of *production-oriented* politics of the nineteenth century and *distribution-oriented* politics that increasingly marked public sector activity in the twentieth century.

To be sure, a new national political movement had come to life at the very end of the nineteenth century in the United States. But the Populist movement, in many ways a successor to the state-based Grangers, had met with only small successes in passing the reformist laws that were so frequently overruled by "substantive due process" cases in the Supreme Court. Though the Populists failed in their attempt to place the cognitively synthetic demands of the worker, and even of the consumer, under national, public sector protection, their failure did represent a testing of the institutional balances between the state and the federal government as well as between legislatures and the Supreme Court. They also tested the imbalance between the private and the public sectors. If these movements failed, the Populists at least served as the precursors of a far more successful reformist movement, the Progressive movement. The twentieth century would contest the imbalance of the private and public sectors from a very different perspective than the nineteenth century. The synthetic cognitive form, now largely drained from the private contract in its traditional production-assisted role, would slowly return to the contract as a product of a distribution-concerned and now more clearly oppositional public sector. Put another way, the invitation of the private sector to the public sector's productivity-oriented syntheses is substantially replaced by the unwanted challenge to the private sector of distribution and customer protection public sector syntheses.

CHAPTER NINE

The Reformers

Roots

Where, then, would the next battle between the private and public domains be joined? Recall that in the late nineteenth century Congress had passed the Sherman Act (1890), an admonition against whatever a court could be persuaded was a "restraint of trade." But some argue that, rather than being a truly reformist piece of legislation, the Sherman Act was a product of already established industries' desire to protect themselves from new, potentially damaging competition. At its best, as Hans Thorelli argues, "the bills reported by Sherman in the 51st Congress but also the bill finally passed, were intended . . . to be [but] federal codifications of the common law of England and the several states."[1] Nothing more. Richard Hofstadter quotes Senator Nelson W. Aldrich to the effect that the Sherman legislation was "a delusion and a sham . . . an empty menace to the great interests made to answer the clamour of the ignorant and the unreasoning."[2]

If William McKinley promised anything after his 1896 triumph over the Populist William Jennings Bryan, it was to continue the Republican (and to an embarrassing degree Grover Cleveland "Gold Democrat") policies of the nineteenth century into the twentieth. But after McKinley's first term a political compromise at the 1900 Republican Convention brought the progressive, former New York police commissioner Theodore Roosevelt to the national Republican ticket. The following year an assassin's bullet dramatically changed the ideological direction of American politics, a goodly part of that change being accomplished by a Roosevelt Supreme Court appointee.

Perhaps more than anything except the 1930s and 1940s presidency of Theodore Roosevelt's distant cousin Franklin, the early-century judgeship of the great Supreme Court Justice Oliver Wendell Holmes Jr. marked the road back from the sectoral and institutional imbalances of the late nineteenth century. A Harvard-educated Brahmin, the former Massachusetts chief justice was a scholar, and sometimes philosopher. Holmes enjoyed describing great patterns in the law during his early scholarly writings, but he warned at the same time that the loftiest patterns, even of his own design, should endure the greatest skepticism. Holmes's mind was supple if it was nothing else.

Holmes's most significant intellectual contribution is his legendary work *The Common Law*. This extraordinary chronicle of the Anglo-American peoples' *grundnorm* reached back to the Roman notions of *Ex Delicto* and *Ex Contractu* where injury and contract laid the foundation for all Western law. Here, Holmes reminded his readers that the principles of contract of the late nineteenth century were nothing more than a jurisprudential distillation of what was already in place by the time of Magna Carta. At the beginning of the twentieth century, the Roman notions of injury and restitution, that natural equity of fairness whether in contractual dealings or in the implicit duty not to injure, was still at the core of Anglo-American jurisprudence.

For all of Holmes's understandings of both the origins and balances of the law, however, writers such as H. L. Pohlman have argued that the great jurist's conceptions of other intellectual arenas, particularly concerning the nature of business associations and productive arrangements, never progressed beyond Holmes's pre–Civil War school days framework.[3] Holmes's early economic opinions, in other words, largely reflected that early common-law heritage which reflected the assumption of those like Adam Smith and other believers in the invisible hand that the natural workings of the economic struggle would invariably reach equilibrium.

The dissenting opinion that Holmes wrote in the 5–4 *Northern Securities* decision (1904),[4] for example, revealed that Holmesian confidence in economic self-equilibration.[5] The opinion infuriated the new president. Why had his new, supposedly Progressive, appointee argued that the Sherman Act did not apply to financiers such as J. P. Morgan and J. J. Hill and their creation of a railroad monopoly for the northwest portion of the country? The answer to that question, I suggest, says a great deal about the layering of private-to-public, institutional, and cognitive form considerations of American jurisprudence shortly after the turn of the century.

The trusts were at their strongest in the early 1900s, and the idea that two large railroads would come together to control a market so that they could set whatever rail rates they wanted, and at the same time monopolize trackside grain storage, was well in keeping with American industry's contemporary norms. The idea that such actions were unjust, at least in the eyes of many who suffered the injustices that came with dealing with the railroads, was a position that one might have expected a jurist like Holmes to share. Only a year later, as a matter of fact, Holmes's dissent in *Lochner* excoriated a conservative Court for declaring a cap on a baker's workweek unconstitutional by proclaiming that the Constitution had "not enacted Mr. Herbert Spencer's social statics."[6]

But in the earlier *Northern Securities* case Holmes had seemed to side with the enemy. Holmes's dissent upheld the right of Morgan and Hill to bind their railroads together. But Holmes's opinion bears closer analysis, for, as Alfred Lief has properly described it, the justice's attitude about the abuses of monopolies, oligopolies, and the like was directed only toward the "unreasonable" restraints of trade which might grow out of the above arrangements. Specific economic activities that might suppress competition through price fixing or market sharing, for example, should indeed be looked at carefully. But, as Holmes himself put it, to suppress competition by "fusion"—that is, by the mere forming of a partnership— might well be permissible under the law.

According to Holmes, the mere lessening of competition was not an unreasonable restraint. It signified nothing more than a natural outcome of business growth, and it even held out the advantage of *preventing* ravenous competition. In his *Northern Securities* reasoning Justice Holmes joyfully noted that Justice Brewer, the fifth vote for the majority, agreed with him and the other dissenters that the Sherman Act outlawed only unreasonable restraints, not every restraint of trade. "I am happy to know that only a minority [four] of my brethren adopt an interpretation of the law which in my opinion would make eternal the *bellum omnium contra omnes* and disintegrate society as far as it could into individual atoms," Holmes wrote.[7] Is this a position that favors the pure, unsocialized contract? Is it a position that would permit such an unbridled level of competition between and among businesses that would further exploit workers and customers? For Holmes the answer was a resounding no, his dissent hanging onto that last bit of social contract which still dressed the law of contract from Magna Carta through the mercantilists and (Holmes assumed) through the nineteenth century. A socialized set of business institutions, Holmes thought, would avert rather than encourage ravenous competition, and perhaps treat its workers better to boot.

Note that Holmes spoke to an extraordinary combination of considerations in his *Northern Securities* opinion. Most important, he spoke of the social order, the need to combat social "atomism," and the desire to prevent what Holmes called "the ferocious extreme of competition with others." It was, therefore, "not the cessation of competition among the partners that was the evil feared" in the Sherman Act, according to Holmes.[8] It was only the actual misuse of a combination's powers that the act spoke to. Thus, though Holmes voted for the railroad merger, his reasoning clearly places him in league with those who would soon have the public sector redress the denuded contract and protect the industrial worker.

Put simply, if the private sector had reached its zenith of power vis-à-vis the public sector by removing virtually all noneconomic factors from the contract, then somehow, whether from the bench or from the legislative hall, these public, social, elements to the contract would have to be restored. The Holmes of 1904 might have been the last scholar, if not the last judicial figure, who believed that the social balance might still be maintained through the device of the business contract. But, although he did not say so explicitly in *Northern Securities*, Holmes also believed, and stated so in writings such as his famous *Lochner* dissent the year following, that when that balance could not be maintained, the public sector should affect redress.

Specifically, Holmes's motive for calling "unreasonable" restraints on trade to task was that the federal Supreme Court should restrain itself in supporting such contrivances and allow state legislatures to grant relief to their citizenry. After those periods of allowing state legislative leeway, during Roger Taney's Court and the immediate post–Civil War period, the Supreme Court in railroad cases such as *Chicago, Burlington & Quincy* (1897)[9] had ushered in a period of judicial activism which troubled a democrat like Holmes. Holmes felt that such judicial activism should end, particularly when the contract that was being protected was as exploitative of the public interest as so many later-century contracts had been.

There were therefore at least two differences between the activist Supreme Court of the late-nineteenth- and early-twentieth-century Court and the Marshall Court. First, the public purpose of the contract was different. The contract of the post-Constitutional period, up through the time of Kent and Story, had largely included the involvement of the public sector in mercantile enterprises such as a national bank, as we have reviewed. Yet something else had changed in the late-nineteenth-century contract. The "robber baron" contract largely excluded that public, productivity-based role. The coming of the Industrial Revolution meant that the *employment* contract was far different from what it had ever been. The factory system meant waged employment, often meager in its return and often accompanied by unhealthy and unsafe conditions. The employer owned the factory, the machinery the worker worked on, as well as the products' components. The worker had only his, or her, labor to sell.

Mercantilism as a doctrine spoke little to the politics of distribution, merely promoting the public works that built post roads, harbors, canals, and whatever else boosted the nation's commonwealth. The ideological argument of that day centered on favors given to certain interests as well as on the crowding out of potential competitors by those who were granted monopolies. But by the twentieth century, as the preceding chapter began to explore, the ideological argument dealt more with the fairness of the contract to those who were immediately impacted by it than the benefit of an industry's productivity. That is why Holmes's opinions in *Northern Securities* and *Lochner*, the former approving a monopoly creating railroad merger and the latter decrying the lengthy hours of a bakery worker, are not inconsistent.

That Teddy Roosevelt did not understand what Holmes intended in *Northern Securities* is no reason that Holmes's full intentions cannot be understood today. The Justice's pejorative vision of the pure private contract signified nothing less than a hope for an industrial age working arrangement that would find its own balance between public and private needs. It was a search for that same kind of private-to-public balance which could be restored by legislators such as those who passed the *Lochner* law. The twentieth century's liberal sense of political economy, recall, had been altered by writers such as Herbert Croly, who had argued for "equality and the average man" rather than "liberty" and "the special individual."[10]

As the soon-to-become Supreme Court Justice Felix Frankfurter once said about Holmes, the justice pinned his redressing of the imbalances of private contract and the public sector on the belief that political rights were simply more important than economic rights.[11] Holmes never had believed that the common law, with its inherent quality of reason, was simply a shield of protection for private prerogatives. Holmes saw the common law much as Sir Edward Coke did, as a regulator of deep social balances and as a promoter of the political democracy that would need to actively maintain such balances.

Is it unlikely, in retrospect, that the great justice would have agreed with Daniel Boorstin's criticism of Sir William Blackstone on the larger issues of jurisprudential form and purpose? I don't think so, for Holmes not only believed in the role of democratic legislatures; he also believed in the need for a Court that respected the growing and adaptive product of those legislatures. Legislatures, Holmes thought, provided a vitality for the law which kept it from being a rigid and potentially irrelevant body of rules. Those legislative notions of the law, again much as both Coke and, later, Boorstin had thought of the law, would enable the private-to-public balance to be regained. Considerations of worker rights were rightfully brought to the doors of legislatures, and the Courts should respect that avenue of legal change, even if it did not always agree with its product.

As Frankfurter put it again, "Holmes attributed very different legal significance to those liberties of the individual which history has attested as the indispensable conditions of a free society from that which he attached to liberties which derived merely from shifting economic arrangements."[12] Whatever the current economic arrangements might be, in other words, the ever-evolving reason of the citizenry—the reason that fell heir to the early days of judge-made common-law experience—could and in great part should be available to the citizen as legislator. A free people could change their laws as needed.

Writing further of Holmes, Frankfurter noted that "the Justice deferred so abundantly to legislative judgment on economic policy because he was profoundly aware of the extent to which social arrangements are conditioned by time and circumstances." Holmes was thus acutely aware of "how fragile . . . is the ultimate validity of a particular economic adjustment," Frankfurter thought.[13] If the nakedly free enterprise–oriented adjustments of the immediate pre-Holmesian period had scraped the contract of whatever the Great Charter contained within it, and if the politics of the judicial appointments of the last decades of the nineteenth century had bade the judiciary to do little more than protect the private sector, the citizenry would have to redress both the form and the content of a contract that was now very different from the mercantilist contracts of only a century earlier.

The Brandeis Contribution

In Oliver Wendell Holmes Jr. the Supreme Court had a justice whose thirty-year career marked an uncompromising attempt to right the distorted balances of both the private with the public sector and legislatures with the judiciary. Along with Holmes, someone on the judicial outside, though a person of great insight and integrity, played to the great justice's own sense of potential contractual unfairness. As it turned out, it would take an innovative lawyer to provide the justice with further ammunition for a war that was very different from what Holmes had fought in his youth. The thrice-wounded veteran of Ball's Bluff and other Civil War skirmishes never suspected that he would be joined in his latter years on the Court by a reformer like Louis D. Brandeis. But, after the case of *Muller v. Oregon* (1908)[14] had been argued, Holmes knew that the young and brilliant lawyer had not only extended the boundaries of the legal brief but had proposed a full reconsideration of the twentieth-century employment contract. Brandeis would persevere, both as a lawyer and later as a justice, until his progressive ideas on labor contracts, health care, and the safety of workers filled out the Constitutionally-protected police powers of a state. Holmes chose to be at his side.

In the so-called Brandeis Brief the young lawyer armed himself with a revolutionary scientific study, a study that gave Holmes the opportunity to turn his usually dissenting opinions on workers' rights into a majority. Brandeis's study described the fatigue and the efficiency of workers using terms such as *anabolism*—that is, the "assimilation, or building up" of cellular material, and *catabolism*, or the "disassimilation, or breaking down [of] material into its simplest chemical forms."[15] Drawing on the experimental work of leading physiologists such as the British Sir Michael Foster and others, Brandeis coherently explained something which had never before been a part of a legal brief.

In short, what Brandeis's presentation demonstrated was that the inordinate accumulation of "acids," those residues of fatigue which an overworked factory worker invariably contracted during the ten-, twelve-, and fourteen-hour days of the industrial contract, destroyed a worker's health and even his or her working efficiency. When the state of Oregon provided that "no female [shall] be employed in any mechanical establishment, or factory, or laundry in this State more than ten hours during any one day,"[16] it challenged the purely economic contract in a manner that now necessitated Supreme Court interpretation.

In the *Muller* case, the most private sense of contract—the wholly noncontextual economic contract—became Brandeis's open target. And it was Justice Brewer, Holmes's ally in that *Northern Securities* position that only *unreasonable* restraints of trade were proscribed by the Sherman Act, who declared Brandeis's evidence of contractual excess to be valid. *Muller* marked a watershed of judicial acceptance of what a legislature might do to graft workers' rights onto the raw contracts of America's robber baron period.

To be sure, Brandeis and Holmes's similar perspectives on the innate unfairness of the industrial contract may well have come from different philosophical perspectives regarding political economy. Whereas Holmes hoped that the natural progression of capitalism would evolve into the stable combinations that we have spoken of, Brandeis openly questioned the natural, often putative, development of contractual law in the industrial context. At a glance, therefore, Brandeis appears to be the more radical of the two figures, something that Samuel Konefsky has argued in his study of these juridical progressives.[17] But, in fact, the differences between Holmes and Brandeis were not great. Konefsky overlooks the antiatomism point of Holmes's *Northern Securities* opinion and forgets that Holmes opposed the distorted usage of the Fourteenth Amendment to protect property and contract in ways that Justice Miller's majority opinion had protested against as early as *Munn v. Illinois* (1877).[18] Brandeis believed in the political and judicial excoriations of the Fourteenth Amendment's slide into substantive due process. He may have differed with Holmes regarding tactics, but not results.

In fact, when it came to the form of the contract, particularly the matter of including social and economic considerations that the barons had excluded from their contracts, Holmes and Brandeis thoroughly converged. Even Konefsky recognized that "part of Mr. Justice Holmes's service to Constitutional Law was to rescue it from the unreal world of absolute concepts." As he put it, though Holmes might have been unable "to extricate himself from the pull of the common law," the justice's deep sense of the progress of history, and of the necessarily tentative nature of even the greatest of philosophical principles, meant that Holmes had no difficulty altering the law of contract as modern circumstances required.[19]

In sum, the early part of the twentieth century brought a new, but hardly unexpected, reconfiguration of ideological positions, institutional (court-to-legislature) positions, and private-to-public positions to the national argument. In the wake of the late-century judicial activism that protected a contractual form (again far different from the mercantile contract of Marshall's era), the movement toward contractual balance did not come from a Taney-like, legislatively directed reliance upon the innate egalitarianism of preindustrial capitalism. Instead, whether from the perspective of Holmes's sense of the calming aspects of combinations and monopolies or from Brandeis's sense of how contracts should carry their costs to the worker on their sleeve, the Taney/Jackson notions of egalitarian contract were replaced by Holmes and Brandeis's broad-ranging acceptance of a political response to contractual excess. To be sure, Holmes and Brandeis were not frequent winners on the Court. Most of the time the Supreme Court of Melville Fuller, Edward White, and William Howard Taft protected those agreements that would extend the nineteenth-century contractual form well into the twentieth century. Again, business and the private sector still won their cases far more times than they lost in the early twentieth century, although occasionally a case such as *Bunting v. Oregon* (1917),[20] which extended Oregon's maximum-hour legislation to men, did marginally temper the excesses of the private contract.

The Federal Government

A brief further point needs to be made in the context of the Holmes/ Brandeis alliance. With the exception of the *Northern Securities* reaction of the young President Roosevelt, I have said little of the impact of the executive branch during this review of early-twentieth-century law. Without question, however, the trust-busting of the Roosevelt and then William Howard Taft presidencies did have an impact on U.S. business. The *Standard Oil*[21] case broke up Rockefeller's petroleum monopoly, while the *American Tobacco*[22] case dispersed that company's monopoly in the cigarette industry. It was not until the presidency of the Democrat Woodrow Wilson, however, that the federal government's political swath was enlarged sufficiently to deal with a variety of private-to-public issues.

Woodrow Wilson took office in 1913. The record of Constitutional amendments and significant statutory innovations during and just before his two terms in office was and still is truly extraordinary. The Sixteenth Amendment, reinstating the income tax which had been ruled unconstitutional in the *Pollock* (1895)[23] case, was placed into the Constitution by a progressive Congress and three-fourths of the state legislatures as Wilson came into office. The Seventeenth Amendment, providing for the direct election of senators, was also ratified in 1913, taking the power of senatorial election away from state legislatures, which were so often under the thumb of mining, ranching, railroad, and financial interests.

Sub-Constitutionally, both the Security and Exchange Commission Act, regulating the equity markets to some degree, and the Federal Reserve Board Act, which stabilized a banking system that had witnessed severe monetary crises during the last years of the nineteenth and first years of the twentieth century, were also passed in 1913. In 1914 the Sherman Anti-Trust Act received two powerful allies: the Clayton Act spelling out prohibitions against discriminatory pricing, price fixing, market sharing, and a variety of other uncompetitive practices; and the Federal Trade Commission Act setting up the nation's first regulatory agency specifically dealing with antitrust matters. In 1920, with Edith Wilson shouldering the now bedridden President Wilson's much scaled-down daily business, the Nineteenth Amendment granted women the right to vote and thus completed the Progressive agenda.

Arguably, the full rebalancing of private-to-public power was not achieved by the Progressive reforms, with later cases such as *Adkins Children's Hospital* (1923)[24] still striking down attempts at the creation of a minimum wage. It was clear, however, that by the end of the Wilson presidency in 1921 the nineteenth-century imbalance between the private and public sectors, as well as between state and federal power, was at least partially redressed. Federal-level public power failed to anticipate, and in the 1920s it surely failed to deal with, the continuing excesses of not only smokestack industries but, more importantly, the financial industries of banking and securities.

The next period of governmental response to private sector excess would need a Depression to legitimize it. But before we review that response in the next chapter, we need to review one more episode in the development of Anglo-American jurisprudence wherein scholars, in the tradition of Glanvil and Bracton, themselves impacted the law.

The Realist Revolution

As the real-world history of the English common law periodically interacted with the great early chroniclers of the law, so too, from time to time, legal history has interacted with those who went beyond mere descriptions of the law. Surely Coke and Blackstone, like Glanvil and Bracton, were not mere chroniclers. Their writings, as their authors intended, moved the law significantly in one direction or other.

Discussions of legal philosophy, or jurisprudence, became increasingly focused early in the twentieth century. They did so, in part, because something quite dramatic happened just after the time when the most pristine (analytic) nature of contracts was exposed both to legislative and judicial attack. What happened is as simple as it is profound, for, with the coming of the "legal realists," the core perspective on the nature of the entire judicial process was challenged, and eventually changed. What happened was that some of the judicial processes' keenest observers during the 1920s and the early 1930s critically examined the neutrality of the judicial decision itself. Those writers argued that the actual process of decision was far different from the dispassionate scientific application of principles which the common law's traditional writers had represented it to be.

The legal realists, including writers such as Karl Llewellyn and Jerome Frank, marked the culmination of what a few jurisprudential scholars throughout the Western world had begun to argue in the first years of the new century. The so-called Sociological School, made up of writers such as Léon Duguit on the continent and Roscoe Pound in the United States, for example, had combined the findings of emerging, respectable disciplines of social science with the argument that the law could ultimately be functional, or purposive, in its direction.[25] Put another way, the Sociological School and its Functionalist predecessors argued that the law could be consciously directed toward the accomplishment of social goals.

This argument that the law could and probably should be purposive turned out to be a perfect introduction for the realists' inquiry into whether the processes of legal decision making were biased all along. The realists had openly grappled with the issue of the law's bias in favor of private interests. Specifically, the realists suggested a bias toward those interests' contracts, even though the realists rarely spoke explicitly of contractual forms. They further argued that, because of the way that judges were trained and selected for the bench, a preference for the private sector grew out of perceptions of how well potential judges fit into the legal-political elite of the country. As Karl Llewellyn put it, judicial remedies always "have a purpose."[26] So far in American history, that purpose had seemed to Llewellyn to be "protections of something else."[27]

In a historical context the legal realists argued that, if it was legitimate for the legislature (that reflection of the public's passions that Madison, Blackstone, Hamilton, and the other protectors of the common law had so worried about) to make changes in the legislated law, it was also legitimate (or had quietly been assumed to be legitimate) for those who adjudicated the law to decide cases according to their own "passions." Within the Anglo-American legal community the response to such a charge was protest. The common-law Anglo-American bench, in contrast to a legislature, was free of bias. The expert, after all, was someone who understood the "scientific" law which Blackstone had not been alone in writing about. As these traditionalists saw it, a judge merely unlocked the law, "discovering" the scientific solution to each case's central question.

It was this reliance on the ostensibly mechanistic, internal reasoning of the common law, in the sense that Blackstone thought of the law according to Boorstin, which underlay the principal justification for judicial review. According to the orthodox view, a court like the United States Supreme Court therefore never struck down legislation because it did not agree with it. The Supreme Court, more expertly than any other, referred to the internal reason of the common law as its underpinning for understanding whatever Constitutional issue was at stake. Any court, if deciding a Constitutional issue, could merely declare that it had "discovered" legislative violations of the Constitution. It had also discovered the reason not only of the common law but also of that "higher law" that the Constitution ostensibly represented.

The fact that the Supreme Court could count the common law's reasoning much as Coke and Blackstone had counted on that reason (although for different purposes), meant that legislative invasions that the

Court felt went too far could be stricken because they violated something fundamental about the law. From the American jurisprudential perspective the Constitution represented the principal bulwark against that kind of violation. The heart of the judicial declaration represented something inherent in the law which could not be violated by legislative fiat. Well into the twentieth century there was still as much of the Englishman Blackstone in the idea of judicial supremacy as there ever was of the Americans Hamilton and Marshall.

Thus, the jurisprudential perspective that is called legal realism ultimately addressed the nearly blind traditional obedience to the supposedly neutral reasoning of the Anglo-American law. It also addressed the supposedly neutral set of legal safeguards of a document such as the U.S. Constitution. Some of the intellectual background for judicial realism, no doubt, came out of the growing psychological awareness of the writings of the Freudian age. Everyone had biases, and these biases were much a part of a more or less static, if still largely unexplored, human personality. A goodly portion of that personality came from a child's socialization, as noted earlier. A family identification with the business community, rather than the working community, for example, would tend to continue throughout a legal career. Without introspection on the part of the jurist, such identification would naturally impact judicial decisions.

If the Anglo-American judiciary had forever maintained the mask of judicial scientism, that is, had the members of the bench forever continued to benefit from having their black robes cover the "black box" of ostensibly unbiased decision making, attacks on the striking down of legislation would have continued at merely a substantive or ideological level. Also, the Supreme Court would more than likely have continued its Marshallian supremacy over the legislature, as Hamilton and the Federalists intended. Not incidentally, the cognitively analytic nature of the late-nineteenth-century contract might also have continued to dominate the law.

We know, for example, that for years after the ratification of the Constitution the dominant perspective on judicial review had remained pretty much that of *Marbury*.[28] Debtors were kept in line by their judge-protected creditors, and the case-by-case meanings given to Madison's and Hamilton's *Federalist* writings meant that judicial review's common-law and ultimately Constitutional law roots continued to protect the bulwarks of contract and property. Those referred to in Madison's quotation concerning the "diversity in the faculties of men from which the rights of property originate" thus continued their dominant position in the political and legal order.

But that period's dominance of the judiciary over the legislature was nothing more than the product of what the Anti-Federalists had already noted regarding the Anglo-American judiciary's protection of the propertied class, well before shots were fired at Lexington and Concord. The advent of the realist's perspective on judicial decision making changed the complexion of the entire argument over the Constitution and its interpretive method. Legal realism changed that argument because it was not the only product of a twentieth-century jurisprudence that was impacted by Roscoe Pound and others. It changed the argument because it was the product of a perspective that called for the law to acknowledge the broadest real-world *impact* of what it was doing whenever a case was adjudicated. Ultimately, the realists' focus on legal impact necessitated a focus on legal purpose. And, since the private law's evolution brought about such great separation from the public law by the close of the nineteenth century, legislated law would need to stand again in the twentieth century as the principal opposition to the private law.

In full colors, therefore, the legal realists' criticism of the alleged neutrality of the common law in the early twentieth century reached to the entire spectrum of the decision process itself. If the Sociological jurisprudential school and its forerunner, the Functionalists, had prescribed for their own substantive agenda, the underlying premise of the twentieth-century legal realists would largely subvert the jurisprudential assumptions of the day's judicial orthodoxy.

Therefore, in the context of challenging the adversarial method's claim as the proper formula for determining truth in the trial format, a writer such as Jerome Frank, for example, could openly challenge the plausibility of the traditional court's "discovery" of reason through combative trial techniques. The idea that courts only referee the squabble between two judicial proponents, neither of whom are dedicated to the finding of truth, appalled Frank. He criticized the accepted common-law methods of cleverly questioning witnesses, coaching witnesses before testimony, preventing damaging facts from reaching a jury, and the like. Frank concluded that the common law's method of trial was "the equivalent of throwing pepper in the eyes of a surgeon when he is performing an operation."[29] Frank went on to quote the law's greatest authority on evidence, Dean Henry Wigmore of Northwestern Law School, who wrote that "the common law, originating in a community of sports and games, was permeated by the instinct of sportsmanship." Such an instinct, according to Frank, led inevitably to "a sporting theory of justice."[30]

Reaching down to a court's decisional method, Frank noted further that there were meaningful parallels between the methodologies of "'classical' laissez-faire economic theory" and the sporting theory of justice. Such a jurisprudential perspective assumed that the combat between a "litigious man" and his opponent will "ensure that court-orders will be grounded on all the practically attainable relevant facts." Frank argued that this notion complemented the conservative William Howard Taft's aspiration that "the poor man" should have "as nearly as possible an opportunity in litigating as the rich man."[31] Of course, the sporting theory meant this rarely happened.

Jerome Frank's specific criticisms of the common law's truth-finding methods were but a prelude to his principal jurisprudential theme, that theme carrying him beyond the question of methodological distortions within the adversarial system. Frank, too, questioned whether judges were free of personal bias, noting specifically that even to mention whether "judges are human," as Frank put it, was a topic that had been "largely tabu" among American lawyers until the twentieth century.[32] "To mention it [the bias of judges], except in an aside and as a joke, even in gatherings of lawyers, was considered bad taste, to say the least."[33]

As one might expect, the assumption of judicial freedom not only dominated the bench throughout the nineteenth century and earlier, but, as Frank particularly noted, the assumption of bias also pervaded formal legal education and accordingly "controlled what lawyers said to non-lawyers in publications and in public addresses."[34] Now, after blind obedience to the supposed neutrality of the Anglo-American legal method, Frank added his voice to those who felt it was time to investigate, and correct, such biases.

Put simply, what realists such as Frank, Llewellyn, and Pound and Duguit before them, argued was that, if the courts, including the Supreme Court, were as imbued with bias as were elected legislators, then not only could the mechanic of the common law be violated by a rapacious legislature (as Blackstone and Madison had warned of) but the entirety of Constitutional, statutory, and case-driven law could be detrimentally altered by judicial ideologies as well.

What turned out to be the significance of the realists' disrobing of the judicial process? What did it mean to contradict the heretofore impervious nature of court decisions with a charge that neutral "reason" did not control the law in the way the practitioners had always pretended? Institutionally, I suggest that two things happened, both of which diminished all courts' legitimacy to a degree, and the Supreme Court's legitimacy perhaps more than any other. The first thing that contributed to a loss of credibility for the Court was that, as the "mysterious science of the law" (Boorstin's phrase), became less mysterious, reverence for the

Court's law declined accordingly. It is no discredit to the great Justice Holmes to note that his role as a dissenter might have been less recognized, and less admired, had the realist perspective never emerged. Holmes's dissents are in no way diminished by an acceptance of the notion that judicial disagreement may well be based on the notion that eminently reasonable men or women might still see things differently. Even reason may be a matter of perspective.

The second impact of legal realism on American jurisprudence grew out of the first, it being that, because the Supreme Court was somehow less regal, it would now not be able to contradict a legislature as convincingly as it had in the past. As Supreme Court decisions looked less and less like scientific decisions, their ideological positioning not only began to resemble the ideological positioning of a legislature, but the old issue of to what degree a Court should be entitled to override the will of popular legislatures also gained a new credibility. If the Court possessed the same passions that Marshall took from Madison's *Federalist* no. 10, why, again, should the Court's passions have preference over those of the people's representatives?

When writings such as Edward Corwin's *Court over Constitution*, for example, attacked the conservative, New Deal–negating Supreme Court of the early Roosevelt years, the book was widely read and, to a considerable degree, agreed with.[35] Its publication in 1938, when the Court was already turning away from its New Deal negation, did not minimize the work's importance. Corwin's book contained a comprehensive jurisprudential argument, summarizing what this Constitutional scholar had been saying for years about the Court and its limitations. When *Court over Constitution* said that there was a "total defect of governmental power" afoot in the land, and that "a governmental 'no man's land'" meant that the "Utopia, the City of the Sun, the Elysian Fields of *laissez-faire*-ism" could exist because "legislative power was pleasantly non-existent,"[36] Corwin was condemning far more than the institutional arrogance of the Supreme Court. His specific condemnation of the imbalance of the United States' private-to-public sectors demonstrated Corwin's understanding of how deeply engrained the bias of the pre-1937 Court was. Corwin's sense of not only the institutional but also the sectoral biases of the pre-1937 Court, coming at the time of the realists' revelations on the true nature of the judicial decision, meant that the stage was set for the alteration in Supreme Court direction which had begun between Corwin's writing of his work and the work's publication.

In the next chapter I will look more closely at the third great period of Supreme Court activism, that of the first years of the Roosevelt New

Deal. For now, it is useful to keep in mind that the period's condemnation of the Court was as widespread as it was among the populace during that time in great part because Constitutional scholars such as Edward Corwin found it easier to attack the Court due to the realist writers who preceded him. These reasons, as well as the depth of America's greatest economic crisis, no doubt contributed to why this third period of judicial activism lasted a far shorter time than either the Marshall or the Field Courts' judicial activism.

CHAPTER TEN

The Third Activist Period

A Pre–New Deal Precursor

Before turning our attention to the Supreme Court of the Depression era, it must be said for the record that, between the judicial activism of the Field-led nineteenth-century Court and the Charles Evans Hughes Court of the first four years of the New Deal, another Court engaged in a fair degree of activism regarding labor, consumer, and welfare legislation. William Howard Taft, though more of a trustbuster as president than Teddy Roosevelt gave him credit for, became increasingly suspicious of progressivism as Woodrow Wilson administration legislation invaded more traditionally private sector arenas. By the time the newly elected Republican president Warren Harding appointed Taft to the Court's chief justiceship in 1921, a Court that was to include not only Brandeis and Holmes but, by the mid-1920s, progressives like Harlan F. Stone as well, Taft had already girded himself to stem the tide of what he deemed excessively reformist legislation.

Numerically, there can be no doubt about Taft's judicial impact. As Alpheus Mason reminds us, Taft's "super-legislature" engaged "in what Dean [Roscoe] Pound spoke of as a 'carnival of constitutionality.'"[1] If until 1920 there had been only fifty-three Congressional actions declared unconstitutional, in the decade of the 1920s, "twelve, or nearly one fourth as many of these adverse rulings were handed down."[2]

In important ways, however, the Taft Court's reversals may not have been as significant as the three Courts I have mentioned as the best examples of private sector–supporting activism. For one thing, though Taft himself was a relatively consistent supporter of those whom Bernard Schwartz properly alludes to as the "Four Horsemen" of the conservative Court (by 1922 Willis Van Devanter, James McReynolds, George Sutherland, and Pierce Butler), Taft at times separated himself from the farthest pole of that conservative perspective.[3] Whereas in *Truax v. Corrigan* (1921)[4] he voted with the conservatives in striking down an Arizona anti-injunction law covering organized labor, for example, he joined with Holmes and Brandeis in a dissenting opinion in the case of *Adkins v. Children's Hospital* (1923),[5] arguing vigorously for the constitutionality of a minimum-wage law.

Second, I cannot place Chief Justice Taft's Court in quite the same ideological, institutional, and sectoral place as the other activist Courts because Taft, in the judgment of his detractors and supporters alike, made his most significant contribution in the area of judicial administration. Though Mason properly notes that Taft was motivated by "stemming the tide of social democracy," Mason notes as well that Taft sincerely favored "leveling gross inequalities between rich and poor at the bar of justice."[6] With all of Taft's wariness regarding progressives, labor unions, and the like, the chief justice, as Mason put it, did not feel that the Court need "block all regulatory legislation; its function was that of a fine filter, carefully discriminating between good and bad laws."[7] For Chief Justice Taft, in other words, judicial acquiescence in a small portion of the "overwhelming mass of ill-digested legislation" might serve adequately to calm the ideological waters.[8]

Third, let me combine two further notions that also suggest why Taft Court activism was not of the significance of Marshall, Field, and the early Hughes Courts. Though, as Justice Felix Frankfurter was to put it later, "the Court had invalidated more legislation than in fifty years preceding," what is also clear is that much of what was invalidated was of less than earth-shaking importance. Laws applying to "standard-weight bread" regulation and "the fixing [of] the resale price of theater tickets by ticket scalpers" are part of the count.[9] Although not all Taft reversals of legislated law were as trivial, to be sure, it must be pointed out, perhaps above all other points here, that the tenor of the times—the ideological tone of the 1920s—was such that conservative Supreme Court rulings simply did not kindle the kind of legislative-to-judicial, and particularly private sector–to–public sector, intensity that other activist Court periods did. Remember that, though there may have been a residue of progressive legislation to be dealt with, the Supreme Court of William Howard Taft reigned during the presidencies of Warren Harding, Calvin Coolidge, and Herbert Hoover, the Congress of the 1920s being a decidedly conservative place as well. The legislative residue of the Wilson era was a good deal less threatening once the era had passed.

The Early New Deal

It was not long, however, until the early-twentieth-century's realist protestations over the biases of an ostensibly neutral law, combined with jurisprudential attacks on the Court like those of Edwin Corwin, soon received their real-world response. If the judicial activism of the late-nineteenth-century period, or even the Taft period, revealed the ideological biases and the sectoral imbalances of America's political and legal systems, the Supreme Court of the twentieth century's fourth decade was a more visible target for those who would redress institutional and sectoral imbalances.

Though a handful of state laws protecting workers from the excesses of "freely negotiated" labor contracts had survived the Court rulings of the early century, *Muller* and *Bunting* being the most prominent among them,[10] the labor contract still remained largely unencumbered at the time of the Great Depression. As a result, the United States, practically alone among the industrial democracies of the time, did not legally protect activities directed toward the formation of labor unions. As a result, the industrial wage was still pretty much what the entrepreneur wished it to be. Neither had old-age insurance come to the United States, as it had to so much of Europe, and even workers' compensation, which had its origins in the guilds of the Middle Ages and was enacted in the modern era by Bismarck in the but recently aggregated Germany of the 1870s, came to a far more democratic nation fully sixty years later.

Of course, the economic collapse of the 1930s had a greater impact upon a larger portion of the American populace than did the bank failures and the monetary crises of the late nineteenth and early twentieth centuries. So, too, the remedies that the public demanded as a cure for the Depression were necessarily more intrusive on the contract than the reforms of previous years. The ideological and institutional arguments of President Franklin Roosevelt's remedy for the Depression were not the only arguments that confirmed the protestations of the legal realists concerning Court recalcitrance. At the time of the "switch in time that saved nine," the Court's chief justice, Charles Evans Hughes, suggested that the law was nothing more than what the Supreme Court said it was. Supreme Court decisions, now more readily seen as the result of judicial passions, were suffering a loss of legitimacy which the Marshall and Field Courts never suffered.

It should be no surprise that the mid-1930s Supreme Court opinions of conservative Justices Willis Van Devanter, James McReynolds, George Sutherland, Pierce Butler, Owen Roberts, and the pre-1937 Charles Evans Hughes still perform their yeoman service within law school presentations on contract and property. Whether in *Panama Refining* (1935),[11] which found a goodly section of the National Recovery Act unconstitutionally vague; in *Schecter Poultry* (1935),[12] which struck down the fair-competition codes of that act; or in *Carter v. Carter Coal Co.* (1936),[13] which struck down the Guffy Coal Act, the rejection of the public sector's adjustment of the private domain was based on fundamental assumptions concerning the nature of the contract. A relatively pure contract, negotiated wholly by the immediate parties and speaking largely to the economic purposes of those parties, survived as judicial orthodoxy several years into the Depression.

All in all, the Hughes Court fits quite well into the evolutionary pattern of linkages between the economic and the political variables at work in the Marshall and Taney Courts. Whereas Chief Justice Marshall had maintained the primacy of the federal government and the Constitutional order in matters dealing with the new nation's economy, recall that his successor, Chief Justice Roger Taney, weakened the federal sphere with broad endorsement of state-generated economic competition in cases such as *Charles River Bridge*.[14] But again, with Taney, through *Dred Scott*, there was still strong support for the private domain.

Yet, if the economic and the political realms—that is, the private and public sectors—were divided further in the opinions of Taney than they ever were by Marshall, the later Court's attachment to a more competitive private sector was part of the progression that led to the pre-1937 Charles Evans Hughes Court's favor for the private over the public domain. The partial *reintegration* of the public domain with the private domain which began at the state level with Hughes's 1937 opinion in *West Coast Hotel*[15] and at the federal level with *Jones and Laughlin Steel*[16] was clearly a precondition for the *rebalancing* of the private and public domains which Hughes eventually achieved. That reintegration and rebalancing, as I will elaborate on later, also had a great deal to do with what the Warren Court was to do in the 1954 *Brown*[17] opinion, and later Warren Court decisions.

The short of it is that not since the time of John Marshall did the federal government need the kind of authority to deal with the national economy that it did during the Depression. The necessities of a new and internationally vulnerable economy, spoken of passionately by Hamilton in the *Manufactures* and other places, were not altogether different from the necessities of a now broken economy, which many felt would never recover from the Depression without aggressive public action. By reproximating the public and the private sectors in 1937, Hughes and his Court opened the door to a reinvigoration of the entire federal jurisdiction through an activist, responsible government, particularly vis-à-vis the private sector.

As I have noted, this Depression-era crisis forced the Court to succumb to political pressure from a revitalized Congress, and a popular president, in a substantially shorter time than the Supreme Courts of earlier activist periods. In part this responsiveness was facilitated by the legal realist's vision of the Court's biases. John Marshall never succumbed to political pressure over a space of thirty years, still firing his judicial cannons in cases such as *Barron v. Baltimore*, (1833)[18] when many thought a less nationalistic, less Court-dominated orthodoxy was in order. Only Marshall's leaving the Court permitted the legislatively inspired economic competitivism of Taney's *Charles River* to receive judicial sanction. And, in the other significant activist period, the length of Court recalcitrance is similarly long. The tone of the Stephen Field–dominated, substantive due process Court did not come to an end until well after Field left the Court. Only in the twentieth century, following progressive antitrust, banking, and at least minimal worker protection state legislation, did the second activist period even minimally subside. Even then legal protections for the private entrepreneur were but slightly reduced.

But the Hughes Court was different. The realists' and the Corwin-like criticisms of the Court paralleled the Depression trauma. When combined with the overwhelmingly successful presidential and congressional campaigns of Franklin Roosevelt and his legislative allies in 1936, and the threat of Roosevelt's plan to pack the Court with six friendly justices, who would "assist" the over seventy-year-old members (unimaginable in the Marshall or Field eras), the Court acknowledged that four years of foot dragging were enough. As James MacGregor Burns has noted, Roosevelt was convinced that "there would be 'marching' farmers and workers throughout the land if the Court tried to throw out the New Deal."[19] The former presidential candidate Hughes's political instincts had not left him entirely when he was appointed to the Court.

Hughes II

Institutionally, if the federal political jurisdiction—the Congress and its vigorous executive accomplice—was strengthened itself in the mid-1930s vis-à-vis the Supreme Court, what transpired with regard to the private-to-public balance was even more notable. As I have suggested, the reification of private power which justices like Marshall and Field indulged in was largely rationalized by their time's emphasis on economic *productivity*. Neither period's rulings were determined substantially by considerations of distribution or economic "fairness." The private sector's principal charge had always been to produce wealth. That goal could be accomplished with a fair degree of public cooperation, as in England's mercantilist period or America's own Marshall-era, Hamilton-prescribed mercantilism. Or it could be accomplished with minimal public involvement, as in the late nineteenth-century United States. It took the Depression to bring production back into the public limelight, such concerns now being well integrated with those of employment as well as fair wages during employment.

The Hughes Court, in short, was faced with a set of problems different from and more complex than any that had bedeviled Marshall or Field. As the Great Depression became increasingly intractable, it became clear that what President Roosevelt, the New Deal Congress, and Chief Justice Hughes were faced with was a host of economic maladaptations that married the obvious productive deficiencies of the Depression with what Roosevelt more candidly than any presidential predecessor labelled the unfairness of the American economic system.

As a result of this novel production and distribution interlock, the public sector was increasingly relied upon as the proper arena for remedying both the nation's productivity and distributional problems. The public sector could not ascend to a position of vigor, particularly after one hundred years of passivity, without having to deal with two tasks simultaneously. If Keynesian-like economic stimulation programs were being enacted in the hope that they would improve productivity, the public sector would also need to create legislation such as the Wagner Act (ensuring the freedom of labor organization), the Workmen's Compensation Act (ridding the worker of the need for costly and unlikely to be successful private lawsuits for on-the-job injury), the Social Security Act (bringing minimum old-age protection to America's retirees), along with similar pieces of "redistributive" legislation. After a century in the doldrums (note *Charles River Bridge*'s and *Jones and Laughlin Steel*'s dates), the public sector had returned to the economic fray.

In this context the cognitive nature of the Roosevelt-era Supreme Court should be clear. As the private and public sectors reintroduced themselves to each other (though, again, a measure of mercantilism never left the U.S. system), the essential instrumentality of a common law which had had many of its social encumbrances whittled from it since Magna Carta was at least in part returned to its social castings. Though surely a long way from the feudal indistinguishability between the private and public sectors, or even the sixteenth- to early-nineteenth-century-variety of mercantilism, the private contract was unquestionably reintroduced to a larger social context during the New Deal. The cognitively analytic contract now would confront the broader, cognitively synthetic necessities of a very frightened nation.

What does it mean, cognitively, to encourage collective bargaining through a union shop contract? Recognizing the substantive wage and benefit provisions of such a contract, I would also point out that, for the first time in the American experience, the federal government was now sanctioning a *form* of employment agreement in which, quite simply, multiple parties (workers) on one side of a contract were negotiating with but a single interest (management) on the other. Apart from the cognitive quality of the contract's terms, as discussed earlier, this qualitative imbalance of contractual participants is the essence of the union contract's form. Such a form, in cognitive terms, is undeniably synthetic.

Much of the public had been protesting the absence of a fair return for the worker since the coming of the Industrial Revolution to the U.S. economy. But that return would be negotiated in a contractual setting, rather than simply acknowledged within the context of a long-settled feudal understanding. For the historian Sir Henry Maine, modernity after all was the movement from status to contract. But workers, in the plural, were protected in their right to bargain with a single entity, and their new form of contract now frequently included retirement provisions, health care provisions, vacation and seniority guarantees, along with a variety of other "fringe benefits." The cognitively "clean," so-many-hours-for-so-much-money agreement, was increasingly replaced by a complex and necessarily well-negotiated document.

In sum, the pre-Roosevelt-era contract, with its near perfect analytic purity, had become not one but two steps removed from the synthetic form contract that was available during the mercantilist, pre-Taney period. The egalitarian ideal of a nation of farmers, artisans, merchants, and the like, the essence of Thomas Jefferson's bucolic pastoral vision, had been uprooted by both the Industrial Revolution and the distributive realities of America's own industrialism. The assumed egalitarianism of the Jackson/Taney free enterprise ideal, essentially small business and artisan-based, was no longer applicable and even the benign considerations of corporate mergers which Holmes had held onto in *Northern Securities*[20] were outdated by 1937. The contribution to economic justice which the Taney/Jackson preindustrial capitalism promised was increasingly seen (the 1869 Knights of Labor being America's first labor union) as a badly broken pledge by shortly after the Civil War.

By 1937, the "switch" of Chief Justice Hughes, along with the retirements of two of his aging colleagues, meant that the Court that Edward Corwin and others had so harshly condemned would now march in another direction. As mentioned above, the landmark 1937 cases of *West Coast Hotel* and *Jones and Laughlin Steel Co.* signaled what is still widely recognized as both American jurisprudence's greatest retreat of the legal branch in the face of the mandates of the political branches. It is also the most thorough triumph of the public sector over the private sector in the nation's history. At a time of extreme economic dislocation, the issues put before the United States Supreme Court were largely concerned with the failures, both productive and distributive, of the private sector. But, to a degree, they also dealt with the failures of those weak and often prostituted public institutions that had either shielded or ignored the private sector for so long.

Ironically, the *West Coast Hotel* and *Jones and Laughlin* cases have a Marshall-like ring to them. Their decisions, in great part, endorse public sector activities designed to spur the private economy. But, in another sense, these cases and the political ideology that they evidence place private business on the defensive more than at any time since the Anti-Federalists' attacks on privileged mercantilists and the Constitution itself. Perhaps not surprisingly, it was not long before the cases stopped, in large part because private business, like Chief Justice Hughes, knew that it had been beaten. Big business would not trumpet its new weakness, at considerable cost and embarrassment, to the public that had defeated it.

Thus, as the private sector largely withdrew from the courtroom, so too private business withdrew from the sometimes extreme ideological conservatism that had so damaged its image during the early days of the Depression. By 1940 the Grand Old Party supported the internationalist, moderate, and not very Republican Wendell Wilkie for its presidential nomination. In 1944, and again in 1948, another moderate, the New York governor, Thomas E. Dewey, carried the Republican banner. The private sector had retrenched all around, virtually conceding the permanence of the ideological and private-to-public sector reallocations that it endured because of the Depression.

CHAPTER ELEVEN

The Pre-Warren Court

A Very Different Legacy

Of course, no government has ever been free of interinstitutional conflict. No government as decentralized as the United States could have expected anything other than to have more than its share of interinstitutional jostling. But it is fair to say, I think, that the Supreme Court which former California chief prosecutor and then governor Earl Warren began to serve as chief justice in 1953 may well have marked the Court's most institutionally contentious period. So much happened during the sixteen years that Warren led the Court that it is tempting simply to chronicle the achievements of that time and have the mere length of the record speak for the Court's innovative brilliance, or its juridical perversity, depending on one's point of view. But, if anything is clear about the Warren Court, it is that its institutional independence can be understood only when it is contrasted with what the Courts that preceded it did. It is understood still better when it is also contrasted with what the Court that followed it did.

What, then, distinguishes the Warren Court from the Courts that have preceded and followed it? All observers tick off the Court's judicial attention to previously unconsidered issues. From the rights of minorities to the rights of the accused, from the rights of women to the right to fair legislative representation, Earl Warren's Court never shied from addressing that broad range of new and difficult controversies that grew out of a confrontational age.

But without question what was most controversial about the Warren Court's activism was that, ideologically, it was blatantly liberal. In stark contrast to the activism of all three of the activist Courts that preceded it, the Warren Court captured the momentum of that aggregation of the federal government's powers which had begun with Franklin Roosevelt and used it to attain clearly egalitarian, essentially reformist goals.

To be sure, there was more to Earl Warren and his colleagues, such as William O. Douglas, William Brennan, Tom Clark, Arthur Goldberg, and others, than simply a liberal agenda–enhancing Supreme Court. The Warren Court, unlike any Court before it, actually began to look at itself as a legal institution that could, and should, embrace innovative methods of interpreting Anglo-American law as a matter of normal Court practice. In furtherance of its ideologically liberal goals, the institutional and judicial strategies that were designed to further that practice distinguished the Warren Court from any that came along either before it or after. But to understand that distinction we should look first at a foundational jurisprudential structure that was built immediately before the Warren Court came into existence and which the Warren Court most certainly built upon.

The Warren Inheritance

No government, or judiciary, is immune to the times that it inherits. The Warren Court, indeed the entire U.S. federal government, could not have been an exception to that historical truism in the 1950s and 1960s, even had it wanted to be. If federal jurisdictional restoration, Congressional jurisdictional restoration, public sector restoration, along with the cognitively synthetic contractual alterations of the post-1937 period, had laid the groundwork for this unique Supreme Court, nothing that occurred from the time of Chief Justice Hughes's famous "switch" to the coming of Earl Warren to the bench impaired the Court's building on the 1937 framework either.

World War II surely did not lessen the national government's authority or legitimacy. External threats rarely lessen the power of governments. Likewise, the United States' fear of internal communism, along with the fall of China to Mao Zedong's "agrarian reformers" and the subsequent use of Chinese troops against United Nations forces in the prolonged Korean War, further ratified the nation's satisfaction with a strong federal government.

But, apart from the United States' external and internal security dangers (real or perceived), something significant happened within the country during the immediate pre-Warren period which foretold the active role of the central government throughout the postwar 1940s and early 1950s. What happened was that two great migrations took place, one being the actual movement of a peoples within the nation, and the other (though slow to begin) being within the thinking of at least some Americans with regard to the status of this country's African-American citizens.[1]

Consideration of the United States' largest minority, which had begun to move into the great Northern cities in the early twentieth century, was beginning to become more central to this country's politics than at any time since the three-quarter-century-old Hayes-Tilden 1877 Compromise. Many descendants of the former African slaves who had been sold out by the 1877 Compromise now found themselves living in cloistered ghettos within those Northern cities. They found that their fight for full citizenship was not only far from over but that the enemy this time was a far more subtle enslaver.

Some African Americans had begun to come North during World War I and the great Southern agricultural depression of the 1920s. As August Meier and Elliot Rudwich have pointed out, "it was an economic crisis arising from several converging factors that precipitated the [early] population movement."[2] But, even by the time of the immediate pre–World War II period, most African Americans still lived as second-class citizens in the South, rarely far from where their forbears had been slaves. These citizens' employment as tenant farmers or sharecroppers had upgraded their status from slavery to a kind of serfdom, but little farther. Yet the accumulation of many years of migrations by Black citizens who abandoned their sharecropping and tenancies, along with the mental migrations of those Whites whose consciences were finally wrenched by the squalor of the Black condition, North and South, took place at roughly the same time.

Black soldiers, after all, had fought and fought well in World War II. If their blood spilled within our own borders during a time of lynchings and shootings had not brought expectations for better treatment, their blood spilled overseas brought expectations of meaningful change for Blacks within their own community and within a growing community of White allies. In the same year that a young Minneapolis mayor, Hubert Humphrey, spoke for a strong civil rights plank at the Democratic convention (1948), a middle-class Black family that had recently purchased a home in St. Louis reached out to the United States Supreme Court for redress from what was known as a "restrictive covenant."

The kind of restrictive covenant that the family sought to override was candidly designed to keep Blacks—and sometimes Asians, Jews, or whomever else seemed "undesirable"—from moving to neighborhoods that they could financially afford but that were inhabited by those who did not want them as neighbors. The Shelley family was symbolic of those Black families that had either moved to the North during World War I (when factory jobs first opened to Blacks), during that Southern agricultural depression of the 1920s, or during World War II's manpower-short years. They had worked hard, saved their money, and they felt entitled to the better life that African Americans could in at least some cases afford.

In short, the *Shelley v. Kraemer* (1948)[3] case spoke to a good deal more than the argument that arose between one Black family's living in a St. Louis neighborhood with neighbors who had recently drawn up a standard restrictive covenant in order to keep "negroes" out of the neighborhood. Just as might be expected in any number of neighborhoods with similar covenants, one of Shelley's new white neighbors, Kraemer, attempted to enforce the covenant against Shelley and his white seller, a woman named Sophie Fitzgerald. At first glance the Fred Vinson Supreme Court's ruling appears not to build itself on an overwhelmingly important legal point. Yes, the Fourteenth Amendment's "state action" doctrine was altered by the case. Its ruling overturned an earlier decision that had established the mere *judicial* enforcement of what was an equity pleading as something short of state action.[4] But the case stood for more than that.

Restrictive covenants, of course, have been a tried-and-true equity instrument for hundreds of years. They are still fully enforceable when their provisions relate to setbacks (equalizing house distances from the street within a neighborhood), minimum square footage (protecting property values by ensuring comparable housing in a neighborhood), or whatever else might reasonably preserve property value amongst a group of landowners. But the ruling of the *Shelley* case reflected the notion that something as important as the modern descendant of England's land law could still be altered by a court, without the "activism" of a legislative body. More broadly, it reflected the fact that the common law, even without Coke-like political encouragement, could still enlighten a hotly contested area of public policy. It also, sadly, marks the limits of what the private law can accomplish in the furtherance of social goals.

At one level, *Shelley* seems to be a less than overwhelming ruling on the law of equity, the ruling only rejecting the state action concept, which shielded all but undeniably political actions from judicial interference. But it is, in a soft-handed but important way, a latter-day confirmation of how the common law, without legislative embellishment, would always continue to grow. Whereas the traditional line of state action cases had required a *political* institution of the state to engage in outright discrimination before the Fourteenth Amendment's state action doctrine could be applied, *Shelley* ruled that a *judicial* institution could be held to a state action standard if it enforced a doctrine that was discriminatory in its *impact*. By so holding, it demonstrated how the Supreme Court, in its role as a common-law court as well as a branch of the U.S. government, could rule in a publicly important equity matter. It could deny Kraemer's request for an injunction and thus continue to grow the law.

Clement Vose's classic 1959 work on the *Shelley* case, *Caucasians Only,*[5] may still be the best book which deals with the preparation and trial of a case before the United States Supreme Court. The absence of even the slightest mention of a legislative role in the strategies that led to the St. Louis covenant's overturning makes the book even a bit more interesting. From their selection of plaintiffs to their raising of money for the case's prosecution to the divining of strategies for the arguing of the case, the National Association for the Advancement of Colored People (NAACP) and its allies engineered their victory without the slightest thought of seeking a legislative remedy for their clients.

In spite of the political drama that *Shelley* brought, and in spite of the judicial ruling that saw a pre-Warren Supreme Court begin to assume an activist role in the absence of legislative activity, the *Shelley* case might still have been hidden among the Court's but moderately significant Constitutional rulings. Yet when one considers what was really done in *Shelley*—that is, that *Shelley* did not respond in any way to legislatively created law (because there wasn't any that prohibited housing integration and there wasn't going to be any)—the case becomes more important than it first seems. Whereas a holding that directly responded to a legislative initiative could have made the case a mere confirmation of an accepted civil right, the fact that *Shelley* created new public law, even though the precedent it grew from was embedded in the common law's protection of the right of property alienation, presages the Warren Court cases that followed it.

Shelley, substantively, protected the American minority that had been so ill treated from the time of the slave ships through the passage of Article 1, section 9, of the Constitution and beyond. That the case was decided largely as a matter of private law, that the common-law freedom to alienate property came to the rescue of a racially discriminated-against group of citizens within the public domain, presaged the exceptional nature of the Warren Court that followed it. The case of *Shelley v. Kraemer* is generally considered to be a minor Constitutional landmark, particularly when compared with the more sweeping civil rights cases of the later Warren Court. But the case, like the Bill of Rights itself, is best seen as having as its larger *purpose* the preservation of a judicial channel of protest for an aggrieved *group*, even though the particular case was decided on private-law principles.

It also, once more, marks that legal place where the private law could go no further in righting the wrongs of racial discrimination. Seen this way, *Shelley* becomes a pathway for the remediation of a variety of conditions, involving Blacks and other "out-group" citizens, which many thought should be remediated. The Warren Court, following this case and the mildly adventuresome Supreme Court of its predecessor Chief Justice Fred Vinson, could now expand on the deeper implications of *Shelley* as well as on the Bill of Rights–protected purposes of those groups that had not been responded to by legislatures.

CHAPTER TWELVE

The Warren Court

Modern Civil Rights

The purpose for discussing *Shelley v. Kraemer*[1] at some length in the preceding short chapter was, once more, that the case's decision foretold, and facilitated, the immediately following ideological and institutional shift in American jurisprudence which is still so controversial. The substantive, ideological notion of *Shelley v. Kraemer* paralleled the larger civil rights consciousness that the year 1948, with the Humphrey speech at the Democratic Convention, the creation of the Truman Civil Rights Commission, and the adoption of the Civil Rights plank by the national Democratic convention, brought to U.S. politics. By the close of 1948 the issue of equal rights for the nation's African-American citizens was on the front burner.

It was not until the Congressional logjam was broken by post–John F. Kennedy assassination sympathy, of course, that legislative actions such as the Civil Rights Act (1964) and the Voting Rights Act (1965) were finally passed. A variety of bills that approximated these two laws had been bottled up in Congressional committees, most often under the control of segregationist Southern chairs, since the time of the second Truman administration. In 1964 a Constitutional amendment outlawing the poll tax was ratified.

The "idea whose time had come," as the mellifluent Illinois Republican senator Everett Dirksen put it when he swung his support behind the first Civil Rights Bill, generated laws that were quickly and unceremoniously ratified by the Supreme Court. The Supreme Court cases of *Katzenbach v. McClung* (1964)[2] and *Heart of Atlanta Motel v. Katzenbach* (1964),[3] specifically, upheld the public accommodations provisions of the 1964 legislation. Both are moderately significant cases. Unlike *Shelley,* however, each merely ratified what the federal legislature had already enacted. Like the judicial holding of Roger Taney's *Charles River Bridge*,[4] they created no new law. Earl Warren's legacy on the Supreme Court did not grow out of cases like *Heart of Atlanta* or *Katzenbach*.

What cases, then, mark Earl Warren's Supreme Court? What distinguishes the Warren Court, I am hardly the first to suggest, are those cases whose rulings grew out of the most innovative strategies for finding new law which any Supreme Court had ever utilized. The three great activist periods of the Court—the John Marshall Court's protection of the mercantilist notions of contract, the Stephen Field Court's protection of the most naked private contract in U.S. history, and the early Hughes Court's protection of the contract against the Roosevelt New Deal—had been well in the spirit of James Madison's position on the "diversity in the faculties of men from which the rights of property originate." They were also much in the spirit of William Blackstone's position on the intrusions of legislated law into the common law, particularly as they reversed intrusions on the private contract. The Warren Court's most innovative cases must be understood, I suggest, for their innovative realignment of not only the traditional positions between the Court and the legislature on which institution protected the private sector and which spoke for the public. They must be understood as well for the creative inclusion of a variety of considerations into what Warren and his brethren wished to reframe as a modern American social contract.

Particularly in the areas of (1) the right of a minority to racial integration in education, (2) the right of an accused to a fair trial, (3) the right of citizens to at least roughly equal formal political access, and (4) the right of women to be freed of traditional gender roles, the Warren Court's actions at first glance seem far from anything having to do with the private-to-public jurisdictional divide. In fact, however, all of these judicial arenas have a great deal to do with that divide. I will look briefly at these arenas as a group before investigating each in detail, recognizing that other areas of judicial outspokenness, such as the establishment of religion cases, for example, might equally well portray the private-to-public jurisdictional alterations of the Warren Court.

First, let us not forget that it was *public* education that Warren ruled on in *Brown v. Board of Education*.[5] The case concerned the obligation of the public sector to prepare its citizens to live within the greater society. Second, it was the role of the law in providing protections for those accused of crime which Warren dealt with in the criminal cases. U.S. states must not, as did the Stuarts, abuse their sovereign powers in the process of protecting themselves from either political dissidents or common criminals. Whether in Fourth Amendment protections against unlawful search and seizure (*Mapp v. Ohio*),[6] Fifth Amendment protections against self-incrimination (*Miranda v. Arizona*),[7] or the right to be represented by an attorney (*Gideon v. Wainwright*),[8] the Court spoke from the perspective of the public sector in protecting fundamental freedoms.

Third, it was the public's access to the political arena which the Warren Court spoke to in both *Baker v. Carr* and *Reynolds v. Sims*.[9] The American promise of equal opportunity was not merely an economic promise. It was also a guarantee of being politically heard. Finally, the Warren Court at least began to respond to the pleas of a majority of women, and their male allies, concerning the still inferior status of women before the law. Particularly with regard to the control of their own bodies, the *Griswold* case[10] shows the Court beginning to act in opposition to the private moralities that had bridled women who, though a numerical majority, had traditionally been prevented from acting as a majority. In short, the private-to-public battle was deeply rooted in the key Warren Court opinions. The detailed examinations of the four judicial arenas that appear in the next two chapters will elaborate on these roots.

Majorities and Minorities—Calhoun Inverted

Before examining these judicial arenas, however, it may be helpful to review what the core preconditional understandings were which dealt with the political and legal authority that the Warren Court utilized in its opinions. Within the context of the Warren Court's nearly revolutionary institutional role, an issue that once again became salient during the Warren era was that of political majoritarianism versus minoritarianism.

To be sure, America's arguments over the correct place of majorities and minorities in the political order go back before Madison's *Federalist* no. 10. The Constitution's original seven articles clearly reflected Madison and the Federalists' fear of unruly state majorities. But throughout the three previous periods of America's Supreme Court activism, along with those more quiescent periods when the Court largely ratified what legislatures were doing, a fundamental alignment of legislatures with the majoritarian position, and a corresponding alignment of the Supreme Court with the minoritarian position, habitually reappeared.

What Madison saw as so troubling—essentially, state legislatures' habitual favoring of debtors over creditors—had so firmly cemented the alignment of legislative-to-judicial and private-to-public allegiances that this alignment lasted all the way through the Roosevelt, and even Truman, presidencies. Usually representing majorities, legislatures traditionally challenged the prerogatives of the private sector. As Hamilton had argued so convincingly in *Federalist* no. 78, the power of judicial review was necessary to preserve the "real" law, that is the private law, and particularly the cornerstones of property and contract and the debts that have been enforced as part of the law since the time of Edward I.

With the Warren Court, everything changed. That is, the ideological-to-institutional alignments not only changed (the Court now being the generator of innovative law), but they changed in response to the pleas of active political groupings that were roughly analogous to liberal groupings like the Jacksonian Democrats which had benefited from, and contributed to, an increasingly democratic political system. Put another way, not only had the Supreme Court switched roles with the institution of the legislature for the first time in American history, thus becoming the creator of new laws and not the negator of legislated law; the Court switched ideological preferences as well.

In its switching of ideology, the Supreme Court, as *Shelley v. Kraemer* foreshadowed in a private-law case, filled in for the *silence* of legislatures on public issues in which groups that might have constituted a winning political majority, or groups that were aspiring to be majorities during the Constitutional period, had not achieved their goals within the legislative domain. In the matter of an accused's rights, the Warren Court's sensitivity to the sometimes routine intrusions of law enforcement onto street criminals parallel Court sensitivity for the analogous position of those like the defendants in the free speech case of *Yates v. United States* (1957)[11] who were accused of political crimes. All who were accused of crime deserved the full protection of the Bill of Rights.

Regarding political majorities and minorities, in other words, the Supreme Court under Warren abandoned the judiciary's traditional minoritarian, private law–protecting position. Again, even when functioning, current majorities may not have existed, as in the cases involving the rights of the accused or in, say, First Amendment cases regarding religious instruction in the schools, the Warren Court ruled for the political position analogous to that of a political opposition. Why did the Warren Court consistently rule in such a way? And why were such rulings neither as unpredictable nor as devastating to the traditions of Anglo-American jurisprudence as some believed they were?

Obviously, I think the rationale for the Warren Court's boldness belies the conclusion that it distorted either the nation's jurisprudential heritage or the institutional arrangements of the American Constitutional system. And a historical and ideological perspective on the majoritarian-to-minoritarian issue is what helps demonstrate how the distinctions between Warren Court activism and the three major periods of activism which preceded it did not rend that system.

I have already referred to the fears of majoritarianism which are found in the writings of James Madison and Alexander Hamilton, as well as Blackstone in the *Commentaries*. The unique relationship of individual groups to the political whole is the essence of Warren Court interpretation. But the question of to what extent stifled majorities, or stifled aspiring majorities, should be assisted by the Court when legislative impediments stand in their way, is also the essence of Warren. In chapter 7 I described the nature of John C. Calhoun's response to the intensifying regional frictions of the pre–Civil War period. Calhoun's proposal for the reduction of these frictions was substantially to disengage the regions. His idea of nullification, or the concurrent majority, would give what Calhoun candidly called a "veto" to each state over the majoritarian rule making of the general government.

Calhoun's prescription, of course, showed how any minority might adopt a highly decentralized or structurally centrifugal response to that Calhoun-like sense of an inability to secure that group's rights. What is significant about the four arenas of Warren Court judicial interpretation which I will review, however, is that, with one minor exception (the Black Nationalist exception), no segment of the involved groups ever advocated the Calhounian, structurally centrifugal route for the achievement of their political goals. Indeed, each group overwhelmingly endorsed the notion of having the national government, if anything a strong national government, come to their aid. What is also significant about these groups is that they came to the Court, not the political institutions of the Congress and the presidency, for assistance.

The willingness of Warren-era plaintive groups to have the national Supreme Court become their principal instrument of political and legal change is understandable, I suggest, when two considerations are put into context. The first deals with the problem of legislation generally within the U.S. political process. Without engaging in a detailed review of U.S. legislative history, I merely point out that American government scholars overwhelmingly agree that the passage of significant legislation in this country has always required more than the support of a simple majority of all Americans or their legislators.

The structures of the Congress—its bicameral houses; its powerful committees and committee chairs; its parliamentary obstructions which often stifle popularly favored legislation such as the cloture rule of "the world's greatest deliberative body," the Senate—all place a higher burden on the proponents of federal legislation than on any legislation's opponents. The founding fathers knew what they were doing. For the record, legislation is almost as difficult to pass in the states, all of them (except Nebraska with its unicameral arrangement) mimicking at least the institutional if not precisely the procedural arrangements of the federal government.

In short, the difficulty of passing legislation had hindered Warren Court–era groups which sought change through their own inclusion under Bill of Rights freedoms. The Calhoun position, and the pre–Civil War position of the Southern aristocracy, as we have reviewed, combatted the tide of history that would have politically empowered the growing, upland commercial interests of their own states. The procedural hurdles of the national system worked to the South's advantage for a good while. The Missouri Compromise, the Fugitive Slave Laws, the Kansas-Nebraska Bill, along with the compromise-at-any-price presidencies of Taylor, Fillmore, Pierce, and Buchanan, all demonstrated the ability of the Southern leadership to parry the aspiringly majoritarian thrusts of antislavery sentiment.

The same hurdles that assisted Calhoun and his constituents in the decades before the Civil War were still in place opposing those groups that sought political relief in the 1950s and 1960s. These groups did not, in Calhounian fashion, suggest a structural disassembling. When their quest for legislation faltered, for reasons that they considered to be antimajoritarian, they came to the Supreme Court. But they came to a Supreme Court, as we shall review in the succeeding two chapters, which had a keen sense of the role of the public sector in resolving the conflicts of the 1960s.

There was another reason for why Earl Warren's Supreme Court succeeded to the position of the nation's rule maker when attempts at remedial legislation had either failed or had been discouraged. This reason, in a general way, had to do with the complementary interaction of (1) the character of the issues that were brought before the Court in the 1950s and 1960s, and (2) the demographic configuration of the population that was being asked to consider these issues. By the 1950s it was clear that the economically based New Deal coalition that might have supported reform had already begun to erode. As Ira Katznelson has noted, the New Deal coalition's loss of the South to the racial issues of the 1950s and 1960s, along with the decline in organized labor's strength and the resultant placement of labor into the national political calculus as more of an "interest group," severely crippled the kind of politics which might have advanced the rights of Blacks, those accused of crime, women, and unfairly apportioned urban citizens.[12]

The political impact of all of the above was unmistakable. As Jonathan Reider put it, "millions of voters, pried loose from their habitual loyalty to the Democratic Party," were at best a "volatile force" in American politics. Besides Southerners, "ethnic Catholics in the Northeast and Midwest, blue-collar workers, union members, [and] even a sprinkling of lower-middle class Jews" had begun to stray from the New Deal coalition.[13] Even if the supermajority demands of the legislative process at both levels of America's governments had not been sufficient to deter legislative activity, significant shifts in the kinds of issues that were now at stake, along with the new social and economic configuration of the American populace, effectively blocked legislative redress. The political and social realities of the post–World War II period thus complicated the burdens of all aspiring groups that were not a part of that middle-class, largely white, and increasingly suburban portion of the American populace.

Thus, whereas the working-class interests that had sought to improve their condition during the Great Depression eventually found a measure of relief from a sympathetic president and an accommodating Congress (that relief not being ratified by the Supreme Court until 1937) the pure numbers that put Roosevelt into the White House and strong Democratic majorities into the Congress during the 1930s were overwhelming. Blue-collar, no-collar, and unemployed workers, as well as those who feared that they would soon be unemployed in the Depression, made up a hefty majority of the population. Once energized, that majority worked its will, even in the judicial branch of the government.

Looked at spatially, what I am suggesting here is that though the demographic distribution of economic and social strata in the 1930s still pretty much resembled a classical distributional pyramid, no doubt with a dip in the pyramid's bottom line, the proportion of citizens who could be called middle class in the 1930s was nowhere near as great as it was by the 1950s or 1960s.[14] The Roosevelt New Deal coalition, with its labor support, urban support, Southern support, and the support of other "have-not" groups, was energized by a Democratic Party that made itself stronger than it had been at any time since the Jacksonian period. By the 1950s and 1960s, the demographic configuration was more like a diamond than a pyramid. Its suburban, white-collar makeup, along with the noneconomic nature of issues surrounding Blacks, women, reapportionment, and the rights of the accused, among others, made legislative redress for the aggrieved less likely.

What happened between the 1930s and the 1950s and 1960s, of course, spoke to the success, not the failure, of both the U.S. political system and the American Dream itself. A substantial segment of American families had successfully escaped the working identity of the smelting furnace, the knitting room, the stockyard, or the mine, and moved behind a desk, usually although not always at a higher level of pay, and with an identification of social class and ultimately political ideology which was wholly different from what it had yet known. No, it was often not the same individual who moved from factory to office. It was more likely the son, not yet a daughter. But, politically, this shift in the next generation's occupational identity, along with the physical movement of that family from the city to the suburbs, made all the political difference in the world. In short, since the majority required for legislative action within the U.S. political system had always been a supermajority, and the nation's demographics had now experienced a sea change from a more or less pyramidal configuration of economic distribution to a more or less diamond-shaped configuration, the task that at least some aggrieved groups faced in order to achieve their political goals became far more difficult than it would have been only twenty years earlier.

But again, when faced with a prolonged lack of political response to their condition, those groupings that sought justice from the American political system did not (contra Calhoun) suggest either the balkanization of the political system or the retardation of history. All they suggested was that a different national institution, a court instead of a legislature, take up their cause. They suggested that the institution that had stood for so long in opposition to the majoritarian, redistributive politics, now hear their pleas. The Warren Court was prepared to accommodate those pleas and the nature of that accommodation led to a different arrangement of ideology and institutions and, ultimately, to a wholly different way of looking at the boundary between the private and public domains than the American Republic had yet witnessed. As I review the specifics of these core Supreme court cases, I shall of course accent the private-to-public lines that the Warren Court drew within them.

In closing this chapter, let me suggest that, just as the Depression-era American citizen's loss of confidence in the self-regulating nature of the American economy was a catalyst for the Court's acceptance of innovative roles for the presidency and the Congress, the Warren Court was addressing nothing less than what it perceived to be the failure of the self-regulating nature of the two Constitutionally *political* branches of the government. The Warren Court, like those that it favored in its opinions, despaired of the ability of the Congress, the state governments, and to a degree even the president to do what it believed they ought to do for those citizens who were not so able to access the levers of political power.

It is important, I think, that the Warren Court's activism occurred not long after the legal realists had let the cat out of the bag about what judges really did in deciding cases. Earl Warren and his compatriots on the Court were viewed as so different from what any chief justice and Court had ever been in part because what they were doing could be less hidden behind judicial robes than the property and contract-oriented Marshall, Field, and early Hughes Courts had ever tried to hide. Under Warren what the realists had identified as very human judges were making what were now increasingly human, not economic, decisions, about sometimes more intimate areas of concern than Anglo-American judges had ever considered. Criticized though it may have been, the Warren Court's brand of legal realism made its greatest real-world contribution to the liberal political agenda.

CHAPTER THIRTEEN

Civil Rights
and the Rights of the Accused

Race and the Schools

Of the four substantive arenas of Warren Court rulings which I have suggested best illustrate the primacy of the private-to-public divide, let us begin our analysis with the rights of the United States' principal racial minority. The roughly 13 percent of America's ethnic mix that the African-American community comprises is roughly what it was at the time of the Emancipation. The minority status of the African American is unlikely ever to change. Though the Black community enjoyed the support of a good portion of the White community throughout the civil rights struggle, the burden of that struggle fell then, and continues today to fall, where it has always fallen—on the Black community itself.

Also, among the four arenas I will review, America's racial divide alone produced that small contingent within the minority population which, for a time, openly advocated an essentially Calhounian, structurally centrifugal, solution to America's racial tension. The Black Nationalist community's membership was never large, but it constituted a vociferous, and sometimes disproportionately listened to, dissident group for a while. The Nationalists pointedly argued that the solution to America's racial tensions should include a "return" of some portion of the country (most commonly the area of five Deep South states) to the Black community. In these states African Americans would supposedly live peacefully near, but separately from, the remainder of the U.S. citizenry.

The Black Nationalists, of course, were not persuasive within most of the Black community, much less within the larger American populace. The mark of the Warren Supreme Court, indeed the mark of the national political system as a whole throughout the still partial resolution of the racial crisis, was a movement toward an essentially centripetal, integrationist solution. By integrationist I refer not only to the racial admixture of White and Black citizens. I refer principally to the dominant institutional view of the Black community, as well as of supportive Whites, that the U.S. political system must collectively accommodate the Black request for full inclusion within the larger nation. The Black Nationalists' (or separatists') loss meant a victory for the true nationalists, both Black and White. What was accomplished for the Black citizen, inadequate though it may still be in some areas, was accomplished by eventually engaging all of the institutions of the national government in a candidly public exercise. But in so many areas, the courts had to come first.

Armed with the ideological perspective that America's great ethnic groupings should be included within one another's experience, the first task of the Warren Court became a matter of resetting the institutional imbalances that had only recently facilitated the separation of the races. In the case that Earl Warren cited at his retirement as one of the two most important he had ruled on (*Baker v. Carr* being the other), the Court opened its opinion with a discussion of the unique position of the South, that portion of the country in which racial segregation was still the most institutionalized.

Important though it was, *Brown* itself is correctly labeled by legal scholars as a "tombstone" case. It precluded any further usage of the separate but equal doctrine, a doctrine that was already contradicted by cases such as *McLaurin v. Oklahoma* (1950),[1] prohibiting separate seating for an African American in a graduate school classroom, and *Sweatt v. Painter* (1950),[2] prohibiting an allegedly equal (it was not) but separate Black law school to fall under a *Plessy*-like protection in Texas. The cases prior to *Brown* were heard in the last days of the Vinson Court, a Court that was quietly mimicking the purposive spirit of *Shelley* in situations that stood out as outrageous violations of fundamental American freedoms. Uniting with *all* of his fellow justices (the new chief justice's patience in forging unanimity in *Brown* is one of the great stories of intra-Court politics), Warren completed the segregation-ending job of *McLaurin* and *Sweatt* admirably. As a member of the public, and as one exercising a public right, a Black schoolchild was held to be entitled to associate with those of the dominant race during his, or her, schooling.

Implicitly, the Court began its argument for admitting Black children to integrated schools by acknowledging that the legal rights of a minority had been diminished by the post–Civil War Compromise of 1877. This compromise, once more, had granted the South a kind of regional semiautonomy. The Supreme Court's first task was therefore to reassert the supremacy of the national government over the state governments. Significantly, the landmark case of *Brown v. Board of Education*,[3] before it said a word about race or schools, or even about integration generally, ruled on something of immense historical and ideological significance. It revoked the post–Civil War compromise.

Although Warren conceded that the circumstances in each of the four cases combined under *Brown* reflected some "different local conditions," there was no question that what the Court ruled on formed "a *common* legal question."[4] Conceding as well that the Fourteenth Amendment's equal protection provisions were invariably subject to interpretation, generally along the line extending from those who had a property and contract-based view of the amendment's civil rights to those who would boldly "remove all distinctions among 'all persons born or naturalized in the United States,'" Warren revealed the scope of his own perspective on the amendment, declaring that "we must consider public education in the light of its full development and its present place in American life throughout the Nation."[5] Though the northern region of the United States was hardly free of racial bias, and though its racial problems might therefore need to be addressed by the Court at some future time, what *Brown* insisted upon, before anything else, was that a single, national standard for educational arrangements across the races be put in place. By implication *Brown* insisted that, when a national standard is not being met, the national government may see to it that it is.

With regard to the institutional dichotomy, the tension between the courts and the legislatures, the position of Warren and his Court is again quite clear. Reviewing the status of education North and South at the time of the Fourteenth Amendment's passage, Warren carefully noted such historical realities as that, "in the South, the movement toward free common schools, supported by general taxation, had not yet taken hold." He noted as well that "the effect of the [Fourteenth] Amendment on Northern States was generally ignored in the congressional debates."[6] So much for what the legislatures, state and federal, had been doing. They hadn't been doing much of anything, and the Court, in the case's early going, would make note of their lassitude.

Noting that the Court had proscribed "state-imposed discriminations against the Negro race" from the time of the Fourteenth Amendment's passage, something that had been lost sight of in much of the argument over school integration, Warren carefully reminded everyone that the "separate but equal" interpretation of the amendment did not become part of the Court's lexicon until the 1896 ruling in *Plessy v.*

Ferguson.[7] And this ruling, Warren was quick to point out, did not concern education. It concerned transportation. The jurisdictional grounding for *Brown*'s decision was being carefully laid.

To the merits: Warren, the tactician as well as strategist, properly noted that, in the cases the Court had dealt with since its creation of the separate but equal doctrine, "the doctrine itself was not challenged." But "in more recent cases," according to Warren, "inequality was found in that specific benefits enjoyed by white students were denied to Negro students of the same educational qualifications."[8] Even the cruel bargain of separate but equal had clearly not been kept.

Further noting that it was not necessary to "reexamine the [separate but equal] doctrine" in such cases, because the inequality was so patent, Warren insisted that "that question is [now] directly presented."[9] Is there any doubt that the Court was deeply aware of the ideological and historical nature of the separate but equal doctrine? Is there any doubt, after Warren's descriptions of what was done and not done in the past by legislatures (and done or not done by earlier Supreme Courts), that the Court wanted to have the last word on this issue? Quite apart from the decision in the case, there is no question about who was going to decide the issue. The justification for the Court's boldness was well stated in Warren's review of the prior cases, "there [having] been six cases involving the 'separate but equal' doctrine in the field of public education" already.[10] Warren, of course, was not so subtly reminding everyone that the Supreme Court had never relinquished jurisdiction over Fourteenth Amendment interpretations. He was also reminding everyone that there had been few arguments over the Court's right to be such an interpreter when the cases were decided in the opposite direction.

Yet there is one more dichotomy in *Brown*. Within much of the Fourteenth Amendment's interpretation the institutional battling was so often a part of the political discussions that followed the case that the issue of the private-to-public balance within this arena, briefly discussed in the last chapter, had largely been lost. We need not engage in guesswork concerning this most important of school integration opinions to find its private-to-public jurisdictional line. Neither do we need to engage in hyperbole to describe how far that line was moved in *Brown*.

The fact is that the words *private* and *public* are used frequently throughout the *Brown* opinion. And these terms are invariably placed into a historical context, as they should have been. They largely concern early education in the South, education that Warren properly noted "was largely in the hands of private groups."[11] But Warren pointed out that, though public school education had "advanced further in the North" at the time of the Fourteenth Amendment's passage, "the effect of the Amendment" on those states "was generally ignored in the congressional debates."[12]

Clearly, at the time of the Fourteenth Amendment's passage, Warren said that "even in the North, the conditions of public education did not approximate those existing today."[13] This comment preceded Warren's previously cited observation that "We must consider education in the light of its full development and its present place in American life throughout the Nation."[14] The following sentence, almost inevitably, returned to the private-public theme again, noting that only within the context of this "full development" of education could the Court determine "if segregation in public schools deprives these plaintiffs of the equal protection of the laws."[15]

Putting the central question of this case directly and poignantly, Warren concluded his "warmup" institutional and sectoral review in *Brown* by saying that "we come then to the question presented. Does segregation of children in public schools solely on the basis of race . . . deprive the children of the minority group of equal educational opportunities?"[16] The answer is obvious, I suggest, once the sectoral preconditions are laid out. Of course, if this matter lies within the public sector (just as it lies within the federal and not the state government's jurisdiction), there can be no discrimination. Declaring "we believe that it does" (deprive minority children of equal opportunity) was the predictable response to the Court's question. The schools had denied Black children publicly guaranteed equal protection.[17]

In sum, once the sectorally and institutionally relevant questions in *Brown v. Board of Education* were addressed, the actual ruling that marked the end of legal discrimination in U.S. public schools was inevitable. From the Courts' ideological willingness to repair to the public jurisdiction in a dispute over whether the federal government was to impose national standards as opposed to state standards, to the Court's willingness to engage in legislative-like action when legislatures were unwilling to remedy what an aggrieved group of citizens suffered, and, most important, to the Court's sense that the entire matter properly belonged within the public sector, the decisional path in *Brown* was clear. In its structure, it was a path that would be followed again and again by Earl Warren's Supreme Court.

Rights of the Accused

The second group of cases which illustrates the significance of the Warren court private-to-public boundary concerns the rights of the accused. Here, also moving into the void of legislative inactivity, the Warren Court is properly known for its extension of practically all the accused-related sections of the Bill of Rights beyond what state jurisdictions had yet permitted. Whether in *Mapp v. Ohio* (1964)[18], in which Fourth Amendment protections against unreasonable searches and seizures were applied to the states, or in *Miranda v. Arizona* (1966)[19], which extended the right against self-incrimination to include an obligation to inform the accused of her rights upon arrest, or in *Gideon v. Wainwright* (1963),[20] in which a small-time criminal received free Sixth Amendment counsel from one of Washington's most prominent attorneys, the Warren Court opened huge new territories of protection for those accused of crime.

The standard term used to describe the Fourteenth Amendment's application to the states is *incorporation*. What Chief Justice John Marshall had made so clear in *Barron v. Baltimore* (1833)[21] was that the Bill of Rights, that creature of the Constitutionally suspicious Anti-Federalists, applied only to citizen protections from what the *federal* government might do. If Barron's docking slips in the port of Baltimore were silted out by the paving of Baltimore's streets, thus putting him out of business, Barron could only complain to his state. No appeal to the federal government through the Bill of Rights that Marshall still detested in 1833 would be available.

But in spite of *Barron*, the middle third of the twentieth century saw the federal Supreme Court begin to incorporate certain Bill of Rights protections in order to prevent state governments from continuing to engage in what had often been outrageous invasions of citizens' rights. In the early years of incorporation only truly heavy-handed state conduct could arouse the Supreme Court to declare that the state was violating the federal Bill of Rights. The outrage that the case of *Powell v. Alabama* (1932)[22] brought before the Court qualified as such conduct.

Powell, recall, was a case in which the so-called Scottsboro boys, seven uneducated Black youths, were convicted and given a death sentence for their highly unlikely crime of rape. The case was more than a travesty of justice; it was infamous for its bringing of the Communist Party into the fray as a credible protector of minority citizens' rights. The idea of presenting such a group with an issue of this magnitude no doubt had a good deal to do with why the federal Supreme Court broke the *Barron* rule. In any case, it is important to note that this pathbreaking criminal case preceded the "switch in time that saved nine" economic cases of *West Coast Hotel* (1937)[23] and *Jones & Laughlin Steel Corp.* (1937).[24] A still generally conservative Court in *Powell* reluctantly but firmly countermanded the grotesque abuses of an embarrassing criminal trial.

With the state-to-federal ice broken in Alabama regarding the rights of the accused, it was surely easier for the Warren Court of the 1950s and 1960s to diminish, if not transcend, the state-federal distinction regarding other criminal case protections. A brief look at the arguments of the three criminal cases cited earlier should be helpful.

Virtually all of the major cases on the rights of the accused arose from instances in which state legislatures or local jurisdictions had not fostered improvement in the conduct of police with regard to suspects. Neither had such jurisdictions fostered improvement in the conduct of trial judges with regard to the admission of evidence. Improvement would have to come from the courts, and cases such as *Mapp*, *Miranda*, and *Gideon* would mark a beginning.

Mapp v. Ohio is the third of that trilogy of search and seizure cases which even undergraduate pre-law students are all dutifully subjected to. Originally, the *Weeks* case,[25] decided in 1914, had confirmed the federal restrictions on unreasonable searches and seizures. But the *Wolf* case[26] of 1949 assured states that they would not be subjected to the federal standard. *Barron v. Baltimore* would be whittled at only in extreme circumstances such as those in *Powell*. This maintenance of a double standard for state and federal searches and seizures permitted what became known as "the silver platter doctrine." Federal law enforcement officers could crash through a door at three o'clock in the morning, and, though not able to use their evidence in a federal court, they could readily lend that evidence to state prosecutors.

Earl Warren assigned the writing of *Mapp* to Associate Justice Tom Clark, the former attorney general speaking for the Court's narrow, five-to-four, majority by touching all the appropriate jurisdictional and sectoral bases. As in *Brown*, the states were first subjected to a federal standard. Clark noted, consistently with *Wolf*, that "a federal prosecutor may make no use of evidence illegally seized but a State's attorney across the street may."[27] Such hypocrisy, Clark contended, "encourage[s] disobedience to the Federal Constitution which it [the state] is bound to uphold."[28]

Regarding the state-to-federal distinction, Clark's argument even went so far as to raise the issue of loyalty. A century after the beginning of America's Civil War, the Court's majority continued what *Brown* began, the federal standard being held out as the standard to be obeyed. Regarding courts and legislatures, Clark's argument was rooted in the supremacy of the law over political preference. Quoting the noted federal judge Benjamin Cardozo with regard to "judicial integrity," Clark admitted with Cardozo that the application of the exclusionary rule meant that a criminal may indeed go free.[29] But, Clark argued, "it is the law that sets him free."[30]

Continuing, he reminded doubters that "nothing can destroy a government more quickly than its failure to observe its own laws."[31] That law, and most particularly the higher law of the Constitution, is superior to laws promulgated by state legislatures. And, since *Marbury* had settled the issue of who, under the federal Constitution, would interpret that document, and since the right to be "secure against rude invasions" was no less than "constitutional in origin," Clark said,[32] that right was fully protected.

Finally, with regard to the private-to-public nature of the *Mapp* case, the lesson is every bit as powerful, if somewhat less boldly stated in the opinion. In the purely legal sense, protections against governmental intrusions may well be private, even individual. Recall again that the locus of the Bill of Rights protections is, as Amar described it, the individual citizen. But, in the larger sense of the telos, or in the sense of the purpose of the Bill's protections which I have referred to in the context of Amar's reflections, the public nature of any citizens' rights rings clear, even in those cases that deal with citizens who are not politically active.

Note the linkage of sectoral and substantive political rights, therefore, in Clark's opinion above. Reminiscent of the political abuses of the Stuarts were the kinds of government actions which Clark was seeking to prohibit. No government should be allowed to make an "unconstitutional seizure of goods, papers, effects, documents, etc.," nor should any government attempt to gain a "coerced confession," nor may "the rights to notice and to a fair public trial" of anyone accused of crime be violated by a government.[33] These protections, according to Clark, were the essence of "the true administration of justice" in this country.[34] Then, in the strongest tone yet, Clark admonished law enforcement officers not to be guilty of "official lawlessness," calling it "a flagrant abuse" of basic American rights.[35]

Upon reflection, is there much difference between Clark's language and the language of Sir Edward Coke or of all those who opposed the Stuarts in the seventeenth century? And is it not also a direct expression of Cokeian reasoning when Clark candidly admits that "our decision [is] founded in reason and truth"?[36] Reason, more than anything else, is what Coke loaned to the legislature, and to the public sector, as that reason came from the private sector and from that sector's traditional jurisdictional ally, the courts. It is the member of the public, the citizen, whether accused of political crimes in the seventeenth century or solely of criminal activities in the twentieth, whom these rights have always protected.

In the still controversial Fifth Amendment case of *Miranda v. Arizona*,[37] Chief Justice Warren assigned himself the writing of the majority opinion. The pattern of the opinion's general argument, however, is nearly a mirror image of Clark's reasoning in *Mapp*. By extending the rights of those subjected to police interrogation, *Miranda* declared that the *entire* period of police custody was covered by fundamental constitutional protections. By taking that position, the ruling extended the *Escobedo v. Illinois* case (1964),[38] which had set the initiation of Fifth Amendment protections at the time when police questioning turned from being generally inquisitorial to being directly accusatory of whomever was being held. Warren's jurisdiction, predictably, was national, reminding his reader of "our concepts of American criminal jurisprudence."[39] He spoke disparagingly of "procedures observed and noted around the country" and declared that "the current practice of incommunicado interrogation was at odds with one of our nation's most cherished principles."[40]

In view of legislative insensitivity it was the courts, Warren argued, which now had to do something about such improprieties. Indeed, it was proper, he said, that "we [the Court] encourage Congress and the States to continue their laudable search for increasingly effective ways of protecting the rights of the individual while promoting efficient enforcement of our criminal laws."[41] The former prosecutor argued that "the Fifth Amendment privilege is so fundamental to our system of constitutional rule" that the Supreme Court will not even "pause to inquire in individual cases whether the defendant was aware of his rights without a warning being given."[42] This will be done, Warren could not help but mention, without help from the legislatures. "In this Court," he observed, "the privilege has consistently been accorded a liberal construction."[43] Courts, unlike an acquiescent legislature's favored police interrogation rooms, would stand as impartial observers to guard against intimidation or trickery."[44]

Finally, as in *Mapp*, the private versus the public battleground figured prominently in *Miranda*. In the police rooms, Warren said, "interrogation still takes place in privacy"; it was there, where "privacy results in secrecy and this in turn results in a gap in our knowledge as to what in fact goes on in the interrogation rooms," that the public needs its greatest protection.[45] The public nature of the protection, in other words, was the key to the shield.

Three years before *Miranda*, in the case of *Gideon v. Wainwright* (1963), the same juridical elements appeared again in the protection of Sixth Amendment rights.[46] This case declared that the right to be represented by an attorney in a felony proceeding was a federally protected "fundamental right." As such, the right must be strictly observed by the states. Harkening back to *Powell*, Associate Justice Hugo Black found that "the fundamental nature of the right to counsel is unmistakable,"[47] A lesser-known case decided four years after *Powell*, declaring that such fundamental rights were "safeguarded by the first eight amendments against federal action, [and] were also safeguarded against state action by the due process of law clause of the Fourteenth Amendment."[48] The growing incorporation of the Bill of Rights within the states, the piecemeal revocation of *Barron v. Baltimore*, would also embrace the Sixth Amendment.

With regard to the sectoral role of the Court, the *Gideon* opinion is predictable. In searching for "constitutional principles established to achieve a fair system of justice," the Court would rely upon "reason and reflection," both of which "require us to recognize that anyone . . . cannot be assured a fair trial unless counsel is provided for him."[49] Touching on the legislative record, Black noted that "governments, both state and federal, quite properly spend vast sums of money to establish machinery to try defendants of crime."[50] The fact that "government hires lawyers to prosecute and defendants who have the money hire lawyers to defend are the strongest indications of the widespread belief that lawyers in criminal courts are necessities, not luxuries."[51] The courts, particularly the Supreme Court, therefore, should "assure fair trials before impartial tribunals in which every defendant stands equal before the law."[52] This, I suggest, marks a clear extension of the public nature of the Bill of Right's protection. Without it "the poor man [or woman] has to face his accusers without a lawyer to assist him."[53]

In sum, the three areas of the Bill of Rights summarized here clearly demonstrate the kinds of protections which Earl Warren's Supreme Court thought should be available to those accused of crime. All citizens should enjoy Bill of Rights protections at the state level, by direction of the federal courts. This should be the case because they have not been protected by their state legislatures or by the Congress. Most important, citizens should be protected because they are public citizens, not solitary individuals who have their cases brought before a court.

As I've mentioned, the *Gideon* case was presented to the Court with a pencil-written jailhouse lawyer's plea for counsel. The Court responded to assigning one of Washington's leading K Street lawyers, Abe Fortas, to the case. Gideon's case, quite obviously, was representative of a class of similar conflicts, but, more important, it was representative of a class of American citizens whom the Court felt would never be properly heard within the public sector's legislative halls. Just as the Shelley family stood for those who were hemmed in by legislative impotency as much as within their Northern city ghetto, Mapp, Miranda, and Gideon all stood in the place of a large group of citizens who might be accused of crime and who would almost certainly never enjoy legislative redress for the procedural improprieties that took place in the investigation and trial of their alleged crimes.

From a historical perspective, on which side of the ideological argument were those who asked the Supreme Court for such protections? Though their motivations were not directly political, were they not still the heirs to Coke and his commercial and political allies as well as to the politically active Anti-Federalists who insisted on a Bill of Rights at the federal level? Were they not also heirs to the Jacksonians, who greatly democratized the American political system, as well as to the Populists and the Progressives, who spoke loudly to economic injustice, and, finally, to the New Deal advocates, who spoke so powerfully to economic deprivation?

Though unique with regard to its ideological and institutional alliance, as I have suggested from the beginning, the fact is that the Warren Court was the direct heir to a richly ideological political and legal lineage. It is a lineage that could easily embrace issues such as those facing accused criminals in Ohio, Arizona, or Florida (who would never muster a political majority) just as it had embraced issues concerning the integration of the public schools. Though it was the very permanence of their minority status (even with their liberal, non-accused allies) which drove the accused to the courts, it was these defendants' lineage within the long history of reasoned and increasingly democratic justice which allowed them to prevail in an activist court of law just as their predecessors (when they held the majority) had prevailed within legislatures.

In the next chapter I will consider two additional arenas of Warren Court judicial creativity. Each of these areas should illustrate, perhaps more dramatically than the two examples of this chapter, how the Earl Warren Supreme Court fits within the historical and ideological lineage of the emerging democratic traditions of both seventeenth-century England and nineteenth- and twentieth-century America. Before discussing these two categories of cases, however, I should refer again to one key consideration within the context of the criminal cases cited here. In the final analysis it is not possible to consider the criminal cases that I have just reviewed without considering the admonitions of Edward Coke, not only about justice and reason but also about the nature of Anglo-American law itself.

Recall that in *Mapp* the paean to "reason and truth" was proudly declared. In *Miranda* it was those things that are "fundamental to our system of constitutional rule" which Warren reminded us of. And in *Gideon* it was that "fair system of justice," those things besides precedents which "reason and reflection require," which was paramount. Even before Warren *Shelley v. Kraemer* clearly said that it was "the enjoyment of basic civil and political rights" which was at stake.[54]

I close this chapter with one suggestion. It concerns Sir Edward Coke, and particularly the private-to-public, and institutional, dimensions within Coke's writings as well as within so many of the significant writings within Anglo-American jurisprudence which followed him. Coke was originally a creature of the private law, though the greatest impact of his life's work fell ultimately within the public law and both its legislative and judicial creations. I argued earlier that in a very important sense Coke loaned the reason of the private, judge-made law to those like him who fought against the political tyranny of the day. In that sense Coke's originally private law was inherently democratic all along. The bold suggestion that Charles I consider the wishes of the constituency in making an appointment, for example, resonantly rang the bell for both legal reason and political democracy.

What, in our time, led Earl Warren and his Court back to Coke's kind of reasoning? The simple fact is that three hundred and fifty years after Coke, Chief Justice Earl Warren did no more, but at the same time, did no less, than reappropriate the Coke-enriched common law, or perhaps more accurately stated, the *reason* of the common law, back to its original home. Earl Warren did no less than the jurisdictional authority of an institution that, not unlike the independent courts of Coke's day, had fought against the injustices of unreasoned law. When seventeenth-century justice required that the private common law's reason (planted in the sea marsh of the laws of property and contract) be implemented, Coke had generously nurtured the law's reason in order to do so. Similarly, when justice required that the American Bill of Rights' reason be implemented throughout this still new land, it was Chief Justice Earl Warren who reborrowed a healthy dose of reason from the private law and gave it back to the courts, and to the public citizenry, in such decisions as *Mapp*, *Miranda*, *Gideon*, and, of course, *Brown*.

With Chief Justice Warren it was clear that America's courts, particularly the United States Supreme Court, would confidently do what legislatures might and perhaps should have done but had chosen not to. When legislatures were faced with mere minorities, whether they were minorities who had unsuccessfully aspired to civil protections regardless of their race or to similar protections because they were accused of crime, they, the legislatures, had chosen to remain silent. But a Court responded. And it responded using Coke's and the U.S. Bill of Rights' sense of both judicial and political reason. Those ideas "whose time had come" but which too often had not received legislative hearing thus came to the

Court, and were well received. In the following chapter I will show how two additional groupings of American citizens asked for the protection of the law's reason before the Supreme Court. I shall also continue our inquiry into how the analogically majoritarian strategy of these groups differed so greatly from the minoritarianism of John C. Calhoun. In doing so, I shall continue to trace the private-to-public sectoral line as it too continued to progress through the Warren Court.

CHAPTER FOURTEEN

Apportionment and Women's Rights

Standing and Justiciability

Two additional issues, one concerning representational apportionment and one concerning a woman's control of her reproductive choices proved to be then, and in the latter case still are, highly contentious matters. Accordingly, the cases that dealt with them were in some ways even more revolutionary than the previous chapter's cases on school integration and the rights of the accused.

The apportionment cases grew out of many states' practices of ignoring their own constitution's admonitions concerning the mandatory decennial redistricting of their federal Congressional districts as well as the redistricting of their own legislative houses. Back in the 1940s such dereliction encouraged Northwestern University political science professor Kenneth Colegrove to complain about the unwillingness of the Illinois legislature to reapportion the state's congressional districts. The use of an old apportionment had severely diluted the voting power of the city of Chicago's citizens, and, with each census, that dilution grew more marked.

But the Supreme Court in *Colegrove v. Green* (1946)[1] declined to hear Colegrove's plea, the case standing as no more than a continuation of the principle that states and their legislatures should maintain unfettered control over representative allocations, even when representation at the federal level was at stake. *Colegrove* rankled those who pointed to instances of sometimes ten-to-one and growing representative disparities between urban and suburban areas, on the one hand, and rural and small-town areas, on the other. Although originally thwarted, they did not let the issue rest.

By the 1960s two more censuses had been taken and, in many states, the failure to reapportion had led to greater disparities of representative strength than ever before. Tennessee's *Baker v. Carr* case (1962)[2] thus brought the issue before the Supreme Court again. By the time of the 1960 census the most populous county in Tennessee was being held to a nineteen-to-one disadvantageous allocation ratio when compared to the least populous county. Citizens of the state's five most populous counties accordingly brought suit against the Tennessee legislature for its failure to reapportion legislative districts. The case permitted Earl Warren's Supreme Court to eagerly reexamine the ruling in *Colegrove*.

Narrowly construed, it must be remembered that the *Baker* case generated only a procedural ruling. It made no decision, in other words, on the merits of whether Tennessee's legislature, or any other legislature, was properly or improperly apportioned. But the holding of *Baker* is important for what it led to in later apportionment cases. It led to a more activist Court's interest in the apportionment issue if three crucial concerns were met. These concerns involved (1) the proper jurisdiction for the apportionment issue, (2) whether or not a plaintiff had brought a "justiciable cause of action" to the Court, and (3) whether a plaintiff had "standing" to sue.

Thus, in the *Baker* opinion the rebalancing of the dichotomies that we have been concerned with all along was clearly foretold. With regard to the issue of state versus federal jurisdiction, *Baker* distinguished itself from a previous Tennessee ruling (following *Colegrove*) in which federal intervention in federal representative allocation was held still not to be appropriate. Early on in *Baker*, Associate Justice William Brennan reminded the parties that "the very nature of the controversy was Federal."[3] Because of the federal nature of the issue, Brennan concluded, federal "jurisdiction existed."[4] Besides, Brennan went on, since the federal Constitution was involved, it was "federal judicial power" that had the authority to "redress the deprivation, under color of any State law, statute, [or] ordinance, . . . of any right, [or] privilege or immunity secured by the Constitution of the United States."[5]

Note that Justice Brennan spoke specifically of "judicial power" in *Baker*. He was clearly arguing for a judicial institution's capacity to impinge on previously sacrosanct legislative authority. The great divide between the law's jurisdiction and the government's jurisdiction, *Colegrove* had said, could not be crossed. But Justice Brennan blithely crossed it, saying that the "contours" of the political question doctrine "expose[d] the attributes of the doctrine—attributes which in various settings, diverge, combine, appear, and disappear in seeming disorderliness."[6] Such

contours, therefore, needed significant "review" because it was "the relationship between the judiciary and the coordinate branches of the Federal Government . . . which gives rise to the 'political question'" in the
first place.[7] This case, Justice Brennan recognized, could serve as a "deli-
cate exercise in constitutional interpretation."[8] Even more, it could illustrate how the "responsibility of this Court as ultimate interpreter of the
Constitution" might be employed to ensure proper interpretation.[9]

Let us now look beyond the jurisdictional concerns of Baker. Examined closely, there is substantial evidence in *Baker* of a new Supreme Court
delineation between the private and the public sectors. The case clearly
favored the public sector when, within the context of the "standing" question, it rebalanced the private-to-public line. In a general sense what Chief
Justice Warren's Supreme Court rhetorically asked in *Baker* concerned
the true status of the complainant. Was the plaintiff some abstract seeker
who did not fit into the "case and controversy" requirement of the
Constitution's Article 3? Emphatically no, the Court ruled, specifically
designating the case as an "actual controversy."[10] After all, the complaint
"was filed by residents of Davidson [Nashville], Hamilton [Chattanooga],
Knox [Knoxville], Montgomery [Jackson], and Shelby [Memphis] Counties."[11] These public citizens came before the Court, according to their
pleadings, "on their own behalf and on behalf of all qualified voters of
their respective counties, and further, on behalf of all voters of the State
of Tennessee who are similarly situated."[12] Their argument thus approached that of any argument for legislative majoritarianism—except
that the debate took place in a court.

Continuing along the same line of argument, Justice Brennan pointed
out that the *Baker* case's plaintiffs were seeking relief "in order to protect
or vindicate an interest of their own, and of those similarly situated."[13]
What was that interest? "The injury which appellants assert," Brennan
noted, "is that this classification disfavors the voters in the counties in
which they reside."[14] Again, I would ask, what more public personae could
a citizen claim than his or her identification as a voter? And what more
clear continuation of an evolving democracy, and from those who furthered democracy's progress since the time of Coke in the late sixteenth
and early seventeenth centuries, could there be than the continued en-
larging of the franchise? Is not the essential equality of fairly counting
that extended franchise's product—that is, counting the votes more or
less equally—comfortably part of that lineage?

Put simply, the right to vote is an essential public right for any citizen. Some would argue that it is *the* most significant public right of a
citizen. Arbitrarily diminishing that right for any portion of the citizenry,

the Court felt, would be only slightly less of a burden on democracy than having that vote abrogated altogether. A portion of a potentially majoritarian, urban and suburban public suspected, rightly, that small-town and rural private interests were being given favor under the schemes of malapportionment. As Robert G. Dixon has written, the Court's recognition of "the pathology of small town–oriented malapportionment" led to what he called "a new Statue of Liberty, signaling a new majoritarianism which would yield fresh political force for more effective approaches to the problems of city and suburbia, civil rights and liberties, social welfare and even international relations."[15]

The potentially majoritarian urban and more recently suburban public had long suspected that it was rural private interests that were being protected by having metropolitan participation in that most democratic of all activities diluted. They suspected, as Gordon Baker has put it, that the power of "rural and small-town areas" had long "left urban dwellers in a far weaker political position than constituents from the countryside."[16] But they also suspected, with Baker, that such notions as representing "community interests" clearly were representing "the interests of many distinct communities."[17] As Baker concluded, "Many spokesmen who profess to want only a voice for smaller counties actually want a veto power" for such counties and their interests.[18]

As a result of the political realities of the day, though the reapportionment cases certainly dealt with the relative power of the urban and nonurban interests as they battled with each other in the public arena, these cases should also be seen as setting a public standard of democracy, that is as finally addressing the distortions of having one group's private interests given sway over another's. It was the expansion of the public domain, specifically the expansion of the public jurisdiction's protection of fair representation under the Constitution's equal protection clause, which decided the case. It was the urban and suburban interests' justifiable claim that malapportionment, in the public venue, improperly impacted them, along with their claim that they were therefore entitled to an extension of equal protection's previous juridical boundaries, which made the case what it was. Again, the use of the equal protection claim in *Baker* and subsequent Warren Court reapportionment cases was decidedly public; it was the public sphere of equal protection that readjusted how competing private interests would fight out their differences which was altered in *Baker.*

In its wake *Baker v. Carr* not only opened the jurisdictional doors to a full investigation of whether the dilution of selected portions of the public's vote in favor of private interests had in fact occurred. In doing so, as I have pointed out, the case also touched all the bases of state versus federal power, legislative versus judicial power, and, finally, private versus public power, in order to conclude its argument. Inevitably, decisions on the merits of representative apportionment were sure to follow.

Over the next few years additional apportionment cases were indeed accepted by the Supreme Court. One dealt with the insidious discriminations of the Georgia County Unit System, an institutionalized formula for the promotion of small-town and rural interests over the citizenry of Atlanta's Fulton County. This case was *Gray v. Sanders* (1963).[19] Another finally dealt with the federal Congressional districts that Colegrove had complained of two censuses earlier. This was the case of *Wesberry v. Sanders* (1964).[20]

The most significant ruling in the reapportionment area can be found in the landmark, state-centered judgment of *Reynolds v. Sims* (1964).[21] Here the extension of federal, judicial, and of course public authority reached a level of structural interference with state representational allocations which no federal case, or federal legislative act for that matter, had yet reached. *Reynolds* grew out of Alabama's malapportionment of its state legislature. Like Tennessee and so many other states North and South, Alabama had failed to reapportion its legislature since 1901. In its holding *Reynolds* not only directed the lower house of all state legislatures to represent its citizens proportionately; it went on to decree that the *upper* house of all forty-nine bicameral states be fairly apportioned, that is according to population, as well. The reasoning of the case, if not the result, was as predictable as it was in the previous cases.

Early in the *Reynolds* opinion states were reminded that *Baker* had held their legislatures to be clearly subordinate to federal standards in matters of representation. Chief Justice Warren simply declared that any "state's legislative apportionment scheme" could be subjected to federal scrutiny.[22] How could you tell if a state's malapportionment violated the equal protection provisions of the federal Constitution? The Court answered that the power to "require the restructuring of the geographical distribution of seats in a state legislature" would lie within the Court's jurisdiction if "there has been any discrimination against certain of the State's citizens which constitutes an impermissible impairment of their constitutionally protected right to vote."[23] Such a standard left little room for interpretation.

With regard to the supremacy of the judiciary over the legislature, the Court particularly noted that "the achieving of fair and effective representation for all citizens is concededly the basic aim of legislative apportionment."[24] If the legislature had diluted votes in contrast to others because a "place of residence impairs basic constitutional rights under the Fourteenth Amendment," it did so "just as much as invidious discriminations based upon factors such as race" would have done.[25]

Who, then, should see to it that the dilution of some citizens' votes in favor of the other citizens does not occur? To that question the Court's jurisdictional answer was most artful. "Our constitutional system," the Court said, "amply provides for the protection of minorities by means other than giving them majority control of state legislatures."[26] This was true particularly when the real majority could not gain relief from a legislature precisely because it was apportioned out of fair representation by the entrenched rural and small-town minorities themselves. A fair shot at majority control of a legislature was the essence of the democratic process's promise of fairly enacted laws.

All in the context of these institutional considerations, *Reynolds*, like *Baker*, speaks loudly to the private-to-public division. More emphatically even than in the *Baker* case, *Reynolds* declared that "representative government is in essence self-government through the medium of elected representatives of the people."[27] As a result, every citizen was held to have "an inalienable right to full and effective participation in the political processes of his State's legislative bodies."[28] It was "citizens" whom the chief justice himself, the drafter of the *Reynolds* opinion, spoke of. "Full and effective participation by all citizens in state government requires . . . that each citizen have an equally effective voice in the election of members of his state legislature."[29] This standard, according to the Court, was a public right, and, in this case as with so many others, it was a public right that needed to be brought into balance with the protection of these private interests which had been favored within underpopulated districts throughout the country.

All in all, *Reynolds* is an extraordinary case. Would any of the predecessors of the jurisdictional battle between the American states and the federal government, or the jurisdictional battle of the courts and the legislatures, have dared to force the *restructuring* of a competing institution? Madison's Constitutional design had politically subverted the legislatures of states that he felt were acting irresponsibly toward creditors. But the Constitution's writers would not have dared to restructure those state governments; they merely trumped them. And what of Marshall's opinions in those interpretive years following passage of the Constitution? Brutal though Marshall was to those who would have taxed the federal government's agencies, diminished the common market that he felt was ensured by the interstate commerce clause, or claimed federal protections at the state level, Marshall never sought to alter the institutions of the state governments themselves.

Now, of course, the ideological shoe was on the other foot. What Earl Warren and his federal Supreme Court were saying was that the very legislative majoritarianism that the early federally and judicially biased courts of the land had so much feared was now to be judicially protected. Even when he spoke of minorities, as Warren surely did in *Reynolds*, he was not protecting their purely *legal* or locus-centered right, that is, their right to be shielded as individuals from an overreaching government. He was, again, protecting a part of the telos of the Bill of Rights, the *political* purpose of the bill, or specifically, the right to be a part of a political majority.

Once again, the central holding in *Reynolds*, as in *Baker*, dealt with the citizen-based rights of any portion of the public, in its aggregate, to stand on an equal footing when it came to the legislative making of laws. That expectation, and its realization, was always public and democratic in its nature. It bespoke a right that in its purest meaning, again, protected the most important political prerogative that any free citizen has.

As I said in the previous chapter with regard to the racial integration of the schools and the rights of the accused, what Earl Warren did during his sixteen years on the Supreme Court was nothing less than return the reason of the common law, which Coke had loaned to the political jurisdiction in the seventeenth century, back to the legal jurisdiction. Warren knew where Coke's reason came from, and he knew where it could once more reside, when the political deficiencies of the state required it to be there.

In retrospect, the greatest irony of the *Baker* and the *Reynolds* Supreme Court cases was that, in their seemingly extraordinary judicial reach into the constitutions of America's subsovereignties, calling for nothing less than the restructuring of the governments of forty-nine American state governments, the cases ultimately sought to *enhance*, not deprecate, the role of the legislature as the vanguard of democracy. It was the steps *not* taken by the states to further democracy which rankled the Warren Court. Rather than prepare itself to speak to each political issue brought by various groupings that were analogous to the aspiring majorities of past years, Chief Justice Warren felt that political groupings should be able to achieve majoritarian status within all of their legislatures. For those groupings that could not achieve such status, the analogous reasoning of *Brown v. Board of Education*,[30] or *Mapp*,[31] *Miranda*,[32] or *Gideon*,[33] would need to treat these groups as either existing or aspiring majorities. In order to do that, of course, Coke's robust reason would need to be enforced. But, for those groups that could come to the legislature with a majoritarian claim, their plea should be responded to within the framework of the long Anglo-American evolutionary strain of democracy. This

Warren position, of course, contrasted with that of the antebellum Southern aristocracy, which had dealt with its nonmajoritarian status in the opposite manner.

Politically, what *Baker* and *Reynolds* noted was that, because the Supreme Court would not intercede on behalf of each aggrieved group that could not muster a political majority, the groups that were in a position to form coalitions and utilize the political branches of the government should be allowed to do so. In short, what the Supreme Court could do was to make sure that the United States' political institutions responded to *majoritarianism*, whether or not a specific majority had been formed in each instance. The incentive to majority formation was the judicial complement of the political majority itself.

A final thought: If the cases of *Baker* and *Reynolds* grew out of Tennessee and Alabama, respectively, Earl Warren surely knew that the greatest representational inequities within the public citizenry grew out of discrimination against aspiring majorities in metropolitan areas that were a good deal larger than Memphis and Birmingham. The greatest inequities had long impacted the metropolitan areas of New York, Chicago, Detroit, and Philadelphia. It was in these cities where the want of reapportionment had combined with the turn-of-the-century relaxation of incorporation standards for city-strangling suburbs and the gutting of reasonable annexation laws to draw what is by now America's most guarded political boundary—the boundary between great cities and their suburbs. The decline of America's greatest cities, of course, was the inevitable result of such inequities.

Once again, the *Baker*-to-*Reynolds* line of cases turned out to be an irony, if only because their institutional intrusions into the very makeup of state legislatures was motivated by the attempt to reinforce democracy at the state level. These cases sought to place a state's urban communities into what Chief Justice Warren considered to be their appropriate political positions. Alas, as we know, these decisions came too late to accomplish what the Court had wished for them. By the time of *Reynolds* much of the suburbanization that I referred to in Chapter 12 had moved many former urban citizens into at least temporarily protective municipal cocoons. The racial separations, along with the fiscal, infrastructural, and population decline of the cities, had progressed to the point that conservative, white, suburban legislators (fairly represented because of *Baker* and *Reynolds*) began to vote more frequently with conservative small-town and rural interests in their state legislatures. The cities, isolated and stripped of their middle-class tax base, were increasingly left to fend for themselves.

It is futile to speculate on what might have happened if the Fred Vinson Supreme Court had decided *Colegrove* the other way in 1946, thus giving cities fair apportionment two decennial censuses earlier. But the political significance of the demographic changes that took place between 1946 and 1964 are undeniable. Neither can it be denied that the fragmented metropolitan maps of the United States now differ immeasurably from the metropolitan maps of nearly every other developed country. They certainly differ from what they would have been if the eventually held-to-be-unconstitutional actions of rurally dominated state legislatures had been arrested before 1964.

In sum, although *Reynolds* stands as an extraordinary expansion of federal court power vis-à-vis state and legislative authority and though it stands as well as an expansion of the public sector's right to intercede against private interests on behalf of fair representation, it wound up accomplishing little of what it intended in the real world of politics. The American states' blatant violations of the rule of law, beginning at the turn of the century, had borne its bitter fruit.

Women and Their Choices

Over the years, the Supreme Court has used many strategies to change the law, one of the most effective being illustrated in the two "women's rights" cases of *Griswold v. Connecticut* (1965)[34] and *Roe v. Wade* (1973).[35] Seen together, the linkage of the Warren and the still liberal, immediately post-Warren Courts reveals that the Warren Court first decided a case of almost meaningless substantive grist but decided it in a way that could impact a far more important case later on. Whether the Warren Court at the time of *Griswold* specifically anticipated a later ruling on the hot button issue of abortion is not clear. But the changes in the law which were brought about by *Griswold* certainly made the decision in *Roe* far more plausible than it otherwise would have been.

In *Griswold* the Planned Parenthood League of Connecticut and a contentious obstetrician argued that an unenforced state birth control advice law should be overturned by the Supreme Court. *Griswold* represents something that stretches the law considerably, not only demonstrating the Warren Court's ideological liberalism and its willingness to stand in for a reluctant state legislature. The case, particularly in the majority opinion of one of the Court's most liberal justices, William O. Douglas, also represents perhaps the most synthetic construction that ever made up a Supreme Court case. The nature of the Douglas opinion is evident on at two levels.

The first level deals with the reading of the Bill of Rights itself. In

Roe, Douglas unflinchingly extends the Bill of Rights by referring to what he called its "penumbras," such penumbras growing out of what Douglas terms "emanations."[36] It was, after all, the penumbras and emanations of the law which were responsible for the deeper meanings of Bill of Rights guarantees, Douglas argues. At the second level, beyond a generally expansive reading of the Bill of Rights itself, Douglas engages in an unprecedented amalgamation of five specific rights, suggesting that their combined meaning far exceeds the sum of each part's contribution.

The First, Third, Fourth, Fifth, and, finally, the Ninth Amendments all combine for Douglas to form a right that he argues was "created by several fundamental constitutional guarantees."[37] Douglas's synthesis is clear. And, as in *Muller v. Oregon*,[38] new considerations are consequently added to the law. Newer applications of the original Bill of Rights' concerns with opposition to an oppressive government are thus extended to the right of a woman to consult with her physician and to receive advice on her reproductive choices.

With regard to the private-to-public distinction, Justice Douglas said that birth control advice should be available to women without worrying about what the advocates of any private morality might wish the public sector, that is the government, to impose. In an important sense, and one that is consistent with the original, public sector–enhancing nature of the Bill of Rights, Douglas argued that a woman's right to receive contraceptive advice from a physician is much akin to the public's right to engage in political opposition. Private moralities might indeed have interfered with this right in the past. For Douglas and the Court they no longer should.

Curiously, Douglas's reasoning with regard to the Ninth Amendment, the amendment which states that the enumeration of rights in the first eight amendments does not foreclose the recognition of other rights, is similar to the reasoning of a justice who wrote expansively on the Constitution one hundred and fifty years earlier. It was Chief Justice Marshall who, in the national bank case of *McCulloch v. Maryland*,[39] had created the notion of "implied powers." That case held the enumerated powers of Article 1's section 9 to be such that other, complementary powers could and perhaps should be added to it. Powers such as those used in the furtherance of banking and currency stability were well in keeping with what the Federalists believed to be the heart of the Constitution.

So it was with *Griswold* and the Constitution, only in ideological reverse. The protection of the public from private morality–inspired laws in fact is well in keeping with Anti-Federalist beliefs. It should not be surprising that those of one morality had convinced the Connecticut legislature to impose their morality on the general public a long time ago. But by 1965 the imposition of that singular private morality was no longer acceptable to a Court that was prepared to expand the public sector, stand in for timid or indolent legislatures, and utilize synthetic forms of legal understanding to accomplish public goals. Thus, *Griswold* dispensed with Connecticut's anticontraception law and, far more important from an ideological perspective, also laid the foundation for a more fundamental judgment on women's choices.

Roe v. Wade (1973) was without question the most controversial social case of the still somewhat liberal, immediately post-Warren Supreme Court period. Its controversial nature touched all the nerves of ideology, institutions, sectors, and even the forms of cases. Though Chief Justice Warren had retired four years before the case was decided, much of his flavor remained on the Court, particularly through the influence of liberals such as Thurgood Marshall, William Brennan, and William Douglas as well as moderates such as Byron White and Potter Stewart. The ideological misjudgment of the newly elected president, Richard Nixon, in his appointment of Harry Blackmun to the Court sealed the reality that the Warren direction would not be reversed for a while, at least in selected judicial areas.

In *Swann v. Mecklenburg* (1971),[40] for example, though the case technically was tried as a de jure school segregation case, it extended the integration ruling of *Brown v. Board of Education* to those de facto circumstances in which segregated neighborhoods had more or less naturally fostered segregated schools. That 1971 ruling, with the newly Nixon-appointed and generally conservative Chief Justice Warren Burger writing the majority opinion, held that school districts had an affirmative public duty to achieve integration, not simply refrain from segregation. The publicly funded busing of students could be used to achieve that goal.

But two years after *Swann* the explosive issue of abortion was finally broached by the Supreme Court in the *Roe* case. Justice Blackmun's majority opinion predictably contains highly synthetic language, the justice making it clear, for instance, that he was concerned with things like "population growth, pollution, poverty, and [those] racial overtones [that] tend to complicate and not to simplify the problem."[41] Blackmun was concerned as well about the "psychological harm" that an unwanted pregnancy often caused.[42] Psychological harm was a newfound concern of a Court that had only granted judicial notice to the physical harm inherent in certain working conditions earlier this century.

Yet, having noted Blackmun's ingenuity, I would also argue there is less judicial creation in *Roe* than opponents of the case have sometimes charged. At its core *Roe*'s reasoning is little more than an extension of *Griswold*, the key to the case being found in the language that overrules Texas's private morality–induced position that life begins at conception. In responding to the state's contention that it has an interest in protecting an embryo's and then a fetus's life, Justice Blackmun classified Texas' claim as not controlling on the Court. By noting that "medicine, philosophy, and theology are unable to arrive at any consensus," Blackmun made it clear that the Court should not be forced to forge that consensus.[43] What Blackmun said was that, if these three intellectual and moral wellsprings reflected only private positions, the Court must decline to adopt "one theory of life" over another.[44]

Blackmun's opinion in *Roe*, of course, necessarily concluded that there should be no intrusion on "the rights of the pregnant woman."[45] Yet note that these women first needed to be situated within the public domain in Blackmun's opinion, protecting them from the private moralities that would have restricted their choices. To be sure, Blackmun's opinion did not say that the state of Texas had no interest in Jane Roe. Indeed, Blackmun spoke approvingly of the "State's important and legitimate interest in the health of the mother."[46] But the justice referred to the certainty of publicly recognized "medical knowledge," not the opinions of private philosophies or theologies, when he found that the period of state interest came into existence at the "end of the first trimester."[47]

In this way, as I have suggested, *Roe* did not do much more than reapply the new private-to-public sectoral line that had already been drawn in the substantively far less important case of *Griswold*. And note that the Constitutional amendments that were relevant to *Roe* were all products of that original Anti-Federalist vision that sought to prevent private interests from overwhelming the public. As with so many of the cases reviewed here, there was a return again of Coke's reason from the legislature to the Court under Warren and his immediate progeny. That return was necessitated when nearly four hundred years of legislative, evolvingly democratic borrowing from Coke's reason had come to a dissatisfying halt.

In sum, the U.S. Supreme Court under Earl Warren's influence proclaimed that it would stand as a barrier in the abortion conflict to what a number of male citizens, with some female allies to be sure, might do to prevent a majority in the case of pro-choice women and their male allies from achieving. But if a recalcitrant legislature would not respond to the public need, as was the case both in *Griswold* and *Roe*, then the Court would once more reborrow from Coke's legal reasoning what Coke had so generously lent to the public sector.

Even beyond Coke and his reason, women's rights cases also reborrowed that need for growth in the law which comes from a synthetic understanding of the law's *verum*, or ultimate truth. As we have seen, those like Daniel Boorstin or Louis D. Brandeis understood the need for an ever renewed vision of reason far better than those like the venerable Blackstone, or Justice Field, ever did. Worthy new considerations would never be automatically included within the law, and it was therefore necessary for the Court to include them. Ideally, it may have been better that inclusion take place within a legislative setting. But failing that, reason's continued search for the jurisdiction that will best respond to it might well lead it to the Courts.

Once more, the judicial acceptance of a novel consideration in cases such as *Griswold* and *Roe* was not only like what Brandeis had asked of the Court in 1908 and what Boorstin had expected both courts and legislatures to regularly do. The still comparatively modern notion of a woman's choice regarding maternity is accepted within only certain quarters of the world even today. But the issue of who should decide whether or not to take a pregnancy to term is in form much like those issues concerning (1) the African-American citizen who asked for the same educational opportunities as a white counterpart, or (2) the right of an accused to have a fair trial, and (3) the right of a citizen to be fairly counted in political representation. In each of these arenas of political and legal conflict, the insurgent position was either the unrepresented majority position (as with women), and originally with underrepresented urban voters, or it was, again, analogous to those historically aspiring majority public positions that asked for equitable treatment from a court when a legislature (whether state or federal) would not respond. These modern, Warren-era rulings, I suggest, ultimately sought only the same progress for democracy which Coke, the Anti-Federalists, Andrew Jackson, Holmes, and so many others had sought in their own times.

CHAPTER FIFTEEN

Warren Critiqued

Yale's Professor Bickel

The judicial activism of the Warren Court has always been subjected to strong criticism. While earlier criticisms of judicial activism almost invariably came from those who favored legislative revisions of private common law–influenced principles that underlay property and contract, criticisms of the Warren Court have come from very different places. The three prior significant judicial activisms had upheld the private sector, and by doing so had ratified the Court's Hamiltonian prescriptions on restricting legislative overreach. After Marshall it had maintained the private law's evolvingly analytic forms in the private law over synthetic public law encumbrances. Earl Warren's Court, of course, did precisely the opposite.

It may not be much of a stretch to say that there had always been something comforting about the earlier periods of judicial activism. The Court not only did not create new law; the early activist Courts had merely told legislatures that their distortion of the law, the private common law, was destabilizing the foundations of Anglo-American jurisprudence. From that perspective, it was easy to say that they should desist from doing so. The overturning of one law, legislated law, rarely meant more than a return to a law that was already both more tried and more trusted. Ideology aside, one may concede that such Supreme Court activism was far less frightening in its institutional overreach than a wholesale creation of new and public law by the judicial branch would be. Probably the most widely read critic of the Warren Court's new law was the late and well-regarded Alexander Bickel. Let me suggest, however, that the Yale Law School jurisprudential scholar of the generation before Akhil Amar misunderstood in no small degree what the Warren Court was doing, particularly from a historical and an ideological perspective. At one point in

The Least Dangerous Branch, for example, Bickel recounted the traditional understanding of judicial review. "The root difficulty," he said, was "that judicial review is a counter-majoritarian force in our system."[1] Of course, Bickel was right, if one considers only the pre-Warren activist periods. The judicial activism of the Marshall, Field, and the early Hughes Courts were certainly countermajoritarian, as they were intended to be.

What Bickel failed to understand was that the essence of Earl Warren's Supreme Court was to compensate, as I reviewed earlier, for what could, and what many thought should, have been the majority-driven work of both state legislatures and the Congress. As Robert Dixon said of the reapportionment cases, for example, "the decision to make [issues such as] legislative apportionment a justiciable question was a new Statue of Liberty, signaling a new majoritarianism."[2]

In one all too lonely sentence in his *Least Dangerous Branch,* Bickel momentarily acknowledged the problem of bringing majorities, or aspiring majorities, to a place of legislative acceptance. He conceded, almost as if for the record, that "it is true . . . that the process of reflecting the will of a popular majority in the legislature is deflected by various inequalities of representation and by all sorts of institutional habits and characteristics, which perhaps tend most often in favor of inertia."[3] But Bickel ignored the implications of his insight, even in his very next sentence. "It must be remembered," he went on "that statutes are the product of the legislature and the executive acting in concert, and that the executive represents a very different constituency and thus tends to cure inequities of over and underrepresentation."[4]

The fact is that there is little evidence for such a claim. Was President Dwight Eisenhower, before *Brown,* noticeably disturbed by the lack of Congressional progress on the problem of school integration? He certainly didn't speak to such a concern publicly. Were Eisenhower, or Harry Truman before him or John Kennedy after him for that matter, publicly concerned about the unwillingness of mid-century state legislatures to reverse their early-century duplicity with their continuing failure to reapportion their state's or the federal legislature's districts? Or were these presidents upset by Congress's silence on the issue of legislative malapportionment, even as it affected the fairness of representation at the federal level? The truth is that the apportionment issue was pointedly ignored by presidents and the Congress alike. Similarly, there is little evidence of state executives, the governors, ever going to the mat for fair apportionment in confrontation with their own state legislatures.

In the same vein neither President Eisenhower nor his more liberal successors, Presidents Kennedy and Johnson for that matter, spoke for the rights of the accused in their political campaigns. Certainly these figures, even up to Lyndon Johnson at the time of the birth control case (*Griswold* [1965]) and Richard Nixon at the time of the abortion case (*Roe* [1973]), never expressed concern about the rights of women with regard to reproductive choices. Over a variety of issues of the day, or on the issue of "wider representation" (Bickel's term), which might have brought these issues to the legislative fore, silence was the order of the day.

Bickel's error with regard to the allegedly compensatory majoritarian activities of chief executives, unfortunately, is more than a simple misstatement of reality. Referring back to Madison's *Federalist* no. 10 and to the contemporary writings of "pluralist" political scientists such as David B. Truman and the early Robert A. Dahl, Bickel argued that the essence of the American political system was "the proliferation of what Madison foresaw as 'faction,' what Mr. Truman calls 'groups,' and what in popular parlance has always been deprecated as 'interests' or 'pressure groups.'"[5]

Bickel focused on how those interests or groups "operate forcefully on the electoral processes."[6] Look more closely, and you will find that Bickel almost automatically praised these groups, as did Dahl, Bickel seeing them as "a crucial device for controlling leaders."[7] As Bickel himself admits, these groups do not achieve their political goals of controlling leaders until they successfully coalesce into a majority with other groups. Such is the burden of pluralistic, group-centered understandings of politics.

Returning to consideration of the representational issue in the pluralistic context, my own inquiry would contrast markedly with that of Bickel and the pluralists. It would concern those interests that are "underrepresented" because the system has prevented them from being a majority by themselves, becoming a majority after coalescing with other groups, or acting like a majority, even if they already were one. Women, though 52 percent of the population, still constitute nowhere near 50 percent of formal political representation, or general political influence, within any state legislature, the Congress, or the general public. The group is a numerical majority that has been prevented, for a variety of cultural, historical, and economic reasons, from acting as a political majority.

No, the admonitions of Madison, still applauded by so many political scientists in the 1950s and 1960s, if not still today, were directed against, not in favor of, the forming of political majorities. In fact, the deflecting nature of the Constitutional arrangement in the face of possible majorities is precisely what Bickel referred to when he said that "nothing can finally depreciate the central function that is assigned in democratic theory and practice to the electoral process."[8]

Further, Bickel noted that "it cannot be denied that the policy-making power of representative institutions, born of the electoral process, is the distinguishing characteristic of the system."[9] This position, before Warren at least, was certainly the accepted position. But when Bickel concluded the above quotations with the historically correct notion that "Judicial review works counter to this [policy-making power] characteristic,"[10] he casually ignored his earlier reflections on the deliberate underrepresentation that has frequently undermined the equity of a supposedly majoritarian political process. What, then, was Bickel's solution for the system's antimajoritarian inequities?

Bickel and Thayer

Let me suggest that the argument of one who has been so respected in the jurisprudential community would have been far more powerful if it had not been for the sleight of hand which Bickel used with regard to the entire "majoritarian" issue. For example, in completing his discussion of political majorities and the electoral process, Bickel attempted to bolster his argument by citing a leading jurisprudential writer of the nineteenth century, James Bradley Thayer. Thayer indeed had spoken out against the excesses of judicial review.

At an abstract level Bickel properly noted that Thayer had spoken to the impact that excessive judicial review might have upon the diligence of legislatures that suspected their work was likely to be reviewed. Thayer worried that an atmosphere of judicial "distrust" might accordingly lead legislatures "to shed the considerations of constitutional restraints . . . turning that subject over to the courts."[11] Similarly, the citizenry itself could "become careless as to whom they send to the legislature."[12] The result of these representational difficulties, Thayer figured, would be that the "tendency of a common and easy resort to this great function [judicial review], now lamentably too common, [would] dwarf the political capacity of the people, and . . . deaden its sense of moral responsibility."[13]

Thayer's thoughts were noble thoughts. At an institutional level even Hamilton and Marshall would have found little to disagree with. But there are two not so minor points that Bickel fails to include in his review of Thayer's position, points that give a very different slant to Thayer's real point of view. The first is that Thayer, writing in the 1890s, decried the judicial review of the robber baron, Field-led Supreme Court, a Court which had overturned nearly every state legislative attempt to regulate the railroads and trusts near the close of the nineteenth century. Thayer, in other words, was decrying the effect of an overriding judicial presence on that reform legislation which sought to equalize the private-to-public and the legislative-to-judicial imbalances which favored the powerful interests of his day.

Beyond his not reporting on the ideological, institutional, and private-to-public imbalances that Thayer addressed, however, Bickel also conveniently avoided another point in his misusing of Thayer. Thayer, again, had decried the impact of a negative Supreme Court, a legislature-denying Supreme Court, on the very workability of legislatures, saying that "under no system can the power of courts go far to save a people from ruin; our chief protector lies elsewhere."[14] What Bickel, and Warren Court critics generally, more recently complained about was the positive, instigative nature of Supreme Court activity. It can be argued that an overly activist, law-creating Supreme Court might have an impact upon legislatures which is similar to what Bickel described. But I would argue that the worst that could come from a legislature that had its work anticipated for it, rather than have its work rejected, would be a *ratification* of its own lassitude, or a "let the Court do it" attitude which would permit the Court to continue legislating. More optimistically, the once trumped legislature, pride hurt, might work harder in order to facilitate those majoritarian combinations of interests which could steal thunder back from the courts that had embarrassed them.

Yet, regardless of whether one assumes the worst or the best with regard to judicial intrusions and their effect on legislatures, there can be no doubt that Alexander Bickel's arguments with regard to judicial review clearly reflected Bickel's own ideological preference for having the Court be restrained when the judiciary was promoting public rights through the furtherance of legislatively ignored groups. This of course was what the Warren court was doing. Two pieces of evidence for that assumption are that Bickel did not identify the ideologically pro–public sector position of Thayer in his writings and that Bickel otherwise said nothing about those many times when the Court was opposing legislatures in order to protect private rights. It is revealing of Bickel that he did not speak of the common-law, private domain–protecting activism of the Marshall, Field, or early Hughes periods. It is revealing as well that Bickel at one point admitted that "the creative establishment and renewal of a coherent body of principled rules . . . is what our legislatures have proven themselves ill equipped to give us."[15] I think Earl Warren sensed precisely what Bickel was alluding to when his Court returned to the same kind of "principled rules" that made up Coke's reason.

In the final analysis, so much of Alexander Bickel's argument, like so much of the intense argument over the Warren Court, comes down to the meaning given to the terms *reason*, or *rationality*. In speaking of Thayer,

Bickel argued that "Thayer's rule of the clear mistake should . . . be expanded to read as follows: What is rational, and rests on an unquestioned shared choice of values, is constitutional."[16] Nothing in Bickel's writings on this issue is more dramatically naive. Shared values take care of themselves, in any open society. What is politically and legally difficult is dealing with those differentiated values, values that are *not* shared. It is the political *choice* among values which leads to controversy in open societies, both within their legislative halls and before their bars of justice.

Continuing this same argument in *Politics and the Warren Court*, Bickel vigorously attacked Associate Justice William Brennan's use of the standard of rationality in the *Baker v. Carr* reapportionment case. Bickel argued that the case "concerned not a recent willful malapportionment but rather a sixty-year-old apportionment that had been rendered obsolete and oppressive by sheer inaction in face of radical shifts of population."[17] Such a position was naive only at its best. It was disingenuous at its worst. Malapportionments were never the result of legislative lassitude. They were the result of deliberate and almost uniformly unconstitutional state inactions that purposefully limited the impact of politically unfavored—that is, new and urban—populations. A clear intent to discriminate existed, and the impact, though not fully realized for sixty years to be sure, was precisely the impact the legislature intended.

It is curious, is it not, that Bickel deplored Justice Brennan's use of a sense of rationality in *Baker* at the same time that he lauded Chief Justice Marshall's use of rationality in *McCulloch v. Maryland*. Bickel had already facilely conflated the rationality of Marshall and Thayer, arguing that they were both "loose rather than strict constructionists."[18] In a sense that was true, of course. It was more or less accurate to say that, "more concretely, Marshall and Thayer were talking about a method of constitutional construction—that is, a method of interpreting the written document—which would result in the free exercise by the representative institutions of broad and effective powers of government, but not unlimited ones."[19]

But what were Marshall and Thayer each supporting? Thayer, when faced with the most unbalanced weighing between the legislature and the courts, as well as the most unbalanced weighing between the private and the public sectors of all American history, was begging for both sectoral and institutional rebalancing. Marshall, faced with the threat (and the occasional reality) of legislative action that he felt impaired the Constitution and the private order that the first seven articles of the Constitution protected, was striking down legislative intrusions. In his argument Bickel never mentioned that Marshall and Thayer, like Marshall and the Warren Court, were supporting very different ideological, and sectoral, positions.

To be sure, Alexander Bickel qualified his *Least Dangerous Branch* argument to the effect that the electoral process lay at the core of the democratic experience. Bickel conceded in *Warren Court*, for instance, that "the Supreme Court has at the very least participated in making many . . . fundamental value choices for our society."[20] This he wrote shortly after arguing that the issue was therefore not "merely one of power; it is also a question of liberty."[21] Bickel further conceded that "malapportionments favor rural interests of one sort or another over urban and suburban" interests and that these malapportionments "allocate more strength proportionately to sparsely populated areas than to densely populated ones."[22] Having said that, however, Bickel still had the temerity to ask: "Who can say this is irrational?"[23] Citizens who live in the cities could, I think, as Professor Colegrove had already tried to say on their behalf.

Oddly, in further attempting to justify his position, Bickel sought to compare malapportionment with "a farm policy that favors farmers or an antitrust policy that favors small enterprise."[24] Bickel apparently chose not to recognize that his examples involved exclusively *resultant*, or substantive policy choices. They were not in any way akin to the *procedural* imbalancing of the very legislative apportionment that made the resultant, substantive policy choices so consistently imbalanced as a result. Several pages later, in his *Warren Court*, Bickel went so far as to argue that "it is enough justification for unequal districting that it *sometimes* serves legitimate ends."[25] Such an obvious begging of the question of what constitutes "legitimate ends" should make any reader suspicious. And to think that there might be "shared values" over what constitutes such legitimate ends, to return to an earlier theme, is really a stretch of logic beyond all reason.

To conclude with Bickel I cannot help but refer to that unfortunate extension of Bickel's argument concerning rationality which touched on the issue of race. Here, even more than in the issue of apportionment, Bickel not only failed to overcome the false notion of shared values and the electoral imbalances of America's imperfect democracy. He failed as well to be at all convincing about whether his mentor Herbert Weschler's noncontextual notions of the "neutral principle" did in fact lead to neutrality or even to those "general" principles of the law which Weschler, and Bickel, supposedly held so dear.[26]

With regard to the racial issue, Bickel argued that, though there is "no foundation for . . . a premise in the common experience" that "Negroes are inherently less intelligent than whites," it would be permissible for a legislature to conclude that it was "best to segregate the races, or for a legislature to conclude that most Negroes are not likely to go to a university and that it is therefore not economical to maintain one for them."[27] Such reasoning squared perfectly with Herbert Weschler's notion, Bickel went on to point out, that the *Brown v. Board of Education* decision ultimately rested upon a reversal of a legislature's choice "between abridging Negro freedom to associate and abridging white freedom not to associate."[28] Weschler had based his "neutrality" on the balancing of the "negro" claim to be a part of the larger society with an "integration [that] forces an association upon those for whom it is unpleasant or repugnant."[29] That choice to associate, Bickel pointed out, "is simply to reverse such a legislative choice, not to avoid it or to somehow make it unnecessary for it cannot be avoided."[30] This, sadly, is where neutral principles wound up for Weschler, and Bickel. The bias of their "neutrality" speaks for itself.

Bickel and Ideology

At a minimum the writings of Herbert Weschler and Alexander Bickel cry out for a historical understanding of both the contextual place of the U.S. Constitution within Anglo-American jurisprudence and the institutional and private-to-public sectoral tensions that have made America's Constitutional history what it is. But the writings also cry out for an honestly ideological understanding of the nature of the central argument over the Constitution's ratification and subsequent interpretations. The first seven articles of the Constitution are not, and were never intended to be, ideologically neutral. The Bill of Rights was not intended to be ideologically neutral, either. It was intended to balance the bias of the first articles.

Over the years courts of all ideologies have interpreted the Constitution, and they have done so at the same time that they interpreted the role of the Court itself vis-à-vis the legislatures of the country, both state and federal. They have thus consistently revealed their ideological, and correspondingly sectoral, and institutional preferences. It may always be argued, of course, that the Warren Court went too far ideologically and sectorally. Surely, what it did, ideologically and sectorally, went substantially beyond where any Court before it had ever gone. But to argue that the Warren Court's boldness was out of character with the entire history of the Anglo-American jurisprudential experience simply does not hold water. Alexander Bickel, along with so many common law scholars, was right about the law having a great deal to do with reason, or rationality. But, as an eminent scholar like Daniel Boorstin understood so well, the ideological development of the concept of reason itself, and reason's centuries-old historical positioning within so many areas of Anglo-American law, is at the core not only of the Anglo-American jurisprudential experience but of our own nation's foundational political experience as well. Just as the reason of the law was loaned to the legislature by Sir Edward Coke and those who fought the Stuart interruption of democracy's progress in seventeenth-century England, so too Earl Warren and the Warren Court, as it reborrowed Coke's reason for the Court, utilized that reason in areas that reflected the legislative failure of reason.

With America's most prominent racial minority, everything that happened from the Compromise of 1877 and the subsequent Southern status of semiautonomy up to the legislative neglect that finally led to the private law–based decision in *Shelley v. Kraemer* (1948) had demonstrated that legislatures, state and federal, were not going to protect the descendants of America's Constitutionally designated slave populations. The Supreme Court, well within the spirit of the equity jurisdiction that the fourteenth-century chancellor had substituted for an encrusted common law, was all that was left to ensure that protection.

Regarding the rights of the accused, the everyday crime-fighting tactics of so many arresting police officers and interrogators were such that the treatment of the nonpolitical criminal suspect not only violated what a civilized society required of its government but also jeopardized the treatment of those who might have been or who might someday become involved in the political dissent that is the core of this nation's, and any democracy's, existence.

With regard to women, the majority that could never act as a majority would need to receive the "rational" protection of a Court from those state laws that had denied them, as a group, of their choices concerning maternity. With regard to apportionment, the Court looked well beyond what Bickel falsely represented as the harmless and unintentional neglect of state legislatures. It correctly labeled the political biases of malapportioned legislatures for what they were. The Court knew what the rationalizations for that malapportionment were, and, as in the other areas, it was the Court that finally challenged the irrationality of those actions. As I wrote in the last two chapters, it was the public sector, resurrected by the Court, which reclaimed the ground in all of these areas that the Anti-Federalists might well have stood upon had they been with us during the Earl Warren Supreme Court period.

Let us not forget, incidentally, that there is a fundamental asymmetry to the ideology of the common law. That law appropriately underpinned the commercial development of the Anglo-American experience and is largely an ideologically conservative, sectorally private law. In this environment a judicial body, such as the U.S. Supreme Court, when functioning as an activist court, finds it far simpler—and for some, far more legitimate—to turn to the right and borrow its reasonings from that vast storehouse of private sector protecting law, known as the common law. A turn to the left leaves a court with almost no common law principles and almost no precedents. There is, of course, one considerable exception to this asymmetry, that being the democratically directed adaptations of the common law that come from Sir Edward Coke. It was the spirit of Cokeian adaptation that Chief Justice Warren built upon throughtout his judicial tenure.

CHAPTER SIXTEEN

The Post-Warren Court

A Not-So-Silent Majority

Even if the spirit of the Warren Court continued within a few case areas after the departure of the "Chief," as Supreme Court clerks invariably call America's first justices, the revision of Warren Court doctrine was made inevitable by the election of Richard Nixon to the presidency in 1968. Candidate Nixon had made the Supreme Court a whipping boy throughout his campaign, one of the most divisive in recent history. With the memory of the Chicago Democratic Convention riots and campus antiwar and civil rights demonstrations fresh in the public's minds, Nixon was able to saddle the Supreme Court with much of the responsibility for promoting values that America's "silent majority" did not believe in.

True, cases like *Swann v. Mecklenburg* (1971),[1] ensuring the extension of desegregation to de facto arrangements of neighborhoods and "naturally" drawn school districts, and those like *Roe v. Wade* (1973),[2] ensuring the right of women to choose maternity, as we have reviewed, were still decided in a Warren-like direction during the first years of Warren Burger's Court. But it was not long until the ideological reversal of the Warren Court was in full swing. As some political scientists have said, the decisions of the Warren Court on matters such as race, the rights of the accused, women's rights, and apportionment were never fully reversed by the Supreme Court headed by Chief Justice Burger and increasingly staffed by other Nixon appointees.

Stephen Wasby, for one, argued shortly after the close of the Warren Court that the Burger Court revisions of Warren were merely "revisionist and incremental."[3] But, even if there were no immediate or "sharp departures from the Warren Court's work,"[4] as Wasby put it, the direction of the dominant cases of the Burger era, as well as the first years of

the William Rehnquist Court, changed unmistakably across the full panoply of ideological, institutional, sectoral, and cognitive dimensions that
we have been examining. What should concern us here is the meaning of
that change for the Court's ideological history during the last twenty-five
years.

Let us first look briefly at some of the cases that highlighted the fully
post-Warren era. To begin with race, we need look no farther than *Milliken
v. Bradley* (1974),[5] the case that reversed the tide of the three-year-old
Swann v. Mecklenburg holding on de facto school integration. The continuation of white flight in the Detroit metropolitan area had meant that
the ethnic ratios within the entirety of Detroit's Wayne County necessitated the inclusion of outlying counties in order to reachieve racial balance in the schools. The Nixon/Burger Court said that outlying school
districts need not be subjected to anything like that: if you had "escaped"
beyond the county line, your children would be immune from inclusion
in expanded integration plans that might otherwise have included them.

The Court's reasoning in *Milliken* was straightforward enough. Speaking originally to the prerogatives of courts and legislatures, the Court
made it clear that it had little use for judgments in which a federal district
court would "become first, a *de facto* 'legislative authority' to resolve these
complex questions, and then the 'school superintendent' for the entire
area."[6] With regard to state versus federal authority, the Court rendered
the obligatory caveat that, "of course, no state law is above the constitution."[7] But, from there on, the opinion marches firmly in the other direction, noting primarily that "our prior holdings have been confined to
violations and remedies within a single school district."[8]

Sectorally, without ever using the term, it is clear that the Court
would not permit the public sector to serve as the arena in which mitigation of anything short of "inter-district segregation" would occur.[9] Only
where the racially discriminatory acts of one or more school districts
caused racial segregation in an adjacent district, or "where district lines
have been deliberately drawn on the basis of race," should the courts
intervene.[10] Publicly protected rights, under the Bill of Rights, would
stop, in effect, at the county line. Specifically, Chief Justice Burger said
there were "*de jure* segregated conditions only in the Detroit [city]
schools."[11] Therefore, there could be no remedy for the Blacks who might
ask for legal recognition of de facto segregation, no matter how egre-
gious the imbalances had become.

The decision in the *Milliken* case, I would argue, was reasonably well
foretold by the case of *Moose Lodge No. 107 v. Irvis* (1972),[12] decided two
years earlier. There the private-to-public line was substantially redrawn

by this post-Warren Court when an African-American guest was permitted to stay in a room but not welcome to eat in the lodge's dining room. Irvis claimed that the lodge's need for a liquor license placed all Moose Lodge operations within the public sector. But Associate Justice William Rehnquist was not convinced, saying that "Moose Lodge is a private club in the ordinary meaning of that term."[13] It was free, therefore, to discriminate, racially, among its guests. Cleverly citing *Shelley v. Kraemer*, Rehnquist noted that case's lack of protection against "private conduct, 'however discriminatory or wrongful,' against which that [equal protection] clause 'erects no shield.'"[14] Of course, *Shelley*'s protection of the private sector had aided the Black home buyer, that irony delighting Rehnquist, I'm sure.

After such a redrawing of the private-to-public line, the adjudicatory pathway for the Burger Court in Washington was open. "State action," the crux of Fourteenth Amendment public sector protections, was ruled not to be a part of federally extended "incorporations" of the Bill of Rights.[15] As for institutions, Justice Rehnquist merely stated that "the Court has never held, of course, that discrimination by an otherwise private entity would be violative of the Equal Protection Clause if the private entity receives any sort of benefit or service at all from the State."[16] The question of how much benefit or service would be required for inclusion in the public sector is very much what the ideology of the Court was about.

In a way not unlike the *Swann* and *Roe* cases in the immediate post-Warren Court, one case that was decided soon after Chief Justice Burger's leaving of the Court in 1986 nicely rounds out the race-related area of post–Warren Court opinions. In *Richmond v. Croson Co.* (1989) the first woman on the Supreme Court, Associate Justice Sandra Day O'Connor, wrote that minority business enterprises could insist upon what the construction industry knows as "minority set-asides" only when a clear record of past racial discrimination had existed.[17] Justice O'Connor, like the former Chief Justice Burger and now Chief Justice William Rehnquist, wished for the redirection of Warren Court opinions in much the same vein as *Milliken* and *Moose Lodge*. Thus, in replacing the Court into its traditional, private sector–protecting position, O'Connor denied that the city of Richmond had the "power to define and attack the effects of prior discrimination."[18] The Court thus prevented a private, nonminority construction company from suffering discrimination at the hands of a public sector entity, in this case the city of Richmond.

Pointedly, Justice O'Connor argued that the Court in *Richmond* would not only forbid public entities from engaging in "reverse discrimination" activity; it would specifically forbid remedial discriminatory action on the grounds that "to hold otherwise would be to cede control over the content of the Equal Protection Clause to the 50 state legislatures and their myriad political subdivisions."[19] As with John Marshall's sense of the need for private over public sector dominance, the federal government should be supreme over the state governments when those state governments, according to O'Connor, impinged on the private sector.

Thus, with the racial cases, whether dealing with so-called reverse discrimination or indeed with any remedial proposition that might relieve a previously discriminated-against minority from the residue of such discrimination, the Burger Court diametrically changed the direction of Warren Court cases. Ideologically and sectorally, the Burger Court's alterations were as apparent as they were predictable.

With regard to cognitive distinctions—those distinctions between the analytic and the synthetic cognitive forms we have traced throughout—the general unwillingness of the Burger Court to consider the aggregate position of the African-American citizen as a member of a class distinct from White citizens is clear in the majority *Richmond* opinion. Justice O'Connor's argument cast a jaundiced eye on the judicial use of any racial classification by arguing that "a governmental actor cannot render race a legitimate proxy for a particular condition merely by declaring that the condition exists."[20] That the American society and its political institutions had frequently used group classifications in addition to individual classifications in matters concerning racial bias apparently carried little weight for O'Connor. In this context she argued that "The history of racial classifications in this country suggests that blind judicial deference to legislative or executive pronouncements of necessity has no place in equal protection analysis."[21] It had no place in cases like *Plessy v. Ferguson* (1896) either, but the Court of that day willingly drew up the justices' blindfold when deciding that case, the ironically named "Civil Rights Cases" (1883),[22] and others of a similar stripe.

All in all, the post-Warren period evidences a time when the Supreme Court seemed reluctant to disaggregate the general public—that is, to deal with the apples and oranges of a group's rights at the same time that an individual's rights were at stake. Such reluctance is no more glaringly apparent than in Associate Justice Scalia's part-concurring and part-dissenting opinion in *Richmond*. Disagreeing with the Court's dicta that "state and local governments may in some circumstances discriminate on the basis of race in order [in a broad sense] 'to ameliorate the effects of past discrimination,'" Scalia deplored what he called the "source" of past discrimination, which is the tendency "to classify and judge men and women on the basis of their country of origin or the color of their skin."[23] In so arguing, Scalia cites none other than Alexander Bickel, contending that "'discrimination on the basis of race is illegal, immoral, unconstitutional, inherently wrong and destructive of democratic society.'"[24] Bickel's reasoning, of which Scalia approves, was that a "'racial quota derogates the human dignity and *individuality* of all to whom it is applied.'"[25]

The Rights of the Accused

The same reversal of Warren Court direction that occurred in cases concerning racial discrimination also occurred in cases concerning citizens accused of crime. With regard to Fourth Amendment search and seizure protections, the most telling case is probably that of another early Rehnquist Court opinion, *Skinner v. Railway Labor Executives' Association* (1989).[26] There the Federal Railroad Administration's requirements for random drug testing were held to be Constitutionally acceptable because the "citizens subject to a search or seizure" were not, according to the Court, victims of a "random or arbitrary act of government agents."[27] The public, argued newly appointed Associate Justice Anthony Kennedy, did not have its "justifiable expectation" violated by such a testing.[28]

With regard to the Fourth Amendment, the 1988 case of *California v. Greenwood*[29] hinged on a reduced sense of the public's reasonable expectations as well. According to the Court's senior associate justice, Byron White, the Fourth Amendment's "expectation" does not necessarily "give rise to Fourth Amendment protection . . . unless *society* is prepared to accept that expectation as objectively reasonable."[30] The private-to-public line was moved again, and once more in the direction that would limit what the modern-day Anti-Federalist might find necessary to protect the political dissident.

With regard to the Fifth Amendment freedom from self-incrimination protections, the backtracking upon Warren Court–guaranteed rights similarly altered the private-to-public line. In *Rhode Island v. Innis* (1980)[31] police used the trap of sympathy on a suspect already held in custody. They poignantly appealed to that suspect to keep the murder weapon away from children who might pick it up at a nearby school for the handicapped. The *Miranda* protection that had proscribed interrogation without any appraisal of the right to remain silent was thus revised by Associate Justice Potter Stewart in *Innis*. Stewart argued that *Miranda* ruled out "only express questioning" and that the "police surely cannot be held accountable for the unforeseeable results of their words or actions."[32] Was it unforeseeable that the suspect would be moved by an appeal to locate a weapon that could be lethal again? Why did the police talk to the accused about it if they did not think it would have such an effect? The private-to-public line is indeed moved in *Innis;* after this case an accused could no longer insist on a *Miranda* level of protection when suggestive, or even mildly threatening, interrogatories were initiated by the police.

Finally, with regard to the Sixth Amendment's protection of the right to a fair trial, a Burger Court case similar to *Innis* reversed the Warren Court's direction again. In *Nix v. Williams* (1984)[33] an appeal is again made to a murder suspect's sympathy, this time to lead the police to the victim's body. The suspect is reminded of the victim's family's grief, their not knowing if their loved one was alive or dead. Writing for the majority, Chief Justice Burger argued that when there was an "inevitable discovery" of a murder victim, a discovery that could have been accomplished by "lawful means anyway," the police had not violated the Sixth Amendment.[34] As Burger put it, "the Sixth Amendment Exclusionary Rule is designed to protect the right to a fair trial."[35] But, according to Burger, the trial itself is the place of protection. What happens before the trial should therefore never again be as protected as it had been under Warren. I would suggest that the word *public* be added to Burger's rule, placed directly before the word *right*. Burger was limiting a public right.

In short, the rights of the accused cases that came along in the fully post-Warren, Burger, and early Rehnquist Court era retraced a good deal of the ground that Warren had trod in his incorporations of the Bill of Rights to citizens accused of crime. Note that with the exception of *Skinner,* the drug testing case, each takes place in a state jurisdiction, or jurisdiction in which the progress of the Bill of Rights incorporation to the states is rolled back so that states are more free to act to stem the reality of crime.

The Burger and early Rehnquist Supreme Courts, though not completely vitiating Warren Court protections for persons accused of crime, made an about-face with regard to both the private-to-public sectoral balance and the state-to-federal balance that had restricted a state's ability to intrude upon a public right. As an institution, the post-Warren Supreme Court in its criminal case rulings at least partially returned to its traditional perspective. As a defender of the private realm, it once again expanded the power of those who would limit public rights.

The framers, of course, were not concerned with the common criminal when they wrote those property-protecting segments of the seven articles which dealt with contract, full faith and credit, and the rights of the Revolutionary War bond holders. They wrote those provisions to protect private interests from whatever an empowered public might do to diminish private property within the new American political order.

Naturally, the Court would further protect private citizens from those who might also injure them or steal from them. To do so, the ideology balance of both sectors and institutions during the Burger Court reapproached their previous positions.

Regarding the apportionment cases, the strict application of equal access to political rule making, the near-perfectly apportioned districts that *Reynolds* and its ensuing cases required was also reversed by the Burger Court. In *Mahon v. Howell* (1973)[36] the limits of constitutionality were expanded at the state level to allow for a 16.4 percent deviation among districts in the Virginia lower house. By the time of *Brown v. Thomson* (1983)[37] an average deviation of 16 percent was permitted in the Wyoming lower house, the highest deviation rising to 89 percent. By 1986 the Court said that gerrymandering alone was not a violation of the equal protection provisions of the Constitution. Pointedly, the Court held in *Davis v. Bandemer* (1986) that the Constitution does not even require legislatures to "draw districts to come as near as possible to allocating seats to the contending parties in proportion to what their anticipated vote will be."[38]

Only in the area of women's rights, specifically with regard to *Roe*, does the Warren record stand largely if not wholly uncorrected at this writing. The presidency of the Democrat Bill Clinton, the appointment of two new associate justices of the Supreme Court (one a reasonably liberal woman), along with the maintenance of decidedly majority public support for a woman's right to choose maternity, might prevent the reversal of *Roe*. Nonetheless, two cases must be mentioned, the second more important than the first, as examples of the kind of Burger Court chiseling away at *Roe* which might be continued in subsequent conservative Court opinions.

The first case is *Harris v. McRae*,[39] a 1980 decision that affirmed Congress's so-called Hyde Amendment, which had forbidden the federal funding of abortions. Consistent with the *Maher* case of 1977 which upheld Connecticut's right to fund birth-related expenses but not abortion-related expenses, *Harris* said that the Congress did not violate *Roe* when it chose not to fund abortions federally. In *Harris* Associate Justice Potter Stewart reasoned that *Roe* had not guaranteed that "a woman's freedom of choice carries with it a constitutional entitlement to the financial resources to avail herself of the full range of protected choices."[40]

In an even more significant case than *Harris*, the early Rehnquist Supreme Court ruled in *Webster v. Reproductive Health Services* (1989)[41] that the state of Missouri was entitled not only to prohibit the use of public facilities for abortions but also to mandate "viability" tests, the results of which might serve to restrict abortion. As such tests would rule out an abortion if viability was arguably sustainable, the requirement surely stands as a bar to an absolute abortion right.

The Missouri state law, passed by a legislature that had one female senator out of thirty-four and twenty-five female representatives out of a total of one hundred and sixty-three, was held unconstitutional by a federal court of appeals. It did so on religious grounds, harkening back to the reasoning of the religious establishment cases of *Engele* and *Schempp*. The appeals court had cited an earlier, *Roe*-like Supreme Court dictum saying that "a state may not adopt one theory of when life begins to justify its regulations of abortions," in *Akron v. Akron Center for Reproductive Health, Inc.* (1983).[42]

The Supreme Court in *Webster*, however, overruled the federal court of appeals. It argued that, although "Stare decisis is a cornerstone of our legal system . . . it has less power in constitutional cases, where, save for Constitutional amendments, this Court is the only body able to make needed changes."[43] Justice William Rehnquist offered that "we think the rigid *Roe* framework is hardly consistent with the notion of a Constitution cast in general terms, as ours is, and usually speaking in general principles, as ours does."[44] Justice Harry Blackmun, who wrote *Roe*, certainly would have disagreed, but, then, Blackmun was typically writing of the Bill of Rights and Rehnquist of the original seven articles when they spoke of Constitutional guarantees. The public and private nature of these two halves of the Constitution are more in evidence than usual in cases of this intensity.

In sum, whether the judicial issue has centered around the rights of a racial minority, the accused, those harmed by unfair apportionment, or women who insist upon making the maternity decision themselves, the Burger Supreme Court's movement away from the public sector protections of the Warren Court era has been as persistent as it should have been predictable. Indeed, the ideological lines of both Courts are probably as pure as the lines of any Courts in all of America's high bench history. But, one more time if I may, let me point out how the Burger and early Rehnquist Courts' reversals of the Warren Court, though perhaps still incomplete, as Stephen Wasby and later commentators have properly pointed out, still consistently fall along the sectoral divide in ways that any reversal of that Court would have to fall. If the Warren Court so fundamentally reversed the direction of previous activist courts that even scholars as noted as Alexander Bickel did not fully understand it, then the retreat from the Warren Court should at least be understood as having retraced a similar path, albeit in the opposite direction.

Should we be surprised, for example, that Justice Scalia, in that concurring *Richmond v. Croson* "minority set-aside" opinion cited earlier, squeezed some lines from James Madison's *Federalist* no. 10 between his two quotations of Alexander Bickel? The section of Madison which Scalia used concerned the extension of "the sphere" within the new Republic, that third leg of the Federalist strategy which, along with the separation of powers and federalism, was to retard the formation of private domain–threatening majorities. "Extend the sphere and you take in a greater variety of parties and interests, you make it less probable that a majority of the whole will have a common motive to invade the rights of other citizens," Madison said.[45] Scalia, from the bench, was trying to do just that.

Why would a quotation from Madison still be so relevant to a late-twentieth-century equal protection case, one in which the city that was once the capital of the Confederacy had recently "fallen" to a Black majority? Scalia never mentioned the irony that the city was by then but a part of a much larger Richmond metropolitan area, an area that, if unified would have prevented Black dominance of the area. But, after citing Madison's no. 10 notions on "extending the sphere," Scalia continued Madison's quotation to include the founder's admonition that, "if such a common motive exists, it will [through the extension of the sphere] be more difficult for all who feel it to discover their own strength and to act in unison with each other."[46]

The phrase, of course, is one of the most significant in all of the *Federalist Papers*. It not only made the extension of the sphere a key element in the antimajoritarian strategy, but, unlike the devices of the separation of powers and federalism, it revealed that deep suspicion of the public sector which Madison and the Federalists held to so dearly.

Yet, if what Justice Scalia quoted is so revealing not only of the Federalists of 1787 but of their followers among America's jurisprudential modern conservatives, how much more revealing it is, within a modern context, for Scalia to follow the Madisonian citation by saying that "the *prophecy* of these words came to fruition in Richmond in the enactment of a set-aside clearly and directly beneficial to the dominant political group."[47] The dreadful Madisonian prophecy of the public sector's ascendance, according to Scalia, had been realized. Now the line could be held only by repair to the original Constitution as well as to the most riveting portion of the arguments of those who supported the first seven articles.

Only arguments of such a foundation would displace the public's alteration of "appropriate" private protections, displace a legislative body's folly over judge-made overrulings, and place the federal government's protection over whatever a state's subdivisions might do to imperil private rights. Through what Scalia quotes Bickel as labeling a "racial quota," no state would be allowed to derogate, as I cited earlier, "the human dignity and *individuality* of all to whom [the quota] is applied."[48] The cognitive juxtaposition of "individuality" with a "group" that at last held majority control somewhere in the United States was far too synthetic in its cognitive form for Justice Scalia. Again, the race cases of the Burger Court era frequently repaired to the analytic cognition, race-blind position in overruling "reverse discrimination" actions.

Free Speech

Though I have emphasized the importance of Burger and early Rehnquist Court revisions of the Warren Court in this chapter, I cannot leave the discussion of specific areas of judge-made law without at least a brief reference to what so many, perhaps rightly, consider to be the heart of the Bill of Rights: the First Amendment. The push and pull of real-world political events and the ideologies of the Supreme Court's different justices have shaped our vision of the First Amendment from the time of its earliest interpretations. As might be expected, the influence of different justices is perhaps best evidenced by the broken line of decisions that mark the free speech area of the law.

Justice Holmes's use of a largely objective test to determine the limits of free speech limits in *Schenck v. United States* (1919),[49] contains the famous admonition not to yell fire in a theater, and contrasts with the more stringent, largely subjective test of Justice Sanford in *Gitlow v. New York* (1925).[50] Sanford ruled that the mere intent to undermine the World War I draft law was sufficient for culpability. Similarly, the anticommunist fears that affected strict enforcement of the Smith Act in the *Dennis v. United States* case[51] in 1951 must be contrasted with the abating fears of communism that were evident in the 1957 Warren Court decision which exculpated a political dissenter in the previously cited *Yates v. United States* case.[52]

In free speech cases the private-to-public line of jurisdictional demarcation is every bit as obvious as it is in the families of cases discussed earlier. In each circumstance political insurgents, certainly far from a majority in all of the four cases, sought the broadest interpretation of the Anti-Federalists' First Amendment purposes. They sought public sector protection, in effect, for their political activities.

Somewhat less obviously, the private-to-public line is observable within the so-called freedom of religion cases. The free exercise cases speak for themselves, the liberty to practice one's religion is the only *resultant*—that is, nonpolitically vectored–protection of the First Amendment. Even Supreme Court cases such as the early Warren Burger Court *Yoder* case (1972)[53], which protected an Amish child's freedom from compulsory education after the eighth grade, or even the latter-day Burger Court cases such as *Thomas v. Georgia* (1981),[54] which protected a Jehovah's Witnesses' right not to produce weaponry, properly shielded minority religious beliefs from governmental intrusion. But, once more, these protections were free exercise–related—that is, resultant in the sense that they ran to the benefit of private, minority-religioned individuals who wanted relief from governmental majoritarianism. In doing so, however, they did not negate the overriding purposes of the remaining First Amendment freedoms.

With regard to the *establishment* of religion, the most controversial Supreme Court cases have dealt with the breadth of public protections against private moralities. The best example of the establishment clause cases, of course, concern school prayer. The Anti-Federalists' desire to ensure governmental neutrality with regard to religious preference spoke generally to the abuses of the established church in England and to the threat of what such a church might do in the United States. In Warren-era Supreme Court cases such as *Engel v. Vitale* (1962),[55] outlawing a state-prescribed prayer, and in *Abbington School District v. Schempp* (1963),[56] outlawing assigned bible readings, the Court was dealing with something that was directly in line with the establishment clause's original motives.

The state, according to Warren, should not be even minimally theocratic. *Engel* and *Schempp*, like *Yoder* and *Thomas*, protect the religious dissident from theocracy. But it is *Engel* and *Schempp* which hold the position historically analogous to the dissidents of a previous century such as Thomas Jefferson in the United States or even the Puritans in England. These dissidents had argued for the public's right to be free of religious intrusion or religiously assisted political intrusion, not just a small sect's right to be free of the impact of general laws that adversely affected them. The general public's religious position, at least as ascribed to them by Warren, is analogous to the position of the English political dissidents who opposed the Stuarts and to that of America's Anti-Federalists, who opposed the founders' Constitution.

Yet, along with freedom of religion protections, it was the freedom of speech protections in the First Amendment which rang the loudest for most Americans. Of all the recent cases that have dealt with First Amendment freedom of speech guarantees, none has been more politically significant than the case of *Buckley v. Valeo* (1976).[57] The decision in this case is so important because it demonstrates how the post-Warren Supreme Court of Chief Justice Warren Burger, even with its occasional forbearance in the areas of school integration, women's rights, and the free exercise of religion, clearly reversed the direction of the Warren Court with regard to the protection of public, foundationally political rights. *Buckley* is the most important political case since *Reynolds* reapportioned all state legislative houses not allocated by population. It may yet become more important than *Reynolds* when the long-term impact of the decision is recorded.

If nothing else, *Buckley* evidences the reversal in the recent history of the U.S. electoral process of the democratizing trend that the majority of American political history has celebrated. Though money has always been the "mother's milk" of politics, the resources now required to run for federal office, particularly within a heavily populated state such as California, have gone beyond anything that the founding fathers, or even Americans of only a generation earlier, could ever have imagined.

The 1992 presidential campaign saw an extraordinarily wealthy independent candidate, Ross Perot, garner fully 19 percent of the popular vote for president. This percentage was greater than any third candidate had achieved since a former Republican president, Teddy Roosevelt, ran in 1912. Meanwhile, a candidate named Michael Huffington narrowly lost a Senate seat from California after spending twenty-five million dollars of his own money. Currently, Malcomb Forbes Jr. generously finances a presidential run. Merely twenty years ago *Buckley v. Valeo* brought about a test of the 1971 and 1974 Federal Election Campaign Acts, which had been enacted in response to what now seem to be the mild accelerations of campaign expenditures which television advertising originally caused. Wealthy individuals such as the Chicago insurance magnate W. Clement Stone had given as much as two million dollars to federal candidates (presidential candidate Richard Nixon in Stone's case). More than anyone, Stone alerted the public to the need for restrictions on private expenditures in the country's elections.

The decision in *Buckley* is a lengthy one, taking up nearly one hundred and fifty pages in the standard reporter volumes. It is lengthy partly because of the multisectioned provisions of the act, which covers all manner of campaign assistance. But it is also lengthy because five separate opinions diverged to a greater or lesser degree from the per curiam, that is unsigned, opinion on a variety of central political issues.

Most of the act's provisions were found unconstitutional by the Court, illustrating the allocation of the case's private-to-public domains all too well. Essentially, the Court approved only those *contribution* limitations that dealt with what individuals and political action committees (PACs) actually might give to a federal campaign. But the Court disapproved of those provisions that dealt with a candidate's *expenditure* of his, or her, own funds as well as the capping of *total* campaign expenditures or even the capping of what an individual might choose to contribute *independently* to a campaign, that is without coordination with the candidate or the candidate's campaign committees. These three areas, the Court in *Buckley* found, were to be protected by First Amendment, free speech, rights. But note how the First Amendment was interpreted in order to afford that protection.

As part of the fine distinction that the Court made between contributions that individuals or groups could give to a federal campaign and expenditures that a campaign might make to advance an aspirant's candidacy, the Court found only expenditures to be within the public domain, thereby permitting the Congress to exact limitations on such payments. The Court found contributions to be outside the public domain, thereby reading the First Amendment, contrary to an Anti-Federalist presumption, so as to give carte blanche to individuals who might wish to spend as much as they wanted on their own campaigns, or on a candidate's campaigns, as long, again, as there is no contact with the campaign. Similarly, it was held to be in the private domain for campaigns to spend as much as they wanted.

Given these conclusions regarding the private and public sectors, the reasoning of the Court in those areas in which the act was declared unconstitutional was almost inevitable. With regard to independent expenditures, the Court found it "wholly foreign to the First Amendment" to "restrict the speech of some elements of our society in order to enhance the relative voice of others."[58] Of course, it might be argued that the Congress was only listening to the public's outcry with regard to the unbalanced campaign influence created by a few wealthy donors. This public outcry was well within the protections of free speech which the Anti-Federalists placed within the public domain. If this latter approach were taken, contrary to the approach of the Court, each member of the general public would have been treated, like *Reynolds*, as a more equal partner in the election process. Contributions such as those made by Stone, even if they had been spent independently of various campaign committees, would therefore have been forbidden.

Indeed, even the Burger Court's citation of a previous case's argument seems counterinstructive when viewed within the context of the core Federalist/Anti-Federalist, private-to-public sector debate. The per curiam opinion notes that the First Amendment is already on record as wishing "to secure the widest possible dissemination of information from diverse and antagonistic sources."[59] But the issue in *Buckley*, and within the entire area of big money's influence in U.S. campaigns, was not one of "wideness." A fair proportion of the population is usually able to contribute, and does contribute, twenty-five, fifty, or one hundred dollars either to a political campaign or, far less frequently, to an independent endorsement of a candidate.

The issue that the Congress addressed in its Reform Acts dealt with the *size* of a *few* contributions. In its ruling the Court ensured the relative ineffectiveness of those smaller contributions that come from the wider or general public vis-à-vis the powerful contributions of a handful, or perhaps only one, individual. This is hardly the kind of democratic protection which the Anti-Federalists would have given to the voting members of their contemporary population when they proposed what became the First Amendment.

On the second issue, that of a candidate's expenditures on his, or her, own campaign, the Court has been equally disrespectful of the historically ideological direction of the First Amendment. The Court's proclaiming the importance of candidates having "the unfettered opportunity to make their views known so that the electorate may intelligently evaluate the candidates' personal qualities and their positions on vital public issues"[60] wholly ignored what the Congress was trying to do. The Congress was not attempting to curtail any eligible citizen's ability to run for office. Indeed, it was hoping to encourage broad candidacy. The danger it hoped to avert was, instead, now vividly portrayed in the recent candidacies of Perot, Huffington, Forbes, and a growing host of wealthy candidates who have achieved unnatural advantage over their real or prospective less-wealthy opponents by the sheer dint of their resources. What the Anti-Federalists would have said about this should hardly be difficult to figure.

Third, the Court in *Buckley* spoke to the issue of total campaign expenditures. What the Court said was that "in the free society ordained by our Constitution it is not the government, but the people—individually as citizens and candidates and collectively as associations and political committees—who must retain control over the quantity and range of debate on public issues in a political campaign."[61] Such an argument is disingenuous. The fact is that the citizenry had already spoken through their elected, legislative representatives. They spoke through the Congress, and with vigor, in the Federal Election Campaign Acts of 1971 and 1974. Within the limits of the Constitution's provisions, and within the limits of the protections provided in the first seven articles, they spoke as a citizenry deeply troubled by the abuses of excessive money in U.S. political campaigns. To deny the central First Amendment protections that permit the populace to control the ground rules of its nation's politics, rather than have our politics be controlled by a handful of wealthy individuals, misses the point of the First Amendment entirely.

In my view, although the case of *Buckley v. Valeo* is widely written of as a First Amendment protecting case, it is in fact the opposite. *Buckley* is an anti–First Amendment case. It denies the well-considered judgment of the public electorate at large, that denial no doubt leading to the ever-growing cynicism that Americans express regarding their political system and its links to big money. Whether the politics of this country now only serves those few who can afford a very high stakes poker game may still be debatable in the minds of some, but the perception of something very close to this is increasingly credible among large portions of the citizenry. A smaller and smaller number of citizens play an increasingly larger, disproportionate, role in the country's national political campaigns.

One cannot help but wonder, in view of Perot, Huffington, Forbes, and the still skyrocketing cost of U.S. political campaigns, whether the Supreme Court would like to have another chance at *Buckley.* The mere existence of five partially concurring and partially dissenting opinions demonstrates that, even at the time of the decision, serious reservations about the wisdom of the case's holding already existed.

Within these signed opinions Associate Justice Harry Blackmun, for example, revealed that he was never "persuaded that the Court makes or indeed is able to make a principled constitutional distinction between the contribution limitations on the one hand and the expenditure limitations on the other."[62] Associate Justice Thurgood Marshall noted that not only is "the candidate with a substantial personal fortune at his disposal . . . off to a significant 'headstart'" but also the "ability to generate contributions may itself depend upon a showing of a financial base for the campaign or some demonstration of pre-existing support."[63] That reality subverted what Marshall saw as the Congress's appropriate "interest in promoting the reality and appearance of equal access to the political arena."[64]

Perhaps most telling of the Court's confusion was the brief concurring opinion of the centrist Associate Justice Byron White. Accepting the "congressional judgment" that "other steps must be taken to counter the corrosive effects of money in federal election campaigns," White noted that "it would make little sense to me, and apparently made none to Congress, to limit the amounts an individual may give to a candidate or spend with his approval but fail to limit the amounts that could be spent on his behalf."[65]

To review, where was the private-to-public jurisdictional line drawn in *Buckley v. Valeo?* Again, the Supreme Court drew its line along that perilous distinction between contributions and expenditures, specifically begging all who read the opinion to ask if anyone had heard of a contribution to a political campaign which, short of candidate theft or accumulation for retirement, wasn't intended to be used as, and actually was used as, an expenditure. The Supreme Court, in denying the legislative response to the nation's First Amendment–based protest against the corruption of large campaign expenditures, drew that line well to the private side of where, say, *Reynolds* drew it in the reapportionment area. In doing so, the Burger Supreme Court also clearly returned to the Supreme Court's original ideological position vis-à-vis the legislature. It struck down what a liberal legislature had done in responding to the wishes of the populace.

In sum, *Buckley v. Valeo* returned the configuration of Court-to-Congress and judicial-to-legislative jurisdictions to their classical, that is Marshallian, position. If the public thought that it could successfully counterbalance the influence of the wealthy, private few on the nation's politics two hundred years after Marshall, it received the very form of institutional response which Marshall gave to analogous positions in his decisions.

With regard to the drawing of the private-to-public sectoral line, *Buckley v. Valeo* is consistent, ideologically, with Marshall's rulings in *McCulloch v. Maryland, Gibbons v. Ogden*, and a variety of other cases. Though not directly protecting the interests of a national bank or those businesses engaged in interstate commerce, it did directly protect those modern-day private interests that speak with inordinately disproportional voices in U.S. politics. Those voices increased their volume and their coverage, at the same time that they protected those private, corporate institutions that gave them their ability to speak so loudly within the public domain. Again, *Buckley*'s misuse of the First Amendment to protect those interests' disproportionate governmental access was clearly contrary to the core ideological meaning of America's Bill of Rights.

More than any of the so-called civil liberties cases that modified, if they did not reverse, the principal holdings of the Warren Court, *Buckley* thus marked perhaps the clearest ideological departure of the Burger Court from the Warren and immediately post-Warren era. Though the locus of the Bill of Rights' individual protections was impacted but little, the telos of the Bill of Rights—its deeper, political direction—was clearly violated. Perhaps it was fitting that a case that struck so deeply into the essence of America's democracy should have housed such a clear demarcation between the Warren and the Burger Courts. With *Buckley* the Warren era was over for good.

CHAPTER SEVENTEEN

Burger Critiqued

Harvard's Professor Tribe

Considering the extent of the criticism of Earl Warren and the Warren Court's Constitutional interpretations of the 1950s and 1960s, it would
seem only natural that the Warren Burger Court might receive at least
some criticism for its revisions of Warren Court rulings. But there has
been a good deal less criticism of the Burger, post-Warren Court than
there ever was of the Warren Court.

Why was there so little criticism of the immediate post-Warren
Court? An easy answer is that the Burger Court did not engage in the
remarkable, pathbreaking cases that the Warren panel did. But there's
more to it than that. A great deal of the difference between criticism of
the Burger Court as opposed to the Warren Court has to do with that
return of the Burger Court to a methodological status quo *ante*, or a
place where many commentators, as I have mentioned, felt the Court
should have been all along. Wholly apart from the ideology of the Warren Court, the idea of a Supreme Court that makes public law rather
than protects private law from governmental overreach contradicts what
every American schoolchild is taught concerning the Court and its proper
Constitutional role. From the earliest days of America's Platonic socialization, the rubric that "the Congress makes the laws, the President en-
forces the laws, and the Supreme Court interprets the laws" is about as
universally trumpeted as is the founding myth of the young Washington
and his father's cherry tree.

Yet even this explanation for the relative lack of criticism of the Burger
Court as compared to the Warren Court falls short of full description. At
the ideological level, as I have suggested throughout, the place that the
Supreme Court repaired to in its first three periods of activism included

the familiar notions of freedom of contract, freedom to own property, and freedom to partake of those wealth-producing activities that many Americans grant the same level of sanctity that they do to the tripartite allocation of Constitutional authority. What caused consternation among Warren Court critics had a great deal to do with the notion that there had been a clear line of separation between the political playing field, also broadly defined, and the legal playing field, broadly defined, within Constitutional interpretation up to the time of the Court. The political-legal distinction, to be sure, had been intruded upon from time to time throughout the development of English and American law. Such intrusions, after all, were what so upset Blackstone when he bemoaned that the English statute book had "swelled to ten times a larger bulk."

As long as the ideology and the institutional arrangements of the first three activist periods (plus Taft) protected within the private sector only what many thought should never have been threatened within it, however, it would be more difficult to argue that judicial involvement, whether in health, safety, or welfare matters (nineteenth century), or racial equity, women's rights, or equitable representational matters (twentieth century), was soundly within the American tradition. Though the substance of so much of what the Warren Court did in these arenas was surely accepted in some quarters, the Warren Court is still seen by many as moving the Court's jurisdictional boundaries beyond where any Court had previously gone.

What the critics of the Warren Court pointed to and still point to as part of that moving of boundaries was that there was something about the Supreme Court, as a court, which was supposed to make it relatively free not only of legislative-like behavior but also of those sweeping political movements in either ideological direction which courts, as courts, simply should not make. The word that I think best fits their notion is borrowed from physics. It is *viscosity*, a term that simply means "resistance to change." What the term suggests in a jurisprudential context is that, even beyond the "proper" jurisdictional balances between the Supreme Court and the political branches which are so frequently argued over, there is the matter of the relative susceptibility of any public institution to radical change in any direction. The legal jurisdiction's "high-viscosity" tradition has typically been viewed by the citizenry as meaning that, whatever direction the Supreme Court might decide to move, it should not move precipitously.

In short, it was in great part because America's courts have been widely accepted as the ultimate interpreter of the law, something that the framers clearly wished for, and that the Supreme Court has been relatively "judicious" (read ponderous) about the law throughout most of its history, that there was less criticism of the Court when it did make pathbreaking rulings. It has been the Burger Court's incrementalism in eating away at Warren Court rulings, as much as the fact that it returned to something familiar both institutionally and ideologically, which has in part saved it from so much criticism.

Having said all of this, however, the fact remains that the Burger Court has not escaped criticism entirely. Much of that criticism has been mild, and some of it has been misdirected, as I shall try to illustrate. One of the leading critics of the Burger Court has been Harvard law professor Laurence Tribe, who has chastised the Court generally for what he thinks was its overly vigilant scrutiny of legislative initiative. Tribe, I'm sorry to say, misses the larger point concerning the Burger Court.

To be fair, Tribe, in *Constitutional Choices*, demonstrates a keen awareness of the ultimate reflectiveness of the legal understanding.[1] Assuring his readers that he is "not writing for those who feel confident that canons of appropriate constitutional construction may be convincingly derived from some neutral source," on the one hand, and assuring his readers as well that he is not a "cynic" or a "legal nihilist," on the other hand, Tribe acknowledges that the legal enterprise is what he calls "inescapably subjective."[2]

Yet, though Tribe's discussion includes reminders concerning the "stubbornly subjective character of so many of the Constitution's most crucial commitments,"[3] Tribe first mentions the Bill of Rights, not the seven Constitutional articles, in that context. In attempts at balance he does subsequently mention the contract clause and its purpose of protecting "the transactions and expectations to which the institutions of private property give rise."[4] He fully recognizes that the framers clearly wished to "help secure the institution of private property."[5]

Overall, the burden of Tribe's argument thus deals encouragingly with the importance of what he delineates as fundamental "substantive commitments" in the Constitution. His position contrasts with the argument of so many that the Constitution is overwhelmingly a procedural document. Tribe's position on the substance of the Constitution leads to his notion that both legal and political rights must be protected by courts and not just by legislatures. Political rights, "including *substantive rights to participate*," are the necessary complement to the substantive rights of property and contract which Tribe discussed.[6] It was the Burger Court's passivity in protecting such political rights which troubles Tribe, arguing that such passivity can lead to a false sense of security about what he calls a "dangerously ambitious judiciary."[7]

Yet what does Tribe mean when he refers to a dangerously ambitious judiciary? For him such a judiciary is not concerned with issues concerning the environment, women's rights, or the continuation of the civil rights agenda, all of which the Harvard professor has consistently supported. A Court like the Burger Court is too much concerned with procedural matters, according to Tribe, those concerns not advancing the law as the Warren Court did. Such a Court may, in its arrogance, reverse the progress of the Warren Court through the strategy of excessive proceduralism. In short, Tribe's position is that the Supreme Court must either continue to move the law forward—that is, into those difficult political fields that ensure its fundamental substantive commitments—or it must demur to the legislature to do what is necessary to uphold such commitments. So far so good from Tribe's liberal perspective.

But after Tribe's introductory depiction of what he believes the appropriate role of the Constitution's various institutions to be, he next focuses in *Constitutional Choices* on what he thinks the Court has done under Chief Justice Burger to retard rather than advance the law. He selects three cases that he believes highlight the Court's movement in the wrong direction. The first is the *Immigration and Naturalization Service (INS) v. Chadha* (1983) case,[8] which brought forth a decision in which the Supreme Court outlawed the practice of the legislative veto. The post-law-making legislative vetoing of executive action had been used since the waning days of the Hoover administration, when a newly Democratic Congress wished to keep an eye on what a frustrated but still business-friendly president might do to remedy the Depression.

What the Burger Court ruled in *Chadha* was that the House of Representatives' veto of an immigrant's status as a permanent resident alien violated two of the sacraments of the Constitution. The denial of residency came from only one house, not two, and the denial was not presented to the president for signature as statutory bills must be. These were clear Constitutional omissions, the Court said—even though such omissions had been routinely overlooked in at least two hundred pieces of extant legislation. For the Burger Court, perhaps the Congress (overwhelmingly controlled by Democrats for four decades before the 1994 election) had been getting too big for its britches. For the sitting president, the conservative Republican Ronald Reagan, that was certainly the case with the kind of liberal political intrusion which permitted one chamber of the Congress to pull the string on administrative actions when that chamber thought Congressional intent was violated. Tribe found this clipping of Congress's wings to be precisely what a dangerously ambitious judiciary shouldn't do.

Well before the Supreme Court rebuff of the legislative veto in *Chadha* angered Tribe in 1983, he had been troubled by the Court's ruling in *Buckley v. Valeo* (1976).[9] *Buckley*, as I discussed in the previous chapter, declared that much of the Federal Election Campaign Acts were unconstitutional. Unlike *Chadha*'s concern with the separation of powers, the *Buckley* issue, again, was one of free speech, but, institutionally, it was also a matter of the Court's preventing the Congress from limiting the influence of large contributions in America's political campaigns. Tribe was appalled that Congress was rebuked in its trying to do something so worthwhile.

The third Supreme Court case that angered Tribe, and one that was reversed nearly at the moment of Tribe's book's publication, held that the Congress did not have the power to apply federal minimum wage and maximum hour legislation to state governments. That case was *National League of Cities v. Usery* (1976).[10] The reversal case, *Garcia v. San Antonio Metropolitan Transit Authority* (1985),[11] incidentally, resulted from Justice Harry Blackmun's changing his mind and holding that the federal government did in fact have the power to enforce federal work-related rules on state employees.

At an ideological level, then, Laurence Tribe's *Constitutional Choices* reveals his deep and growing hostility to a Supreme Court that had fallen away from the ideological biases of the Warren Court. Tribe sensed that Warren Burger's Court was unmistakably changing the direction of the Warren Court, and he argued that "what emerges from *Buckley*, *National League of Cities*, and *Chadha* taken as a group is less a coherent picture of checks and balances than a sense of judicial frustration and desire."[12] The desire, Tribe claims, is born of a felt judicial need "to reclaim—for the judiciary as the 'least dangerous' branch, or for the states as the most modest—some measure of the power that, under the exigencies of modernity, Congress has sought to centralize along the banks of the Potomac."[13]

All in all, Tribe's is an interesting, if not wholly original, argument. But to get a fair fix on Tribe, it is only appropriate to ask if he was similarly upset with the Supreme Court, and its reining in of the Congress during Earl Warren's time as chief justice. Unfortunately, he wasn't. Indeed, when the Warren Court was *supporting* what Tribe advocated, he willingly championed an "ambitious judiciary." His positions on the full panoply of the Constitutional issues of the Warren Court day, along with the role of the Court in dealing with those issues, were all found to be appropriate.

On issues relating to race, for example, Tribe argued in *Constitutional*

Choices that "to eliminate the persistent effects of racial prejudice and oppression, courts must often take race explicitly into account both in assessing constitutional violations and in formulating adequate remedies."[14] With regard to the rights of the accused under the Fourteenth Amendment, Tribe specifically decried anything that would reduce the protection of the accused under the Fourth Amendment or any "other superficially procedural provisions of the Constitution, such as the rights to counsel, confrontation, bail, and jury trial."[15]

With regard to apportionment, Tribe was no more mysterious, applauding "a growing awareness of political equality as a legitimating foundation for our form of government."[16] As for women's rights, Tribe lamented the continued "discrimination against women."[17] He "would identify their persisting legal disabilities as parts of a subtle mosaic of oppression that is not genuinely framed by human nature, even though it is typically 'justified' by invoking precisely such considerations."[18]

Tribe's ideological record, therefore, is clear and consistent, as a political campaigner might put it. But what is not clear in Tribe's writings, as it was not clear in the writings of Bickel, Weschler, or most conservative Court commentators either, was any reflective sense of the relationship of the ideologies of these writers to their institutional preferences. Bickel abhorred the Warren Court and the legislature-replacing nature of that Court's decisions. Tribe abhorred the Burger Court, particularly its legislative authority–diminishing rulings, which he felt left the least protected among the citizenry even more vulnerable.

Taken separately, neither the Bickel nor the Tribe position on the matter of institutional prerogatives is remarkable, once the advocate's ideological proclivity is clear. The fact that Tribe so readily switched institutional sides in the overall argument once the Burger Court is at issue is more remarkable, but it is far from the most remarkable thing that must be said about him. The fact is that the Tribe position (and the Bickel position too) turns out to be predictive of little with regard to these writers' institutional leanings once the ideological direction of the Warren Court and Burger Court are taken into account. It was the *Warren* Court that Bickel was criticizing but almost certainly because that Court's activism was so liberal. It was the *Burger* Court that Tribe was criticizing, but because that post-Warren Court wasn't sufficiently liberal. Although the ideology-to-institutional preference pattern only exists for these writers when the moon is in the right phase, so to speak, what is even more troublesome about both of their analyses, I suggest, is that neither ventured beyond the level of ideological-to-institutional preference in their analysis. There is, of course, another level.

The Sectoral Level

What I hope is now clear from all that I have suggested is that there is a lot more to an analysis of the political and legal history of the United States, as well as to an analysis of the entirety of Anglo-American jurisprudential history, than reviewing the correlations of ideological-to-institutional preference. From the beginning the burden of this work has been that there is a pattern to far more than the institutional histories that have accompanied the ideologies of the English and American political systems. It has been my contention that there has also been a pattern to the private-to-public balances that have accompanied the ideological history of Anglo-American jurisprudence and that this latter pattern is ultimately more explanatory than the institutionally based patterns. As I said at the outset, the private-to-public sectoral divide has always been both a deeper *and a more consistent* demarcation of the liberal-to-conservative political/legal argument than has been the institutional distinction.

What is undeniable, and what I think casts an almost uncontestable level of doubt over the reliability of merely institutional analysis, is that after one hundred and fifty years of consistency the ideological-to-institutional alignment of our nation's judicial and legislative branches clearly *shifted not once but twice* within the space of merely forty years. From the liberal/legislative and conservative/Court alignments of the pre-Warren period to the liberal/Court and conservative/legislative alignments of the Warren Court and then back to the liberal/legislative and conservative/Court alignments of the Burger Court, these alterations are unmistakable. And that two of the most renowned jurisprudential commentators in this century focused solely on the institutional realignments fashioned by the Courts and legislatures in full view of these unmistakable shifts (admittedly, Bickel saw only one full reversal) is really quite extraordinary. It is even more extraordinary when one considers that the principal ideological distinction throughout the entire history of Anglo-American jurisprudence consistently fell along the same private-to-public divide that remained ideologically consistent throughout the institutional shifts.

To say it again, neither Alexander Bickel at Yale nor Laurence Tribe at Harvard ever reached the Archimedean theoretical point at which they looked beyond the ideological-to-institutional configuration that they both wrote about so passionately. Neither, to say it again, saw that the ideological-to-institutional demarcation was *not* the fundamental demarcation of the American Constitutional argument, just as it had never been the fundamental demarcation during the last nearly eight hundred years of the Anglo-American experience. The ideological-to-institutional *reversal* of the entire previous Anglo-American experience which marked the Warren court, followed by the *re-reversal* of institutional affections which occurred within a very few years after the Warren Supreme Court, should have alerted at least Tribe to the weakness of his merely institutional analysis. Somehow it never did.

What I suggest is that it may now be necessary to embrace an entirely different theoretical perspective on America's Constitutional history. If one wishes fully to understand not only the essence of the U.S. political and legal systems' most divisive disputes but also the nature of the *intellectual argument* that has, since at least the time of Glanvil, underpinned such disputes, the sectoral divide must now receive its proper place in the analysis.

Do not misunderstand. I have never suggested that institutions have been of no significance within the ideological battles that always have and always will continue to be a part of America's public versus private sector debates. Of course, the choice of the arena of any conflict has a bearing on that conflict, in politics and law just as in sport. But we can now see clearly, if we know where to look, that the principal jurisprudential battle was never principally between the institutional jurisdictions, court and legislature, or any more broadly defined legal and political jurisdictions within the larger struggle.

If anything, I think it is fair to say that it is becoming evident in the evolution of American Constitutional interpretation that the ideological differentiation between America's political institutions which did exist, if secondarily, within American jurisprudence from its inception has become increasingly blurred in recent years. Though it is hoped that the viscosity, or resistance to change, of U.S. courts, and particularly the United States Supreme Court, will always substantially exceed that of the nation's legislatures, it is now obvious that virtually all significant political issues are fought out today in both the legislative and the judicial arenas. Is there a single salient contemporary issue, from abortion to school prayer to the issues surrounding affirmative action or those surrounding the prevention and adjudication of criminality, which is not being argued over within both the courts and the legislatures?

If anything, the private-to-public sectoral argument more clearly marks the Constitutional divide than it ever has, and it more clearly marks that divide in great part because those who support the jurisdictional authority of the private and the public sectors respectively fight their battles almost indiscriminately within both the legal and the political institutional jurisdictions. To put it another way, the line of institutional differentiation was not only never the central ideological defining point in American legal history, but that line has been lately blurred by the still consistent placement of the principal—that is, sectoral—differentiation with its natural ideological home, along with the "cleaning out," if you will, of the analytic and synthetic cognitive forms within the two sectors, over the last one hundred years. The private sector now overwhelmingly argues for the pure analytic form and the public sector now argues overwhelmingly for the synthetic form of the contract.

I believe this last reality to be important because, just as it is now clear that the private-to-public sectoral divide is more significant than the judicial-to-legislative institutional divide in the American Constitutional arrangement, so too it should now be clear that our understanding of the American political system is now capable of reaching what I think is best labeled as a subatomic level of understanding.[19] It has reached roughly the same point, in other words, which the discipline of physics reached early in this century, when Neils Bohr and Ernest Rutherford came to understand the nature of the subatomic structure within each atom. Plainly put, what the subatomic understanding means when placed into the Constitutional context is that, if the sectoral separation is the crucial factor in the resolution of political issues that deal with race, the rights of the accused, women's rights, apportionment, and so many other substantive arenas, it should now be clear that the balance of cognitive biases *within* either legislative or judicial institutions—that is, the relative willingness of either legislators or judges to give credence to the extracontractual, usually equity-centered consideration—is crucial to victory in that conflict.

Remember that the Warren Court, with its altogether different "activist" orientation from the previous activist Courts, not only changed the law's substance in a variety of areas; it also began to insist, if implicitly, that Courts consistently consider cognitively synthetic qualities in the law. As the protection of the private sector within the Constitution's original seven articles and the challenge to that private sector within the Anti-Federalists' Bill of Rights' has increasingly placed the subatomic, analytic-to-synthetic structure of ideological debate *within* each of America's legislative and judicial institutions, the structure of that debate means that preferences for the private and public sectoral arenas, including their attendant cognitive qualities and regardless of whether they are found in the legislative or judicial jurisdiction, can now be well understood as the true battlefield of America's ideological debate.

To put it simply, I offer that the deep alliance of conservative ideology with the private sector is not well understood unless the element of the *cognitive form* of any legal and political argument is irretrievably made a part of the ideology-to-sector equation. Just as there is a pattern to the sectoral alliances of activism which marked the Marshall, Field, and early Hughes Courts, so too the Warren Court, and of course the Burger Court, each revealed a clear preference for what had become the evolvingly purer cognitive forms that lay at the core of the different sector-based ideologies since the turn of the twentieth century. Similarly, the relative willingness or unwillingness of legislatures of all stripes throughout the Anglo-American experience to either entertain or not entertain the novel, challenging, and so often equity-based consideration reveals legislative preferences for either the analytic or the synthetic cognitions as those cognitions were increasingly represented by the private and public sectors respectively.

The history of the cognitive evolution, therefore, is clear. The synthetic form of the sectorally mixed feudal order was what the early post-Conquest days of English law and government slowly began to emerge out of. The private contract, still anything but pure in form by the time of Henry II and Edward I, was nonetheless beginning its often-interrupted journey away from the multitudinous exigencies of the social contract to the almost exclusively economic, hence cognitively analytic, contract of the late-nineteenth-century American experience. As we've seen, the time of the framing of the American Republic found Alexander Hamilton's mercantilist perspective to encourage the productivity of a new and still vulnerable nation by endorsing still mildly synthetic government-to-business arrangements. Even Thomas Jefferson, though ending the landed residues of feudalism with his abolition of primogeniture and entail in Virginia, dealt with far less than a purely analytic private contract when he purchased Louisiana, continued support for "manufactures," and even tolerated Hamilton's national bank. Nonetheless, the private contract continued to work its way toward ever purer analytic forms as the nineteenth century progressed.

From the long perspective of history, Sir Edward Coke's ability to ensure the triumph of alienable property in *Shelley's Case* (1584) was not unrelated to Andrew Jackson and Roger Taney's ability in the nineteenth century's fourth decade to wring a healthy portion of cognitively synthetic American mercantilism out of most, though never all, of pre–Civil War America. But all such acts contributed not only to the separation of the public and the private sectors. They contributed as well to the separation of those forms of enterprise which could, and would, exist within these increasingly separate—that is, private and public—domains.

Recall that America's eminent librarian of Congress, Daniel Boorstin, criticized Sir William Blackstone over a half-century ago because Blackstone's balance between the *certum* of the law, that is the law's cognitively analytic internal consistency and predictability, and the *verum* of the law, the law's cognitively synthetic adaptability and proximity to a moving standard of justice, was too heavily weighted toward the former quality. The analytic victory within the private law was that inevitable by the middle of the eighteenth century, in spite of Hamilton's advocacy of synthetic mercantile forms at the close of the century.

What is essential to our understanding is the realization that the sub-atomic ideological dispute, the dispute that invariably goes on *intra*institutionally, and not just *inter*institutionally, deals more than any-thing else with relative ascendancies of analytic or synthetic forms of law. Where do those forms reside? Again, what is clear is that the *certum* of the law has increasingly become the province of the purely private con-tract and the contract's largely analytic cognition. Similarly, the *verum* of the law has become almost exclusively the province of the public sector, as it was been the province of synthetic, Roosevelt-like, legislatively in-spired additions to the private law, Warren Court–inspired additions to the private law, or recent legislatively required mandates concerning con-sumer protection, the environment, and the like.

My suggestion is that the study of Anglo-American jurisprudence, nearly a millennium after the Conquest, should now elevate itself one full level of abstraction in its analysis of the ideological preferences, the institutional dominances, and the sectoral ebbs and flows that have al-ways existed within the law's ideological preferences and institutional dominances. If the standard of justice, whether political or legal, is a stan-dard that consciously seeks balances that lie deep in the substructuring of both real-world institutions and intellectual world arguments, then the balance of cognitive forms within law and politics, Court and Congress, must now become part of the baseline for legal and political justice.

As I have argued, the twin cognitions, analytic and synthetic, have increasingly found their homes within the private and the public sectors respectively. Arguments over the law and arguments over politics invari-ably reflect the forms of their positions as much as they reflect their sub-stance. Just as advocates on both sides of the ideological spectrum will continue to utilize whatever institutions benefit them in whatever issues they present to the polity, those same advocates will continue to use what-ever stratagems they can within their favored private and public sectors to jockey for the ascendence of the judicial or the legislative institutions as those institutions favor the different sectors and their accompanying cognitive forms.

The private sector naturally prefers the analytic cognition because a more purely analytic form of contract shields property owners, and contractors for the purchase and sale of property, from at least many of the things the public might wish to have included within their sector. Matters concerning the environment, the safety of workers, women's rights in the workplace, the safety of products, the quality of products, job security, job retraining, and a host of other considerations all synthetically encumber, or do not encumber, the pure notion of contract, depending on the outcome of the political argument.

In short, as a deeper understanding of the largely sectoral nature of the Anglo-American jurisprudential dispute should be added to, if it should not supersede, our understandings of the institutional disputes among the structures of the American Constitutional order, a deeper understanding of the cognitive nature of so much of the dispute among America's Constitutional institutions is also long overdue. That cognitions lie deeply within the sectors they reside in, regardless of their institutional housing, should now be clear to all. To understand the cognitive nature of the sectoral dispute, regardless of which institution is mediating the sectoral dispute, is to possess the subatomic understanding.

Why have I insisted that the subatomic understanding be so much a part of this sectoral history of American law? My answer is that I strongly believe the relationship between form and sector to not only fortify understanding of the importance of sector to American legal history, but that the form-to-sector relationship ultimately has a great deal to do with the progress of democracy throughout the Anglo-American experience.

As we have reviewed, Sir Edward Coke made the contribution that he did by first moving the reason of the common law into the public sector. But Coke's contribution grew out of a more than a sectoral transference of a well-reasoned private law to what was a highly transitional arena of public law. Coke's moving of reason into the public sector permitted reason to become far more complex than it had ever been in the private arena. Concepts of political representation, among others, began to deal with those issues surrounding the proper relationship of governmental institutions to each other, and, more importantly, the relationship of all governmental institutions to the public.

Without embellishing the history of Anglo-American law unduly, I think it appropriate to argue that a kind of democratic dialectic took place with Coke. Though this is hardly the place for higher philosophy, let me remind my reader that the incorporation of novel complexity into the way that a society thinks about things is what the great dialecticians have always written of. Put simply, historical progress is only accomplished by first understanding, and then implementing, what in its form is a synthetic cognition, a more complex idea followed by a more complex material reality.

Just as Coke broached the complexities of democracy from the perspective of a newly public sense of reason, I suggest that Earl Warren broached what he judged to be necessary advancements in American democracy from the perspective of the newly acquired public position of the heretofore aggrieved group. Only from such a perspective could American society incorporate the democratic innovations of Warren's rulings.

African Americans were placed into their public role, as students in public schools, before they could be better incorporated into society through the device of integrated schools. The accused were rescued from their singular difficulties with the law and were granted the same expectations of due process that all public citizens justifiably expect.

Urban dwellers, who suffered representational discrimination in large part because of the ethnic and religious complexity that they brought to America, were placed onto an equal footing with other public citizens before their complexity received representative equality. And women, though nominally a majority all along, were placed into that public place which eventually liberated them from both the private moralities that had enslaved them and the private status that had partially retained their contractual relationship to father and husband well into this century.

Even the reasoning of the key cases in each of these areas reveals the gathering complexity of the democratic dialectic. The "penumbras" of *Griswold*, the Warren extension of African-American concerns beyond the contractual rights of *Shelley*, the Clark and Warren concerns with citizens' knowledge of the law in *Mapp* and *Miranda*, and the outright institutional restructuring of *Reynolds*, all manifest the synthetic cognitive form.

Contrast Taney in *Dred Scott*, wherein not only is Scott reduced to his private, contractual self, the mere object of a slave sale, but wherein the synthetic notions of both multiracial Constitutional-era citizenship and those public sector compromises that permitted contradictory approaches to slavery to exist side by side were obliterated.

My biases should be clear by now. I believe in that democratic progress that incorporates even what might not have been a majoritarian view at the precise time of its judicial acceptance into an ongoing process of historically assimilated democratic complexity. This, I believe, is how civilization has advanced, as Coke and Warren, as well as historians like Toynbee and philosophers like Hegel, have understood and chronicled it.

Periods during which analytic, essentially simplifying, notions of law and politics hold sway surely alternate with those moments of synthetic aggregation that Coke and Warren represent. In American law the prunings of Warren that are evident in the rulings of the Burger and early Rehnquist Courts were perhaps inevitable. History stretches, and then it rests. And, to be fair, the resting periods are important too, the routinization of recently accepted complexities being necessary in all societies. But the great leaps of historical progress, particularly in the arenas of politics and the law, have almost invariably been leaps of the synthetic cognition. And they have almost always been made within the public sector, the sector that carries the burden of aggregating the demand of the aggrieved and heretofore excluded interest, as that interest turns from what the private sector could or would not do for it.

To review, the overriding purpose of this work was to point out that traditional, institutionally based descriptions of U.S. Constitutional history are at best inadequate. Domains, the private and public sectors, have defined the principle ideological divide of Anglo-American constitutional political and legal history, just as domains marked the principal divide within the American Constitution. A chronicling of those domains' almost perfectly consistent historical alignment with their evolving internal forms, as well as with the ideological position that was commodious to those forms at key points in Anglo-American history, was what I attempted here. In one sense the framers' placement of the governmental structure within the first seven articles of the Constitution was deceptive. Between the original seven articles and the Bill of Rights, as I have mentioned, the former is the more private portion of the document, the latter the more public. Cognitively, the former is the more analytic, the latter the more synthetic. And, just as the ideological history described here has shown that the movement from the Articles of Confederation to the Constitution was principally a movement of the private-to-public line in favor of the private sector, so too recent history has shown that private-to-public domains have largely remained true to their ideological alliances, while institutions have readily changed their ideological stripes.

There have been moments, to be sure, when the private sector furthered egalitarian goals. Coke's predemocratic writings relied on private sector, common-law principles. For a time the Jacksonian period gave preindustrial capitalism an egalitarian, mildly redistributionist bent. Very occasionally, as with the case of *Shelley v. Kraemer,* judicial currents cross in such a way that upholding of the private law advances the cause of the political underdog. But the paucity of exceptions proves the rule. The limits of the private sector in promoting democratic reform that both *Shelley* cases represent beg for the successor contribution of the public sector, synthetic form, that included *Dr. Bonham's case,* the 1616 standing up to James I, and the *Petition of Right* in Coke's case, and *Brown, Reynolds* and so much more in Warren's case. It was always the middle stage of the dialectic, the contradictory stage, which utilized the synthetic incorporation of the new perspective. The private sector, armed with its preference for increasingly analytic contracts and a sacrosanct sense of property, has almost universally favored those whom Madison saw as benefiting from the "diversity in the faculties of men." The public sector has served as the arena for complementary, essentially egalitarian political and legal activity throughout most of Anglo-American history, and throughout virtually all of American Constitutional law.

EPILOGUE

A final word. I have written this work in memory of a friend and valued colleague, M. Glenn Abernathy. Glenn was an extraordinary Constitutional scholar. He was also a distinguished citizen of the scholarly community. An officer in the Southern Political Science Association and the creator of the Faculty Senate as well as the faculty-run Tenure and Promotion process at the University of South Carolina, this Birmingham native was invariably patient with a young colleague from Chicago with whom he frequently differed on matters of law generally and the Constitution in particular.

It is a great sadness for me that Glenn could not have read this work. Whether Glenn would have agreed with so much as a word of what I have written is, of course, something I cannot speculate on. I can only be sure that Glenn would have read it carefully, asked me about it, criticized it civilly when he disagreed as well as applauded whatever he could find to be of value. Over a period of almost twenty years Glenn and I discussed many things. In rare moments he would allow himself a reference to the topic that was surprisingly to me still so painful for him—the Civil War. One of my most vivid, and last, memories of him was his joyfully telling me that he had read the great biography of Holmes, *Yankee from Olympus*, and liked it.

If I have been harsh in my criticisms of the secessionists, I assure my reader that I hold no antipathy for the region of the country I have lived in for over a quarter of a century. My vigorous criticism of the slave-owning secessionists is rooted in my belief that the selfishness of these relatively few people not only burdened our country greatly for a time but to some degree still burdens this region.

My judgment, necessarily, extends to those who intellectually facilitated the secession. John C. Calhoun was not originally a part of South Carolina's aristocracy, but, as he curried favor with it, like so many who have curried favor throughout history, he made it easy for the selfish men to do what they did. For his servility John Caldwell Calhoun received a Justinian due, his birth in upstate Abbeville, South Carolina, contrasting with a ceremonious interring in St. Phillip's Cemetery, on Church Street,

in Charleston. The pain that afflicted possibly the most decent man I
have ever met—over one hundred years after the war—was but one re-
minder of what an expensive indulgence Calhoun's writings turned out
to be.

NOTES

Introduction

1. Cf. Forrest McDonald, *Novus Ordo Seclorum* (Lawrence: University Press of Kansas, 1985); Edward S. Corwin, *Court over Constitution: A Study of Judicial Review as an Instrument of Popular Government* (Gloucester, Mass.: Peter Smith, 1957); Alexander Bickel, *The Least Dangerous Branch: The Supreme Court at the Bar of Politics* (Indianapolis: Bobbs-Merrill, 1962); Laurence Tribe, *Constitutional Choices* (Cambridge, Mass.: Harvard University Press, 1985).
2. Herbert J. Storing, *The Complete Anti-Federalist* (Chicago: University of Chicago Press, 1981).
3. Charles Beard, *An Economic Interpretation of the Constitution* (New York: Macmillan, 1925).

Chapter 1: A Framework for Analysis

1. *Schecter Poultry Corporation v. United States*, 295 U.S. 495 (1936).
2. *Carter v. Carter Coal Company*, 298 U.S. 238 (1936).
3. *Muller v. Oregon*, 208 U.S. 412 (1908).
4. *Lochner v. New York*, 198 U.S. 45 (1905).

Chapter 2: The English Contribution

1. Bernard Schwartz, *The Bill of Rights: A Documentary History* (New York: Chelsea House, 1971), 5.
2. Ibid., 6.
3. Ibid.
4. Charles Montgomery Gray, *Copyhold, Equity and the Common Law* (Cambridge, Mass.: Harvard University Press, 1963), 6.
5. Schwartz, *Bill of Rights*, 6.
6. Ibid., 6–7.
7. Sir William Holdsworth, *Some Makers of English Common Law* (Cambridge: Cambridge University Press, 1938), 11.
8. Ibid., 8.
9. Ibid., 17.
10. Arthur Hogue, *Origins of the Common Law* (Bloomington: Indiana University Press, 1966), 204.
11. Holdsworth, *Some Makers of English Common Law*, 406.

12. F. W. Maitland, *Equity: A Course of Lectures* (Cambridge: Cambridge University Press, 1936), 2.
13. Holdsworth, *Some Makers of English Law*, 64.
14. G. W. J. Barrow, *Feudal Britain: The Completion of the Medieval Kingdoms, 1016–1314* (London: Edward Arnold, Ltd., 1956), 304.
15. Hogue, *Origins of the Common Law*, 221.
16. Sir Frederick Pollock, *The Land Laws* (London: Macmillan, 1896), 80.
17. Ibid., 81.
18. Hogue, *Origins of the Common Law*, 221.
19. Maitland, *Equity*, 5.
20. Holdsworth, *Some Makers of English Law*, 57.
21. Maitland, *Equity*, 5.
22. Ibid., 6.
23. Pollock, *Land Laws*, 86.
24. Ibid., 99.
25. Ibid., 102.
26. Hogue, *Origins of the Common Law*, 227.
27. Ibid., 229.
28. Ibid., 231.
29. Ibid.
30. Ibid., 233.

Chapter 3: Revolution and Counterrevolution

1. George M. Trevelyan, *History of England*, vol. 2: *The Tudors and the Stuart Era* (Garden City, N.Y.: Doubleday, 1953), 14–15.
2. Hastings Lyon and Herman Block, *Edward Coke: Oracle of the Law* (Boston: Houghton-Mifflin, Riverside Press, 1929), 357–63.
3. Ibid., 362.
4. *Dr. Bonham's case*, 8 Coke Rep. 118a (C.P.1610), in Ronald D. Rotunda, *Modern Constitutional Law* (St. Paul, Minn.: West Publishing, 1989), 12.
5. Lyon and Block, *Edward Coke*, 198.
6. Ibid., 198–207.
7. Bernard Schwartz, *The Bill of Rights: A Documentary History* (New York: McGraw-Hill, 1971), 18.
8. Ibid.
9. John Fortescue, *De Laudibus Legum Anglie* (Birmingham: Legal Classics Library, 1984).
10. Barrington Moore, *Social Origins of Dictatorship and Democracy: Lord and Peasant in the Making of the Modern World* (Boston: Beacon Press, 1966), 21.
11. Cf. Gary Wills, *Reinventing America: Jefferson's Declaration of Independence* (Garden City, N.Y.: Doubleday, 1978).
12. William Blackstone, *Commentaries* (New York: Augustus M. Kelley, 1969).
13. Ibid., 4.

14. Ibid.
15. Ibid., 5.
16. Ibid., 10.
17. Ibid., 26.
18. Daniel Boorstin, *The Mysterious Science of Law* (Cambridge, Mass.: Harvard University Press, 1941), 70.
19. Ibid., 74.
20. Ibid., 221.
21. Ibid.
22. Ibid., 226.
23. Ibid.
24. Ibid., 63.

Chapter 4: The American Experience

1. James B. Thayer, "The Origin and Scope of the American Doctrine of Constitutional Law," *Harvard Law Review* 7, no. 3 (October 25, 1893): 129–56.
2. Gordon S. Wood, *The Creation of the American Republic: 1776–1787* (New York: W. W. Norton, 1969), 135.
3. Akhil Reed Amar, "The Bill of Rights as a Constitution," *Yale Law Journal* 100 (March 1991).
4. Ibid., 1132.
5. Ibid.
6. Ibid.
7. Christopher Collier and James L. Collier, *Decision in Philadelphia: The Constitutional Convention of 1787* (New York: Random House, 1987), 174.
8. My thanks to George Rogers of the University of South Carolina Department of History, for his assistance on this point.
9. Forrest McDonald, *Novus Ordo Seclorum* (Lawrence: University Press of Kansas, 1985), 268.
10. Ibid., 270.
11. Ibid.
12. Ibid.

Chapter 5: The Federalists and the Anti-Federalists

1. Alexander Hamilton, James Madison, and John Jay, *The Federalist Papers*, ed. Garry Wills (New York: Bantam Books, 1982), no. 10.
2. Ibid.
3. Ibid.
4. Ibid.
5. Ibid.
6. Ibid.
7. *Federalist Papers*, no. 78.
8. Ibid.

9. Amar, "Bill of Rights," 1140.
10. Ibid.
11. Ibid., 1147.
12. Ibid.
13. Ibid.
14. W. B. Allen and Gordon Lloyd, eds., *The Essential Anti- Federalist* (Lanham, Md.: University Press of America, 1985), 5.
15. Ibid., 11.
16. Ibid.
17. Ibid.
18. Ibid., 12.
19. Ibid., 13.
20. Ibid.
21. Ibid.
22. Ibid.
23. Ralph Ketchum, *The Anti-Federalist Papers and the Constitutional Convention Debates* (New York: Mentor Publishers, 1986), 257.
24. Richard Henry Lee, "Letters from a Federal Farmer," in *American Political Thought*, ed. Kenneth M. Dolbeare, 2d ed. (Chatham, N.J.: Chatham House, 1989), 141–54.
25. Ibid., 143.
26. Allen and Lloyd, *Essential Anti-Federalist*, 24.
27. Ibid.
28. Ibid.
29. Ibid., 26.
30. Ibid., 70–71.
31. Dolbeare, *American Political Thought*, 146.
32. Ibid.
33. Ibid.
34. Ibid.

Chapter 6: The Interpretive Period

1. *Marbury v. Madison*, 5 U.S. (1 Cranch) 137 (1803).
2. *McCulloch v. Maryland*, 17 U.S. (Wheat.) 316 (1819).
3. Ibid., 406.
4. Ibid., 406–7.
5. Ibid., 407.
6. *Gibbons v. Ogden*, 9 (Wheat.) 1 (1824).
7. Ibid., 188.
8. Ibid., 206.
9. *Fletcher v. Peck*, 6 U.S. (Cranch) 87 (1810).
10. *Dartmouth v. Woodward*, 17 U.S. (4 Wheat.) 1819.
11. *Fletcher v. Peck*, 134.
12. Ibid., 139.

13. Ibid.
14. Ibid.
15. Ibid.
16. *Dartmouth College v. Woodward*, 627.
17. Ibid.
18. Ibid.
19. *Barron v. Baltimore*, 7 Pet. 243 (1833).
20. Ibid., 250.
21. Ibid.

Chapter 7: The Taney Revision

1. *Dartmouth College v. Woodward*, 17 U.S. (4 Wheat.) 518 (1819); *Fletcher v. Peck.*
2. James Kent, *Commentaries on American Law* (Boston: Little, Brown, 1861), 445–83.
3. Joseph Story, *Commentaries on the Constitution of the United States* (Boston: Hilliard Gray, 1832).
4. George Brown Tindall, *America: A Narrative History* (New York: W. W. Norton, 1984), 363.
5. *Gibbons v. Ogden.* 22 U.S. (9 Wheat.) 1 (1824).
6. Story, *Commentaries*, 118.
7. Ibid., 119.
8. Richard Hofstadter, *The American Political Tradition* (New York: Vintage Books, 1973), 70.
9. Ibid.
10. Sidney Fine, *Laissez Faire and the General Welfare State* (Ann Arbor: University of Michigan Press, 1956), 14.
11. *Barron v. Baltimore*, 7 Pet. 243 (1833).
12. *Dred Scott v. Sandford*, 60 U.S. (19 Howard) 393 (1857).
13. *Charles River Bridge v. Warren Bridge*, 36 U.S. (11 Peters) 420 (1837).
14. Walker Lewis, *Without Fear or Favor* (Boston: Houghton Mifflin, 1965), 337–97.
15. Alexis de Tocqueville, *Democracy in America*, ed. Richard D. Heffner. (New York: Mentor Books, 1956).
16. Clement Eaton, *The Growth of Southern Civilization* (New York: Harper and Row, 1961), 175.
17. Ibid., 298.
18. Ibid., 295.
19. Lacy K. Ford, *Origins of Southern Radicalism* (New York: Oxford University Press, 1988), 45.
20. John C. Inscoe, *Mountain Masters, Slavery, and the Sectoral Crisis in Western North Carolina* (Knoxville: University of Tennessee Press, 1989), 44.
21. Ibid., 59.
22. Ibid., 68.

23. Steven Hahn, *The Roots of Southern Populism* (New York: Oxford University Press, 1983), 43, 40.
24. Note that writings such as Jefferson's *Kentucky Resolutions* responded to procedural impediments to liberty such as found in the Alien and Sedition Acts, not to the holding of minority substantive positions on contemporary issues.

Chapter 8: Dissolution

1. *Dred Scott v. Sandford*, 60 U.S. (19 Howard) 393 b(1857).
2. U.S. Constitution, art. 1, sec. 9.
3. John O'Sullivan and Edward F. Keuchel, *American Economic History: From Abundance to Constraint* (New York: Franklin Watts, 1981), 104.
4. George B. Tindall, *America: A Narrative History* (New York: W. W. Norton, 1984), 826.
5. *Munn v. Illinois*, 94 U.S. 113 (1877).
6. Ibid., 139.
7. *Wabash Rwy Co. v. Illinois*, 118 U.S. 557 (1886); *Chicago, Burlington & Quincy R.R. Company v. Chicago*, 166 U.S. 226 (1897); *United States v. E. C. Knight*, 156 U.S. 1 (1895).
8. Cf. *Wabash Rwy Co. v. Illinois*; *United States v. E. C. Knight*.
9. *Plessy v. Ferguson*, 163 U.S. 537 (1896).

Chapter 9: The Reformers

1. Hans Thorelli, *The Federal Anti-Trust Policy: Origination of an American Tradition* (Baltimore, Md.: Johns Hopkins Press, 1955), 228.
2. Quoted in Hofstadter, *American Political Tradition*, 230.
3. For such an interpretation, cf. H. L. Pohlman, *Justice Oliver Wendell Holmes* (New York: New York University Press, 1991), 112–36.
4. *Northern Securities Co. v. United States*, 193 U.S. 197 (1904).
5. Cf. Alfred Lief, ed., *The Dissenting Opinions of Nr. Justice Holmes* (New York: Vanguard Press, 1929), 163–75.
6. *Lochner v. New York*, 198 U.S. 45 (1905).
7. *Northern Securities Co. v. United States*.
8. Ibid.
9. *Chicago, Burlington & Quincy R.R. Co. v. Chicago*.
10. Felix Frankfurter, *Mr. Justice Holmes and the Supreme Court* (Cambridge, Mass.: Harvard University Press, 1939), 49–54.
11. Ibid., 51.
12. Ibid., 50.
13. Ibid.
14. *Muller v. Oregon*, 243 U.S. 426 (1917).
15. Josephine Claire Goldmark, *Fatigue and Efficiency: A Study in Industry* (New York: Charities Publication Committee, 1912), 12.
16. Ibid., 558.
17. Samuel Konefsky, *The Legacy of Holmes and Brandeis: A Study in the Influence of Ideas* (New York: Macmillan, 1956).

18. *Munn v. Illinois,* 44 U.S. 113 (1877).
19. Konefsky, *Legacy,* 33.
20. *Bunting v. Oregon,* 243 U.S. 426 (1917).
21. *Standard Oil Co. v. United States,* 221 U.S. 203 (1911).
22. *United States v. American Tobacco Co.,* 221 U.S. 106 (1911).
23. *Pollock v. Farmers' Loan & Trust Co.,* 158 U.S. 601 (1895).
24. *Adkins v. Children's Hospital,* 261 U.S. 525 (1923).
25. Cf. Leon Duguit, "Objective Law," *Columbia Law Review* 20 (1920); Roscoe Pound, "A Theory of Social Interests," *Papers and Proceedings of the American Sociological Society* 15 (1921).
26. Karl Llewellyn, "A Realistic Jurisprudence—The Next Step," in *Readings in Jurisprudence,* ed. Jerome Hall (Indianapolis: Bobbs-Merrill, 1938), 1095.
27. Ibid.
28. *Marbury v. Madison.*
29. Jerome Frank, *Courts on Trial: Myth and Reality in American Justice* (Princeton, N.J.: Princeton University Press, 1950), 85.
30. Ibid., 91.
31. Ibid., 92, 98.
32. Ibid., 146.
33. Ibid.
34. Ibid.
35. Edwin S. Corwin, *Court over Constitution: A Study of Judicial Review as an Instrument of Popular Government* (Gloucester, Mass.: Peter Smith, 1957).
36. Ibid., 115–16.

Chapter 10: The Third Activist Period

1. Alpheus Thomas Mason, *The Supreme Court from Taft to Burger* (Baton Rouge: Louisiana State University Press, 1979), 49.
2. Ibid., 70.
3. Bernard Schwartz, *A History of the Supreme Court* (New York: Oxford University Press, 1993), 218.
4. *Truax v. Corrigan,* 257 U.S. 312 (1921).
5. *Adkins v. Children's Hospital,* 261 U.S. 525 (1923).
6. Alpheus Thomas Mason, *William Howard Taft: Chief Justice* (New York: Simon and Schuster, 1964), 14.
7. Ibid., 64.
8. Ibid.
9. Schwartz, *History of the Supreme Court,* 218.
10. *Muller v. Oregon; Bunting v. Oregon.*
11. *Panama Refining Co. v Ryan,* 293 U.S. 388 (1935).
12. *Schecter Poultry Corp. v. United States,* 295 U.S. 495 (1935).
13. *Carter v. Carter Coal Co.,* 298 U.S. 238 (1936).
14. *Charles River Bridge v. Warren Bridge,* 36 U.S. (11 Pet.) 420 (1837).
15. *West Coast Hotel v. Parrish,* 300 U.S. 379 (1937).
16. *National Labor Relations Board v. Jones & Laughlin Steel Corp.,* 301 U.S. 1 (1937).

17. *Brown v. Board of Education*, 347 U.S. 483 (1954).
18. *Barron v. Baltimore*, 32 U.S. (7 Pet.) 243 (1833).
19. James MacGregor Burns, *The Crosswinds of Freedom* (New York: Alfred A. Knopf, 1988), 90.
20. *Northern Securities Co. v. United States*, 193 U.S. 197 (1904).

Chapter 11: The Pre-Warren Court

1. See George Tindall, *America: A Narrative History* (New York: W. W. Norton, 1984), 1002.
2. August Meier and Elliot M. Rudwich, *From Plantation to Ghetto: An Interpretive History of Black America* (New York: Hill and Wang, 1966), 191.
3. *Shelley v. Kraemer*, 334 U.S. 1 (1948).
4. *Corrigan v. Buckley*, 271 U.S. 323 (1926).
5. Cf. Clement Vose, *Caucasians Only* (Berkeley: University of California Press, 1959).

Chapter 12: The Warren Court

1. *Shelley v. Kraemer*.
2. *Katzenbach v. McClung*, 379 U.S. 294 (1964).
3. *Heart of Atlanta Motel v. Katzenbach*, 379 U.S. 241 (1964).
4. *Charles River Bridge v. Warren Bridge*.
5. *Brown v. Board of Education*.
6. *Mapp v. Ohio*, 367 U.S. 643 (1961).
7. *Miranda v. Arizona*, 384 U.S. 436 (1966).
8. *Gideon v. Wainwright*, 372 U.S. 335 (1963).
9. *Baker v. Carr*, 369 U.S. 186 (1962); *Reynolds v. Sims*, 377 U.S. 533 (1964).
10. *Griswold v. Connecticut*, 381 U.S. 479 (1965).
11. *Yates v. United States* 354 U.S. 298 (1957).
12. Ira Katznelson, "Was the Great Society a Lost Opportunity?" in *The Rise and Fall of the New Deal Order, 1930–1980*, ed. Steve Fraser and Gary Gerstle (Princeton, N.J.: Princeton University Press, 1989), 185–211.
13. Jonathan Rieder, "The Rise of the 'Silent Majority,'" in Fraser and Gerstle, *Rise and Fall of the New Deal Order*, 243–68.
14. William Kreml, *The Middle Class Burden* (Durham, N.C.: Carolina Academic Press, 1979).

Chapter 13: Civil Rights and the Rights of the Accused

1. *McLaurin v. Oklahoma*, 339 U.S. 637 (1950).
2. *Sweatt v. Painter*, 339 U.S. 629 (1950).
3. *Brown v. Board of Education*.
4. Ibid., 486; my emphasis.
5. Ibid., 489, 492–93.
6. Ibid., 489–90.
7. Ibid., 491–92.

8. Ibid.
9. Ibid., 492.
10. Ibid., 491.
11. Ibid., 490.
12. Ibid.
13. Ibid., 493.
14. Ibid.
15. Ibid.
16. Ibid.
17. Ibid.
18. *Mapp v. Ohio.*
19. *Miranda v. Arizona.*
20. *Gideon v. Wainwright.*
21. *Barron v. Baltimore*, 7 (Pet.) 243 (1833).
22. *Powell v. Alabama*, 287 U.S. 45 (1932).
23. *West Coast Hotel Co. v. Parrish*, 300 U.S. 379 (1937).
24. *National Labor Relations Board v. Jones & Laughlin Steel Corp*, 301 U.S. 1 (1937).
25. *Weeks v. United States*, 232 U.S. 3383 (1914).
26. *Wolf v. Colorado*, 338 U.S. 25 (1949).
27. Ibid., 659.
28. Ibid.
29. Ibid.
30. Ibid.
31. Ibid.
32. Ibid., 660.
33. Ibid., 665.
34. Ibid.
35. Ibid.
36. Ibid.
37. *Miranda v. Arizona.*
38. *Escobedo v. Illinois*, 387 U.S. 478 (1964).
39. Ibid., 449.
40. Ibid., 457–58.
41. Ibid., 468.
42. Ibid.
43. Ibid., 448.
44. Ibid.
45. Ibid.
46. *Gideon v. Wainwright.*
47. Ibid., 343.
48. Ibid.
49. Ibid., 344.
50. Ibid.
51. Ibid.

52. Ibid.
53. Ibid.
54. *Shelley v. Kraemer,* 23.

Chapter 14: Apportionment and Women's Rights

1. *Colegrove v. Green,* 328 U.S. 549 (1946).
2. *Baker v. Carr.*
3. Ibid., 199.
4. Ibid.
5. Ibid., 200.
6. Ibid., 210.
7. Ibid., 211.
8. Ibid.
9. Ibid.
10. Ibid.
11. Ibid.
12. Ibid., 204.
13. Ibid., 207.
14. Ibid.
15. Robert G. Dixon, *Democratic Representation: Reapportionment in Law and Politics* (New York: Oxford University Press, 1968), 98–99.
16. Gordon E. Baker, *The Reapportionment Revolution: Political Power and the Supreme Court* (New York: Random House, 1966), 5–6.
17. Ibid., 102–3.
18. Ibid., 103.
19. *Gray v. Sanders,* 372 U.S. 368 (1963).
20. *Wesberry v. Sanders,* 376 U.S. 1 (1964).
21. *Reynolds v. Sims.*
22. Ibid., 561.
23. Ibid.
24. Ibid., 565.
25. Ibid., 566.
26. Ibid.
27. Ibid., 565.
28. Ibid.
29. Ibid.
30. *Brown v. Board of Education.*
31. *Mapp v. Ohio.*
32. *Miranda v. Arizona.*
33. *Gideon v. Wainright.*
34. *Griswold v. Connecticut.*
35. *Roe v. Wade,* 410 U.S. 113 (1973).
36. *Griswold v. Connecticut,* 485.
37. Ibid.

38. *Muller v. Oregon.*
39. *McCulloch v. Maryland.*
40. *Swann v. Mecklenburg*, 402 U.S. 1 (1971).
41. *Roe v. Wade*, 116.
42. Ibid.
43. Ibid., 159.
44. Ibid., 162.
45. Ibid.
46. Ibid., 163.
47. Ibid.

Chapter 15: Warren Critiqued

1. Bickel, *Least Dangerous Branch*, 16.
2. Dixon, *Democratic Representation*, 99.
3. Bickel, *Least Dangerous Branch*, 18.
4. Ibid.
5. Ibid.
6. Ibid.
7. Ibid., 19.
8. Ibid.
9. Ibid.
10. Ibid.
11. Ibid., 21.
12. Ibid.
13. Ibid., 147.
14. Thayer, "Origin and Scope," 156.
15. Ibid., 25.
16. Ibid., 43.
17. Alexander Bickel, *Politics and the Warren Court* (New York: Harper and Row, 1965), 176.
18. Bickel, *Least Dangerous Branch*, 36.
19. Bickel, *Politics and the Warren Court*, 178.
20. Ibid., 180.
21. Ibid.
22. Ibid.
23. Ibid.
24. Ibid., 181.
25. Ibid., 185.
26. Cf. Bickel, *Least Dangerous Branch*, 49, passim.
27. Bickel, *Politics and the Warren Court*, 181.
28. Bickel, *Least Dangerous Branch*, 56.
29. As cited in Robert H. Bork, "Neutral Principles and Some First Amendment Problems," *Indiana Law Journal* 47 (Fall 1971): 13.
30. Bickel, *Least Dangerous Branch*, 56.

Chapter 16: The Post-Warren Court

1. *Swann v. Mecklenburg.*
2. *Roe v. Wade.*
3. Stephen Wasby, *Continuity and Change: From the Warren Court to the Burger Court* (Pacific Palisades, Calif.: Goodyear Publishing, 1976), 8.
4. Ibid., 79.
5. *Milliken v. Bradley,* 418 U.S. 717 (1974).
6. Ibid., 743–44.
7. Ibid., 744.
8. Ibid.
9. Ibid., 745.
10. Ibid.
11. Ibid.
12. *Moose Lodge No. 107 v. Irvis,* 407 U.S. 163 (1972).
13. Ibid., 171.
14. Ibid., 172.
15. Ibid., 173.
16. Ibid.
17. *Richmond v. Croson Co.,* 109 S.Ct. 706 (1989).
18. Ibid., 721.
19. Ibid., 720.
20. Ibid., 725.
21. Ibid.
22. *Civil Rights Cases,* 109 U.S. 3. (1883).
23. Ibid., 736.
24. Ibid.
25. Cited in ibid., 739; my emphasis.
26. *Skinner v. Railway Labor Executives Association,* 489 U.S. 602 (1989).
27. Ibid., 621–22.
28. Ibid., 633.
29. *California v. Greenwood,* 486 U.S. 35 (1987).
30. Ibid., 39–40; my emphasis.
31. *Rhode Island v. Innis,* 446 U.S. 291 (1980).
32. Ibid., 300, 302.
33. *Nix v. Williams,* 467 U.S. 431 (1984).
34. Ibid., 439.
35. Ibid., 446.
36. *Mahon v. Howell,* 410 U.S. 315 (1973).
37. *Brown v. Thomson,* 459 U.S. 819 (1983).
38. *Davis v. Bandemer,* 478 U.S. 109, 130 (1986).
39. *Harris v. McRae,* 448 U.S. 297 (1980).
40. Ibid., 316.
41. *Webster v. Reproductive Health Services,* 492 U.S. 490 (1989).
42. *Akron v. Akron Center for Reproductive Health,* 462 U.S. 416, 444 (1983).
43. *Webster v. Reproductive Health Services,* 518.
44. Ibid.

45. Cited in *Richmond v. Croson*, 737.
46. Ibid.
47. Ibid.; my emphasis.
48. Ibid., 739.
49. *Schenk v. United States*, 249 U.S. 47 (1919).
50. *Gitlow v. New York*, 268 U.S. 652 (1925).
51. *Dennis v. United States*, 341 U.S. 494 (1951).
52. *Yates v. United States*, 354 U.S. 298 (1957).
53. *Wisconsin v. Yoder*, 406 U.S. 205 (1972).
54. *Thomas v. Georgia*, 452 U.S. 973.
55. *Engel v. Vitale*, 370 U.S. 421 (1962).
56. *School District of Abbington Township v. Schempp*, 374 U.S. 203 (1963).
57. *Buckley v. Valeo*, 424 U.S. 1 (1976).
58. Ibid., 48–49.
59. Ibid., 49.
60. Ibid., 52–53.
61. Ibid., 57.
62. Ibid., 290.
63. Ibid., 288.
64. Ibid.
65. Ibid., 260–61.

Chapter 17: Burger Critiqued

1. Tribe, *Constitutional Choices.*
2. Ibid., 3, 5.
3. Ibid., 10.
4. Ibid.
5. Ibid., 11.
6. Ibid., 17.
7. Ibid., 21.
8. *Immigration and Naturalization Service v. Chadha*, 462 U.S. 919 (1983).
9. *Buckley v. Valeo.*
10. *National League of Cities v. Usery*, 426 U.S. 833 (1976).
11. *Garcia v. San Antonio Metropolitan Transit Authority*, 469 U.S. 528 (1985).
12. Tribe, *Constitutional Choices*, 67.
13. Ibid.
14. Ibid., 221.
15. Ibid., 13.
16. Ibid., 192.
17. Ibid., 241.
18. Ibid.
19. The development of the notion of the subatomic institutional variable can be found in William Kreml, *Psychology, Relativism and Politics* (New York: New York University Press, 1991). The idea is a key part of a theory of psychological relativism, which can be found in that work.

BIBLIOGRAPHY

Allen, W. B., and Gordon Lloyd, eds. *The Essential Anti-Federalist*. Lanham, Md.: University Press of America, 1985.

Amar, Akhil Reed, "The Bill of Rights as a Constitution." *Yale Law Journal* 100 (March 1991).

Baker, Gordon E. *The Reapportionment Revolution: Political Power and the Supreme Court*. New York: Random House, 1966.

Barrow, G. W. J. *Feudal Britain: The Completion of the Medieval Kingdoms, 1016–1314*. London: Edward Arnold, Ltd., 1956.

Beard, Charles. *An Economic Interpretation of the Constitution*. New York: Macmillan, 1925.

Bickel, Alexander. *The Least Dangerous Branch: The Supreme Court at the Bar of Politics*. Indianapolis: Bobbs-Merrill, 1962.

———. *Politics and the Warren Court*. New York: Harper and Row, 1965.

Blackstone, William. *Commentaries*. New York: Augustus M. Kelley, 1969.

Boorstin, Daniel. *The Mysterious Science of Law*. Boston, Mass.: Harvard University Press, 1941.

Burns, James M. *The Deadlock of Democracy*. Englewood Cliffs: Prentice Hall, 1963.

Burns, James M. *The Crosswinds of Freedom*. New York: Alfred A. Knopf, 1988.

Collier, Christopher, and James L. Collier. *Decision in Philadelphia: The Constitutional Convention of 1787*. New York: Random House, 1987.

Corwin, Edward S. *Court over Constitution: A Study of Judicial Review as an Instrument of Popular Government*. Gloucester, Mass.: Peter Smith, 1957.

De Tocqueville, Alexis. *Democracy in America*. Ed. Richard D. Heffner. New York: Mentor Books, 1956.

Dixon, Robert G. *Democratic Representation: Reapportionment in Law and Politics*. New York: Oxford University Press, 1968.

Duguit, Leon. "Objective Law." *Columbia Law Review* 20 (1920).

Eaton, Clement. *The Growth of Southern Civilization*. New York: Harper and Row, 1961.

Fine, Sidney. *Laissez Faire and the General Welfare State*. Ann Arbor: University of Michigan Press, 1956.

Ford, Lacy K. *Origins of Southern Radicalism*. New York: Oxford University Press, 1988.

Fortescue, John. *De Laudibus Legum Anglie*. Birmingham: Legal Classics Library, 1984).

Frank, Jerome. *Courts on Trial: Myth and Reality in American Justice*. Princeton, N.J.: Princeton University Press, 1950.

Frankfurter, Felix. *Mr. Justice Holmes and the Supreme Court*. Cambridge, Mass.: Harvard University Press, 1939.

Goldmark, Josephine Claire. *Fatigue and Efficiency: A Study in Industry*. New York: Charities Publication Committee, 1912.

Gray, Charles M. *Copyhold, Equity and the Common Law*. Cambridge, Mass.: Harvard University Press, 1963.

Hahn, Steven. *The Roots of Southern Populism*. New York: Oxford University Press, 1983.

Hamilton, Alexander, James Madison, and John Jay. *The Federalist Papers*. Ed. Garry Wills. New York: Bantam Books, 1982.

Hofstadter, Richard. *The American Political Tradition*. New York: Vintage Books, 1973.

Hogue, Arthur. *Origins of the Common Law*. Bloomington: Indiana University Press, 1966.

Holdsworth, Sir William. *Some Makers of English Common Law*. Cambridge: Cambridge University Press, 1938.

Inscoe, John C. *Mountain Masters, Slavery and the Sectoral Crisis in Western North Carolina*. Knoxville: University of Tennessee Press, 1989.

Katznelson, Ira. "Was the Great Society a Lost Opportunity?" in *The Rise and Fall of the New Deal Order 1930–1980*, ed. Steve Fraser and Gary Gerstle. Princeton, N.J.: Princeton University Press, 1989.

Kent, James. *Commentaries on American Law*. Boston: Little, Brown, 1861.

Ketchum, Ralph. *The Anti-Federalist Papers and the Constitutional Convention Debates*. New York: Mentor, 1986.

Konefsky, Samuel. *The Legacy of Holmes and Brandeis: A Study in the Influence of Ideas*. New York: Macmillan, 1956.

Kreml, William. *The Middle Class Burden*. Durham, N.C.: Carolina Academic Press, 1979.

———. *Psychology, Relativism and Politics*. New York: New York University Press, 1991.

Lee, Richard H. "Letters from a Federal Farmer." In *American Political Thought*, ed. Kenneth M. Dolbeare, 2d ed. Chatham, N.J.: Chatham House, 1989.

Lewis, Walker. *Without Fear or Favor*. Boston: Houghton-Mifflin, 1965.

Lief, Alfred, ed. *The Dissenting Opinions of Mr. Justice Holmes*. New York: Vanguard Press, 1929.

Llewellyn, Karl. "A Realistic Jurisprudence—The Next Step." In *Readings in Jurisprudence*, ed. Jerome Hall. Indianapolis: Bobbs-Merrill, 1938.

Lyon, Hastings, and Herman Block. *Edward Coke: Oracle of the Law*. Boston: Houghton-Mifflin, Riverside Press, 1929.

Maitland, F. W. *Equity: A Course of Lectures*. Cambridge: Cambridge University Press, 1936.

Mason, Alpheus T. *The Supreme Court from Taft to Burger*. Baton Rouge: Louisiana State University Press, 1979.

———. *William Howard Taft: Chief Justice.* New York: Simon and Schuster, 1964.

McDonald, Forrest. *Novus Ordo Seelorum.* Lawrence: University Press of Kansas, 1985.

Meier, August, and Elliot M. Rudwich. *From Plantation to Ghetto: An Interpretive History of Black America.* New York: Hill and Wang, 1966.

Moore, Barrington. *Social Origins of Dictatorship and Democracy: Lord and Peasant in the Making of the Modern World.* Boston: Beacon Press, 1966.

O'Sullivan, John, and Edward F. Keuchel. *American Economic History: From Abundance to Constraint.* New York: Franklin Watts, 1981.

Pohlman, H. L. *Justice Oliver Wendell Holmes.* New York: New York University Press, 1991.

Pollock, Sir Frederick. *The Land Laws.* London: Macmillan, 1896.

Pound, Roscoe. "A Theory of Social Interests." *Papers and Proceedings of the American Sociological Society* 15 (1921).

Rieder, Jonathan. "The Rise of the 'Silent Majority.'" In *The Rise and Fall of the New Deal Order*, ed. Steve Fraser and Gary Gerstle. Princeton, N.J.: Princeton University Press, 1989.

Schwartz, Bernard. *The Bill of Rights: A Documentary History.* New York: Chelsea House, in association with McGraw-Hill, 1971.

———. *A History of the Supreme Court.* New York: Oxford University Press, 1993.

Storing, Herbert J. *The Complete Anti-Federalist.* Chicago: University of Chicago Press, 1981.

Story, Joseph. *Commentaries on the Constitution of the United States.* Boston: Hilliard Gray, 1832.

Thayer, James. "The Origin and Scope of the American Doctrine of Constitutional Law." *Harvard Law Review* 7, no. 3 (October 25, 1893).

Thorelli, Hans. *The Federal Anti-Trust Policy: Origination of an American Tradition.* Baltimore, Md.: Johns Hopkins Press, 1955.

Tindall, George B. *America: A Narrative History.* New York: W. W. Norton, 1984.

Trevelyan, George M. *History of England.* Vol. 2: *The Tudors and the Stuart Era.* Garden City, N.Y.: Doubleday, 1953.

Tribe, Laurence. *Constitutional Choices.* Cambridge, Mass.: Harvard University Press, 1985.

Vose, Clement. *Caucasians Only.* Berkeley: University of California Press, 1959.

Wasby, Stephen. *Continuity and Change: From the Warren Court to the Burger Court.* Pacific Palisades, Calif.: Goodyear Publishing, 1976.

Wills, Garry. *Reinventing America: Jefferson's Declaration of Independence.* Garden City, N.Y.: Doubleday, 1978.

Wood, Gordon S. *The Creation of the American Republic: 1776–1787.* New York: W. W. Norton, 1969.

INDEX